THE
EVOLUTION OF MODERN LIBERTY

THE EVOLUTION
OF MODERN LIBERTY

AN INSIGHTFUL STORY OF THE BIRTH OF AMERICAN FREEDOM AND HOW IT SPREAD OVERSEAS

BY
GEORGE L. SCHERGER

Skyhorse Publishing

Copyright © 1904 George L. Scherger
First Skyhorse edition 2014

Skyhorse Publishing books may be purchased in bulk at special discounts for sales promotion, corporate gifts, fund-raising, or educational purposes. Special editions can also be created to specifications. For details, contact the Special Sales Department, Skyhorse Publishing, 307 West 36th Street, 11th Floor, New York, NY 10018 or info@skyhorsepublishing.com.

Skyhorse® and Skyhorse Publishing® are registered trademarks of Skyhorse Publishing, Inc.®, a Delaware corporation.

Visit our website at www.skyhorsepublishing.com.

10 9 8 7 6 5 4 3 2 1

Library of Congress Cataloging-in-Publication Data is available on file.

Cover design by Danielle Ceccolini
Cover photo credit Thinkstock

Print ISBN: 978-1-62914-390-3
Ebook ISBN: 978-1-62914-939-4

Printed in the United States of America

PREFACE

THE study of political theories seems to be attracting considerable attention at present, a number of able writers, such as Dunning, Willoughby, Merriam, Osgood, and others having recently made contributions to this branch of research. Political theories are not only of theoretical interest, but have at times greatly influenced historical development. This is true in marked degree of those ideas whose genesis is traced in the following pages. They have been put forward repeatedly as a protest against oppression and arbitrary power. Their greatest influence, however, has made itself felt since the American Revolution. They have in large measure contributed to make our American political institutions what they are to-day. They are often spoken of as American principles. Though they did not originate in this country, they were here for the first time incorporated in the political programme of a great nation, and have been more completely realized here than in any other country.

The following dissertation was begun at the suggestion of Professor Max Lenz of the University of Berlin. It was originally my intention to limit my study to a consideration of the relation between the principles of the French Revolution as expressed in the Declaration of the Rights of Man and of the Citizen, and the principles of the American Revolution, as expressed in the

State papers of that time, especially in the Bills of Rights
of the individual States. The recent monograph of
Professor Jellinek of Heidelberg, entitled *Die Erklärung der Menschen- und Bürgerrechte,* translated into
English by Professor Farrand, does not seem to me to
be entirely satisfactory. Jellinek conveys the impression that the French Declaration of the Rights of Man
is a literal transcription of clauses contained in the Bills
of Rights of the American States. He fails to show how
the French people became acquainted with the principles contained in the American Bills of Rights. He
does not consider the discussions that took place in the
Constituent Assembly on the Declaration of the Rights
of Man. The very fact that these discussions lasted
longer than a month and that more than a score of
drafts were considered, proves, it seems to me, that a
literal transcription of the Bills of Rights is out of the
question. In tracing the genesis of the American Bills
of Rights, Jellinek overrates the influence of the struggle for religious toleration and undervalues the influence
of the theory of Natural Law.

Though differing from Professor Jellinek on many
points, I do not agree with the view taken by E. Boutmy
of the French Institute, who fiercely attacks Jellinek
in an article to be found in the *Annales des Sciences
Politiques* of the 15th of July, 1902, in which he argues
against any American influence whatever, attributing
the origin of the Declaration to Rousseau's influence,
and considering that document to be an exclusively
French production. Though acknowledging the fact
that the people of France, yes, of all the civilized countries of Europe, were well acquainted with the political
principles in question before the American Revolution
occurred, it seems to me that the American people first

proclaimed them in the form of a Declaration of Rights. The idea of a Declaration of the Rights of Man is specifically American.   There is no trace of such an idea in Rousseau or any other French writer.   Indeed, though the political theories the Declaration of the Rights of Man announces are to be found in Rousseau's writings, the idea of drawing up a declaration of individual rights with which the State shall not interfere, is hostile to the entire course of Rousseau's reasoning.   The members of the Constituent Assembly in discussing the principles of the Declaration constantly speak of American precedent and refer to the idea of such a declaration as coming from the New World.   It was because the well-known theories of the liberal writers seemed to have been triumphantly carried out in America, that the influence of the American Revolution upon Europe was so great.   The identical principles embodied in a political programme or declaration according to the manner of the Americans are prefixed to the first French constitution.   They were now scattered broadcast throughout Europe, and have contributed more than anything else to the transformation of society and of government along the lines of democracy and individual liberty.

It has been my purpose to trace the genesis and development of the political theories embodied in the Bills of Rights and in the French Declaration of the Rights of Man, and to show that these documents are the results of a long development. I have confined myself to an historical treatment of the subject.   For critical discussions I refer to Ritchie, *Natural Rights;* Willoughby, *The Nature of the State;* Lyman Abbott, *The Rights of Man;* Tiedemann, *The Unwritten Constitution of the United States;* Blum, *La Déclaration des*

Droits de l'Homme et du Citoyen, and to Bertrand's book on the same subject.

Thanks are due to Professor Max Lenz of the University of Berlin; to Professors J. W. Jenks and G. L. Burr of Cornell University; to Professor H. Morse Stephens of California University; and to President F. W. Gunsaulus of the Armour Institute of Technology, for suggestions and assistance in the preparation of this monograph.

September, 1903.

CONTENTS

INTRODUCTION

PART I

THE HISTORY AND DEVELOPMENT OF NATURAL LAW

CHAPTER I

ANTIQUITY AND THE MIDDLE AGES

CHAPTER II

THE SIXTEENTH AND SEVENTEENTH CENTURIES

CHAPTER III

THE EIGHTEENTH CENTURY

PART II

HISTORY OF THE DOCTRINE OF THE SOVEREIGNTY OF THE PEOPLE

CHAPTER IV

ANTIQUITY AND THE MIDDLE AGES

CHAPTER V

THE REFORMATION AND THE MONARCHOMACHISTS

CHAPTER VI

INDEPENDENTS, LEVELLERS, AND WHIGS

CHAPTER VII

ROUSSEAU

PART III

THE AMERICAN BILLS OF RIGHTS

CHAPTER VIII

THE POLITICAL INSTITUTIONS AND DOCTRINES OF THE AMERICAN COLONISTS

CHAPTER IX

THE AMERICAN REVOLUTION AND THE BILLS OF RIGHTS

PART IV

THE FRENCH DECLARATION OF THE RIGHTS OF MAN AND OF THE CITIZEN

CHAPTER X

FRANCE AND THE PRINCIPLES OF THE AMERICAN REVOLUTION

CHAPTER XI

THE CONSTITUENT ASSEMBLY AND THE DECLARATION OF THE RIGHTS OF MAN AND OF THE CITIZEN

CHAPTER XII

THE EFFECTS OF THE DECLARATION OF THE RIGHTS OF MAN

THE

EVOLUTION OF MODERN LIBERTY

INTRODUCTION

ONE of the most characteristic features of modern systems of government is the importance attached to individual liberty.

It is a fascinating as well as an important undertaking to trace the gradual evolution of modern liberty.

In the despotisms of the Orient personal liberty was entirely unknown, the life, actions, and property of the individual being completely at the mercy of the ruler.

The Greeks were familiar with the idea of liberty, but they confounded liberty with popular sovereignty. They possessed political liberty, but lacked personal freedom in the modern sense. In the Greek city-republics the citizens (excluding of course the slaves, who had no legal rights of any sort) made the laws, decided upon peace or war, elected magistrates, served as judges, and performed the duties resting upon them as partakers of the sovereignty of the State. But there was no sphere of life to which the interference of the government might not be extended. The despotism of the State prevented the growth of private rights. The Greek was primarily a citizen. He existed for the

State, not the State for him. The family life, the religion, the property, the time, yes, all actions of the individual, were under the control of the State. The Greek State ostracized Aristides and put Socrates to death.

To the Roman jurists we owe the distinction between public and private rights. "Public Right," they said, "serves the Roman State, Private Right, the interests of individuals." [1]

But among the Romans as among the Greeks we notice the same despotism of the State, the same confusion of sovereignty with liberty, which left the individual at the mercy of the State. The Roman citizen could not choose his own religion, as the persecution of the Christians shows. His speech, dress, manners, and actions were regulated by the censors. [2]

The feudal system of the Middle Ages obliterated the distinction between public and private rights by associating the possession of property with the exercise of sovereignty. Government was regarded, not as a public trust, but as private property. The possession of land carried with it jurisdiction over those dwelling upon the land. Each baron was lord over his domain. The State no longer existed. There were now only rights and duties between lord and vassal, which were based upon contract and were founded upon personal, not political, relations.

In modern times the distinction between private and public rights has again been emphasized. The results

---

[1] Justinian, *Institutes*, I. 1, 4.

[2] See Laurent, *Études sur l'histoire de l'humanité*, t. III (Rome), pp. 265 *et seq.;* Laboulaye, *L'État et ses limites*, pp. 7–17; Benjamin Constant, *De la Liberté des anciens comparée a celle des modernes* (*Cours de politique constit.*, t. II).

of this separation have been beneficial to both. While public rights and duties have become more majestic and authoritative on the one hand, private rights and duties on the other have become more sharply defined, and have been more widely extended and more effectively secured.

It is of great importance that the citizens of any State have a wide degree of individual liberty and that they be secure against an infringement of their liberties, not only on the part of other individuals, but also of the government. The degree of liberty and security a people enjoy will profoundly influence their progress. While degradation has been the rule in despotisms, the strongest and most progressive States have been those in which the sphere of individual liberty was large. The progress of the State is the progress of the individuals who are its members. The State lives in its citizens. Paternalism and arbitrary infringement of private rights weaken the State, because they paralyze the initiative and self-reliance of the individual. There is no more instructive example of this truth than the collapse of the Prussian State in 1806–1807.

The desire of personal freedom which is so characteristic of modern times is the product of two factors mainly; namely, of Christianity and of the nature of the modern, as distinguished from the ancient, State. While the religions of the ancient world were State religions, Christianity is the world religion. It appeals to the individual as a man, not as the member of a particular State or people. The Christian religion has no necessary relation to the State. The God of the Christian is no national deity. From the beginning the Christian religion spread to all parts of the world and found adherents among all peoples. Furthermore, Christianity enjoins that God must be obeyed rather than man. This implies that in case the State should command what is contrary to the law of God, the individual must resist. We thus have the individual rising up against the State; in exercising his religion he feels himself primarily a man, not a citizen. Here a sphere exists within which interference from any external source whatever is not tolerated. History shows in many examples how the attempt to control the consciences of men brought them into conflict with governments and made them conscious of the fact that they were, first of all, men, not citizens.

Then, also, the relation of the individual to the government is necessarily entirely different in the modern State—which comprises a large territory, often with many millions of inhabitants—from what it was in the ancient city-state. In the latter a greater unity was possible and consequently the control of the community over the individual was greater. The immediate control of the State over its citizens is likely to diminish as the extent of territory increases. Since it is impossible in a large State that the people exercise their sovereign power directly in a popular assembly, as they did in the city-state of antiquity, the powers of government must be delegated to one or a few persons who represent the State. This makes the distinction between the government and the people more evident. It is easier for the citizen of a very large State, especially of a monarchy, to become aware of his individuality and set himself over against the State, than was the case in the ancient city-state where each citizen had a share in the government, and where the distinction between individual and State was less manifest.

England led the way for all other countries of modern times in establishing and protecting the liberty of the individual. Magna Charta, the Habeas Corpus Act, and the Bill of Rights are classic examples of declarations of popular rights.

The rights enumerated in these documents are the rights to which Englishmen are entitled as English subjects. The people of the American colonies, Massachusetts and Virginia taking the lead, drew up declarations of certain rights to which they claimed to be entitled as men. These declarations were prefixed to the state constitutions under the name of Bills of Rights. While the political principles these bills contain were not entirely new and did not even originate on American soil, the idea of embodying them in a political programme (an idea of incalculable consequences, since it was in this form those principles exerted their greatest influence) was a distinctively American notion.

This idea was adopted by the French people during their great Revolution. The famous Declaration of the Rights of Man, drawn up by the Constituent Assembly in 1789 and prefixed to the Constitution of 1791, was in its consequences one of the most important instruments ever written. But it was written in conscious imitation of the Bills of Rights of the American States. The so-called principles of 1789 were, as it is one of the aims of this treatise to show, identical with the principles of the American Revolution.

In Germany the Parliament of Frankfort which met in 1849 and attempted prematurely to form a united empire drew up a similar declaration of fundamental rights. The constitutions of many civilized nations now contain similar declarations.

These declarations of the Rights of Man mark a new

era in the history of mankind. The humanitarian spirit underlies them—the conception that each individual citizen is entitled to the concern of the State; that his personality is of infinite worth and is a purpose of creation; that he should be recognized as an individual, as a man. The principles they contain became the creed of Liberalism. The nineteenth century was preeminently the century of Liberalism. Perhaps no other century witnessed greater and more numerous reforms and a greater extension of individual liberty. This century is marked by the abolition of slavery in all civilized countries, by the extension of the elective franchise, by the emancipation of woman, by the popularization of governments, and by countless other reforms.

Great as has been the influence of the declaration of the Rights of Man, this declaration must be regarded only as a factor of historical significance. The permanent value of such a declaration may be questioned. The rights known as Rights of Man are everywhere limited in actual practice and could not be carried out to their full extent without causing the subversion of the State. Thus many of the excesses of the French Revolution arose from attempts to realize an equality that will forever remain a dream. Men are not free and equal. Absolute freedom implies the absence of any restraint whatsoever and would destroy the foundation of the State and of Law. Law in its very nature implies compulsion. Equality pushed to its logical conclusion along economic lines would lead to communism. In every State there must be the distinction between the governing and the governed. The only equality among men is that before God, which is a religious principle; an equality of the formal outlines of human nature, these possessing in each individual a different content, which is a psycho-physiological principle; and equality before the law, which alone is a political principle. The right to life may be forfeited by criminal action, or the State may at need demand the sacrifice of life, as in time of war. The right of property may be abridged by the State. Freedom of speech, as the Duke of Wellington said, is a good thing except on board a man-of-war. None of the so-called Rights of Man are absolute rights. Public expediency may and does demand their restriction. The good of the State must ever go before that of the individual. The State alone can determine what rights its members shall enjoy. It knows them not as men, but as citizens. It cannot allow its citizens to appeal to inalienable natural rights, for in that case the individual, not the State, would be recognized as sovereign.

The Declaration of the Rights of Man was generated by the theories of Natural Law and of the sovereignty of the people. In order to understand its genesis the development of each of these theories must be traced.

The theory of Natural Law is one of the oldest conceptions in the history of human thought. For many centuries it held almost undisputed sway over the minds of men. It has been one of the most important conceptions ever entertained. In our own time Natural Law has fallen into disregard, partly because of the predominence of the historical method of scientific research and the distrust of philosophic speculation, partly because of the exaggeration of its own claims. It was Grotius, the founder of Natural Law in its modern sense, who first committed the mistake of regarding its principles as equally binding with, if not supe-

rior to, the positive laws of the State.[1] Positive law
it is not and cannot be. The State cannot permit its
subjects to appeal to laws which it has not itself issued.

The writers on Natural Law overlooked the fact
that ideal laws are very different from laws which are
actually enforced by the government. There is a great
difference between rights which individuals should,
in their own judgment, possess, and those which they
actually do possess. It was an error, also, to believe
that an ideal code of laws could be framed applicable
to all peoples at all times—laws founded in reason
alone. To have pointed out the fallacy of this conception, so predominent during the eighteenth century
is the merit of the German Historical School of Jurisprudence.

In 1814 Thibaut, a Heidelberg professor, wrote a
pamphlet addressed to the governments and people
of Germany, in which he urged that a general civil code
be drawn up for all Germany, thereby delivering the
people from a multitude of foreign, mostly Roman,
laws. He thought that civil laws were, as a whole,
founded in the human heart and in reason and would
seldom vary with circumstances.[2]

The famous Karl Fried. v. Savigny, professor at
Berlin and head of the German Historical School,
replied to Thibaut's pamphlet by his essay *On the
Vocation of Our Age for Legislation*, in which he maintained that the age was not prepared for the codification of existing laws, inasmuch as jurists lacked
the literary ability and the historical and systematic
understanding necessary for such work. He thought

[1] Stahl, *Philosophie des Rechts*, II. 2d ed., p. 186.
[2] Thibaut, *Über die Notwendigkeit eines allg. bürgerlichen
Rechts für Deutschland*, Heidelberg, 1814.

there was progress in the improvement of laws observable, and that it would therefore be possible to deprive future generations of great benefits by fixing present evils. Though not pronouncing absolutely against codification, Savigny's arguments were not favorable to an undertaking of the kind. The great merit of his essay is to have shown that laws are not evolved from reason, but are a part of, and an outgrowth from, the entire life of a people and the development of its character. As the language of a people, especially in early times, is the necessary product of the spirit of that people, so the laws are evolved from the character of the people according to the daily necessities of life and the popular convictions of right. In more advanced times jurists and law-givers may develop laws, but only in accordance with the national and historical development. They may cause germs already present to grow, but they cannot arbitrarily supply new content. The present is indissolubly linked with the past, from which it develops organically.[1]

Savigny established the predominence of the Historical School, which holds that there is no separate or isolated existence, but that every particular individuality is a member of a higher entity from which it develops. Though Montesquieu in many respects had anticipated Savigny, the latter took a much deeper view of the subject and secured almost general acceptance of his views. Montesquieu's influence was overshadowed by that of Rousseau. Savigny, however, put forth his views at a very favorable moment; namely, at a time when the magnificent work of Niebuhr had given new dignity to the study of history, when

[1] Savigny, *Beruf unserer Zeit für Gesetzgebung u. Rechtswissenschaft.*

Wolf applied historical criticism to the study of philology, at a time also when the stirring uprising against Napoleon and French domination had reawakened the self-consciousness of the European nations and had given them a new interest in the traditions of their past.

What Savigny and others accomplished in Germany was done for the English-speaking world by the Analytic School of Jurisprudence, whose chief representatives are Bentham and Austin. These jurists returned to the system of Hobbes, maintaining that sovereignty is unlimited, and bringing the theory of natural rights into discredit. Until quite recently Austin's views were scarcely questioned and his influence in England and America has been hardly short of the marvellous.

The theory of Natural Rights, which was such a potent factor in bringing about modern liberty, lost its hold upon the minds of men just at the time it had won its greatest triumphs. We are living in an age of democracy, but we are experiencing that democracy and liberty are not synonymous terms and that Demos may become a greater despot than any individual ruler. Demos seems to be rapidly becoming the Leviathan which is swallowing up all power. The liberty of the individual is being more and more restrained. Governmental interference is on the increase. The frequency with which injunctions are issued is becoming a most dangerous menace to individual liberty. The great aggregation of wealth in the hands of a few individuals has made these great capitalists masters over the destinies of millions, who are dependent upon them to a larger degree than the subjects of any despot are upon their ruler. We have discarded many of the principles which were once supposed to form the

very corner-stone of our republic. We have violated
the principle that government is based upon the consent
of the governed by subjugating the Philippines. We
have inflicted greater sufferings upon the Filipinos than
England was inflicting upon the colonists when they
threw off the hated yoke. Again, the heroic struggle
of the Boers for liberty awakened far less interest
among the nations than did the revolt of the American
colonists or the partitions of Poland over a century ago.
Power and wealth, rather than liberty, has become
the ideal of the nations, the United States among the
rest.

The theory of Natural Rights is an exploded theory,
no longer believed in by any scholar of note. There
can, however, be no doubt concerning the fact
that this conception, considering the consequences it
has had upon historical development, has been one of
the most important notions in the history of human
thought. The world would have been very different
but for the influence of this idea. The following are
some of the most important of its consequences:

1. Its influence upon Roman Law was very marked.
The Roman jurists regarded Natural Law as a model
system of perfect laws founded in Reason, to which
positive laws should as far as possible be made to conform. Natural Law was thus conducive in rendering
Roman Law more just, simple, and universal than it
would otherwise have been, and was one of the chief
reasons for the excellence of Roman Law.[1] "The historical significance of Roman Law consists above all
in the fact that it developed the abstract conception
of subjective law, that is, of the general and equal right
of the individual in private law. Therein lies what is

[1] Maine, *Ancient Law*, pp. 76, 77.

called the universal character of Roman Law. This does not mean that Roman Law is the eternal and absolute law for all peoples and ages, or even that a single one of the modern nations can rest satisfied with it, but that an essential and general element of law, which must exist in every system and must in a sense form its foundation, is therein developed in a manner and perfection that it contains the theoretical and practically applicable model for all times and nations." [1]

The French lawyers, too, were ardent students of Natural Law. They regarded it as the panacea for the multitudinous and conflicting laws of their own country, varying as they did with each province and municipality. [2]

The doctrine of Natural Law also influenced the legislation of Frederick the Great and the formation of the Prussian Landrecht, [3] as well as that of the Austrian Civil Code. The latter authorizes judges in cases where positive laws are inapplicable, to decide according to the "natural principles of law." Likewise, the commissioners who prepared a code for India, recommend that in cases not foreseen by law the judges decide "in the manner they deem most consistent with the principles of justice, equity, and good conscience." [4]

2. Natural law more than any other factor was operative in destroying the exclusive spirit which the Romans possessed and in generating the conception of a society of all human beings (*societas hominum*). [5] It is only after Stoic philosophy was introduced into

---

[1] Bruns, in *Holtzendorff, Encycl. d. Rechtswiss.*, p. 81.

[2] Maine, *Ancient Law.*

[3] Trendelenburg, *Naturrecht*, p. 3.

[4] Holland, *Jurisprudence*, p. 35.

[5] Voigt, *Die Lehre vom Jus Naturale der Römer*, I.

Rome, and the Romans adopted the Stoic conceptions of Natural Law and the equality of men, that the change from exclusiveness to cosmopolitanism took place—a change which was of immense influence on subsequent history. This helped to enable the Romans to form that wonderful system of world-empire which was never paralleled except by the English system of our own time. Greeks and Persians regarded conquered peoples as inferior barbarians. "The importance and mission of Rome," says Jhering, "from the standpoint of universal history, expressed in a word, is the victory of the idea of universality over the principle of nationality." [1] The Roman idea of universal empire dominated the entire history of the Middle Ages in Church and State.

3. Modern international law was by its founder, Grotius, built upon the principles of Natural Law, which are founded in reason and conscience. [2]

4. Natural Law has exerted great influence on private law, not only in systematizing it, but also in developing its content, because it concerned itself with the individual and the necessities of his nature. In opposition to the force of custom it ever emphasized the truths of justice, equity, and morals. [3]

5. The principles of Natural Law have exerted their greatest and crowning effect since the last quarter of the eighteenth century. They have transformed the structure of society and of the State by emphasizing the importance of individual liberty. The democratic spirit, which distinguishes the present era, is in no small

[1] *Geist d. röm. Rechts*, I. 1.

[2] Franck, *Réformateurs et publicistes, 17ième siècle*, 320; Bryce, *Studies in History and Jurisprudence*, 1901, Vol. II. pp. 167–69.

[3] Bryce, *op. cit.*, I. pp. 164–67.

degree the consequence of these principles. The Declaration of the Rights of Man, which is their classical expression, became the gospel of the masses. Goethe beautifully expresses in his *Hermann u. Dorothea* the feeling with which these ideas were received by the downtrodden classes of Europe:

"Denn wer läugnet es wohl, dass hoch sich das Herz ihm
  erhoben,
Ihm die freiere Brust mit edleren Pulsen geschlagen,
Als sich der erste Glanz der neuen Sonne heranhob,
Als man hörte vom Rechte der Menschen das Allen gemein ei,
Von der begeisternden Freiheit und der löblichen Gleichheit!
Damals hoffte jeder sich selbst zu genuegen; es schien sich
Aufzulösen das Band, das viele Länder umstrickte,
Das der Müssiggang und der Eigennutz in der Hand hielt."

PART I

THE DEVELOPMENT OF THE THEORY OF NATURAL LAW

THE DEVELOPMENT OF THE THEORY OF NATURAL LAW

CHAPTER I

ANTIQUITY AND THE MIDDLE AGES

BEFORE taking up the history of Natural Law it may be well to show how Natural Law differs from Positive Law on the one hand and from Moral Law on the other.

The Moral Law deals with such actions as tend to promote the interests of society or else to become detrimental to its welfare. Actions are morally right or wrong with reference to the individuals composing society, according as they are good or bad for society as a whole.

Positive Law includes the enactments of a particular government, enjoining certain actions upon the citizens and prohibiting others.

Laws of Nature follow from the nature of things and are not dependent upon any particular form of society or government. They are universal rules of action, discovered by natural reason. They form the ideal according to which men should fashion their actions.

Of these three classes of laws one is set down by society and forms the Right; the second is prescribed by the government and forms the Law; the third is discovered by reason as Good. While in any particu-

17

lar instance all three may coincide, there is the possibility of a conflict.[1]

The ancient Greeks were fond of speculating about the origin and meaning of Law. They first of all peoples developed the conception of Natural Law.

The germs of the conception of Natural Law are contained in the teaching of Heraclitus, whose influence reached its height about 460 B.C. The central thought of his system is the view that all things are in a state of incessant flow. Yet in this world of constant change there prevails an immutable and reasonable law to which all things are subject. This divine law or common reason illumines also the mind of man. All human wisdom is but an imitation of Nature and the Divinity.[2] This divine law should guide not only the individual, but also the State. Human laws are but the efflux of the divine laws.[3] Heraclitus is the first philosopher who believes in the Logos or rational world-soul—the eternal, all-comprehensive order of things. This conception of the Logos has dominated all subsequent philosophy down to the present.[4] Its bearing upon the theory of Natural Law is evident. Higher and more authoritative than the positive laws of the State are the precepts of Universal Reason; the laws which are right, not because they are commanded, but because they are founded in the nature of things.

The views of Heraclitus were attacked by Archelaus and by the Cyrenaican school, who held that right and

[1] Pollock, *Life of Spinoza*, pp. 325–27; Bryce, *Studies in History and Jurisprudence*, II. p. 120 *sq.*

[2] Sextus Empiricus, *Adv. Math.*, VII. 131, 133.

[3] Clem. Alex., *Strom.*, IV. 478b; Stobæus, *Serm.*, III. 84; Diog. Laert., IX. 2.

[4] Kuno Fischer, *Gesch. d. neueren Philos.*, *Einleitung*, 35–38.

wrong do not exist by nature, but are derived from human regulation and convention and are therefore variable.[1]

The Sophists, with whom a new epoch begins in Greek philosophy, return to the view of Heraclitus. While the early Greek philosophers did not question the validity of traditional morality as embodied in the positive laws of the State, the Sophists applied the critical spirit to accepted ethical and religious views. They discriminated between Natural and Positive Law. They taught that positive laws could not be obligatory because they varied so frequently. Positive laws are the arbitrary commands of those in power, framed by rulers for their own advantage. Only such laws can be considered natural or divine as are everywhere observed.[2] But though the Sophists recognized the idea of Natural Law it was not with the purpose of exalting Natural Right. They emphasized rather the subjectivity and relativity of truth. Their object was primarily to prove that existing laws and institutions were conventional and variable.

Socrates, Plato, and Aristotle are not unfamiliar with the conception of Natural Right, though they make little use of it. Socrates distinguishes between written laws which are founded upon custom and unwritten laws which are observed everywhere, being given to the human race by the gods and not framed by the hand of man.[3] Plato's doctrine of ideas, which are supposed to be the essence of things, is closely related

[1] Diog. Laert., II. 6. *Ibid.*, II. 93.

[2] Xenophon, *Memorabilia*, IV. 4, 14; 4, 19; Plato, *Republic*, I. 338 C.; Zeller, *Die Philos. d. Griechen*, 3. ed. I. 921–23; Ritchie, *Natural Rights*, 21–27.

[3] Xenophon, *Memorabilia*, IV. 4, 19; I. 4, 8, 9, 17.

to the conception of Laws of Nature. Aristotle refers
to universal law which conforms to the dictates of
Nature. He speaks of a universal sense of right which,
in a certain degree, all persons possess intuitively. He
refers to the famous utterance of Antigone, who declared
it to be right to bury Polynices, even though she
violated a royal command, because the burial was by
nature a deed of justice, the law enjoining it having
been in force, not for this or the next day, but forever,
no one knowing from whom it proceeded.[1] *Rhetoric*
I. 15 Aristotle speaks of the universal law as being
more absolutely just than the written law, and as
continuing in force forever, whereas written law frequently varies. *Rhetoric* I. 10, 3 he classifies laws as
general and peculiar, the latter being those by whose
written enactments men guide themselves, while the
former consist of those written rules which seem to
be recognized among all men. *Rhetoric* I. 15, 25
Aristotle again refers to universal principles of right.

In the works of the Stoics we find the theory of Natural Law fully developed. It was in accord with their
system of metaphysics. They believed that every
corporate entity is permeated by God, whom they conceived as the *Logos*, that is, as universal reason. They
believed God to be immanent in Nature—to be the
world-soul. According to their view God rules the
universe by means of a universal law.[2] This law they
believed to be the rule of action for every being in existence. The universe is one. The law which is immanent
in Nature and penetrates the being of man, is the absolute
standard, above space and time, independent of human
regulations—the absolute criterion of right and wrong.

[1] *Rhetoric*, I. 13; *Antigone* of Sophocles, 454.
[2] Cicero, *De Natura Deorum*, I. 14; Diog. Laert., VII. 148.

Every person with sound intellect can discover this law.[1] The end of life, the supreme ethical law, is the life according to Nature and the agreement of the human with the divine will.[2] The Stoics taught that law is derived from the common or general reason, its source being God or Nature, and not the will of man. It is Natural Law, and as such unchangeable; the same at all times and in all places.[3] The wise man will use this law as his guide in daily life and as a standard in framing other laws.[4] The divine law was exclusive law in the Golden Age. The depravity of human nature, however, makes positive human laws necessary.[5] Positive laws are not binding when they conflict with Natural Laws. The wise man is free from positive laws. He alone is just in the full sense of the word, since he alone obeys the divine law.[6] The Stoics believed self-preservation to be the chief instinct of all living creatures, the Law of Nature impelling them to ward off that which is injurious and seek that which is beneficial. The Stoics likewise taught that all men are equal and brethren, being citizens of the world and all alike, even slaves, children of the same God.[7] Stoicism anticipated many of the noblest teachings of Christianity. When Stoicism originated the Greek States were breaking up and were being merged in large empires. The distinction between Hellenes and barbarians was being obliterated. Cosmopolitanism was supplanting

[1] Diog. Laert., VII. 88, 128.

[2] Stobæus, *Ecl. Eth.*, II. 132.

[3] Diog. Laert., VII. 128.

[4] Cicero, *De Fin.*, III. 20, 67.

[5] Seneca, *Epist.*, XC.

[6] Diog. Laert., VII. 121, 122; Cicero, *De Fin.*, III. 20, 67; Stobæus, *Ecl. Eth.*, II. 206.

[7] Cicero, *De Finibus*, III. 19, 64; Plutarch, *Moralia*, I. 6.

nationalism. Stoicism was the fruit of this process. "The place of the particular laws of individual states is taken by the general law of the world; the place of members of a nation or city by the human race; the place of native land or city by the entire world." [1]

The Stoic doctrines found many adherents among the Romans, the most notable being Seneca and Cicero. The former teaches the brotherhood of mankind and the equality of all men, including the slaves, more clearly, perhaps, than any other writer of antiquity. The practical influence of these ideas made itself felt after these doctrines began to color Roman jurisprudence. [2]

Cicero adopts the conception of Natural Law from the Stoics, calling it *jus naturale,* or *jus naturae.* [3] He does not consider it as founded upon subjective opinion, but rather as constituted by Nature. It is implanted in reason, being unknown to animals. It forms a sort of conscience, demanding obedience to its dictates. [4] It is the eternal, general, and immutable standard for all lands and peoples, the expression of absolute truth, the highest wisdom of God. Its source is God, Nature, or Reason. It was law before being written. Though every person has some knowledge of it, there exist different degrees of possession. Full possession is the result of an earnest striving after the highest truth. [5] Natural Law is the standard to which positive laws should conform. The latter have for their purpose

[1] Ziegler, *Die Ethik der Griechen u. Roemer,* Bonn, 1881, p. 181.

[2] *Ibid.,* pp. 216, 217; Marquardt, *Handbuch d. roemisch. Alterthums,* VII. 1, 188.

[3] Cicero, *De Inventione,* II. 22, 65, 67; *De Rep.,* I. 5, 12, 17; III. 7, 11; V. 3.

[4] *De Leg.,* I. 10, 28; 5, 16; 7, 22; *De Inventione,* II. 22, 65.

[5] *De Leg.,* I. 6, 19; 17, 46, 47; *Pro Milone,* 4, 10; *De Rep.,* III.

the realization of the former.[1]   In reality positive laws
are but a small and limited circle compared with Natural Law, and but a faint copy of the latter.[2]   Cicero
does not consider the *jus naturale* legally binding upon
all men, that is, identical with the *jus gentium*, but only
potentially and theoretically obligatory; its only political use being to serve as a standard for positive laws
and as an ethical guide for human action.[3]

The *jus naturale* is entirely different from the *jus
gentium* of the Romans.   The latter was the law according to which foreigners were judged at Rome.   It was not
a code applying to States, as does modern international
law, but to individuals, and comprised laws that were
in common usage among various tribes and States.   It
was, in Cicero's time, the universal law of all free men.
The *jus gentium* was not held in great favor, but rather
regarded as a necessary evil.   It had not as yet been
formulated and systematized.   After the introduction
of Stoicism into Rome the *jus naturale* began to penetrate Roman jurisprudence and to influence the *jus
gentium*.   Inasmuch as the two systems had much in
common, they soon coalesced and then came to be
regarded as superior to political laws.[4]

With the adoption of the theory of Natural Law by
the Roman jurists a new phase began in its development.   These jurists did little in the way of broaden-
ing its speculative conception, but they applied the

[1] *De Leg.*, II. 24; 5, 13.

[2] *De Off.*, III. 17, 69.

[3] The influence of the idea of the Law of Nature upon Roman
jurisprudence is very ably discussed by Bryce in Vol. II. of his
Studies in History and Jurisprudence, pp. 128–157.

[4] Voigt, *Die Lehre vom jus naturale, aequum et bonum u. jus
gentium der Römer*, I. pp. 236, 237;   Maine, *Ancient Law*,
pp. 56, 57.

doctrine to positive law and made a practical application of its tenets.

The Stoic doctrine of the natural equality of all men, by coloring Roman jurisprudence, resulted in making laws more general, in weakening the force of race differences, and in improving the lot of the slaves. The latter were by Seneca and his Stoic successors regarded as human beings meriting brotherly treatment.[1]

There are two tendencies among the Roman jurists, the one represented by Ulpian, extending Natural Law to all living creatures, the other represented by Gaius, Paulus, and Marcian, limiting Natural Law to mankind alone.

Ulpian distinguishes two branches of Natural Law, the one including the entire animal world, the other embracing mankind only. The former rests upon instinct and applies to the union of the sexes, the procreation of kind, and the education of offspring.[2] It also stipulates that what is born out of legitimate matrimony follows the mother; that it is just to repel force by force; that all living things have a common ownership of the elements.[3] This is the view of Natural Law adopted by Justinian.[4] Ulpian defines theft and adultery as crimes against Nature.[5]

Gaius and Paulus differ from Marcian in their views on the Law of Nature (*lex naturae*), though all three agree as regards Natural Right or Justice (*jus naturale*). Gaius and Paulus maintain that each thing has an

---

[1] Ziegler, T., *Die Ethik der Griechen und Römer*, pp. 216, 217; Marquardt, *Handbuch des roemischen Altertums*, VIII. p. 188.

[2] *Inst.*, lib. I.

[3] Lib. 27 *ad Sabin.*; lib. 36 *ad Sabin.*; lib. 47 *ad Edict.*

[4] *Inst.*, I. 2, 1.

[5] Lib. 47 *ad Edict.*

essential character, which they call its nature, and that there is an objective intelligence or reason in this nature of things, the Natural Reason (*ratio naturalis*), whose product is Natural Law. This is Montesquieu's view when he defines laws as necessary relations derived from the nature of things. In this sense all beings have their laws.[1] Marcian, however, shares the Stoic view, regarding the Law of Nature as the Law of the entire Universe, extending its scope far beyond simple justice. According to this view, Natural Justice is only a part of Natural Law. Marcian considers God as dwelling in Nature, and as being the source of Natural Law, which is itself Reason, rather than merely a product of Natural Reason. Marcian holds, in common with Gaius and Paulus, that Natural Right is absolute justice applying to all human beings, even to slaves.[2] One of the most striking deductions that were made from Natural Law by the Roman jurists was that according to it all men are from the beginning born free.

Just as Natural Law and the *jus gentium* were fused, though at first distinct, so Natural Law was by the later Roman jurists identified with the principles of equity.[3]

Such were the views of the Greeks and Romans relative to Natural Law. What were the practical consequences of these views? Did they have any appreciable influence upon the evolution of liberty among the ancients? These are questions deserving consideration.

It will be remembered that the Laws of Nature were conceived of by Heraclitus, the Stoics, and their successors, as being derived from the essence or nature of

[1] *Esprit des Lois*, I. 1.

[2] Gaius, *Institutes*, 3, 119.

[3] Voigt, *Die Lehre v. jus naturale, aequum, bonum u. jus gentium d. Römer*, I. 350.

things and as being distinct from the positive laws of the State. These Laws of Nature, though not enforced by material force of any sort, are morally binding upon the individual; indeed, they form the supreme standard of action; all other laws ought to be tested as to whether or not they conform to the Laws of Natural Justice, and positive laws conflicting with them, so the Stoics held, are not to be obeyed. Natural Law thus limits the omnipotence of the State. The despotism of the State was, as we have seen in a previous connection, the chief hindrance to the growth and development of individual liberty in the ancient world. Unfortunately, Natural Law was still in too rudimentary a stage to be of much influence upon the genesis of private rights. It had not yet formulated any specific rights, like that of freedom of conscience, of speech, and other individual rights, to which the citizen should be entitled. The ideas of the natural liberty and equality of all men do, however, seem to have had considerable effect upon Roman laws in the way of rendering them more equal and just than they might otherwise have been.

It is important, nevertheless, that the conception of Natural Law was formed by the ancients, for, after subsequently receiving a wider development, it became in modern times a factor in the enfranchisement of the individual whose importance can scarcely be overestimated.

While the ancients believed in the sovereignty of the State, the German barbarians, who overthrew the Roman empire, believed in the sovereignty of the individual. Our modern liberty goes back to them primarily. Their devotion to personal liberty was so great that it was inimical to all government which was not self-imposed. They hated cities, which the ancients regarded as essential to a complete life, and lived in the forests. They chose their own chieftains. They regarded the payment of taxes as a sign of serfdom. No one can read the *Germania* of Tacitus and the other memorials of this people without being struck by this excess of the individualistic spirit. Thus was the Greek and Roman view of sovereignty supplanted by the German idea of liberty. It must not be supposed that the feudal system annihilated individual freedom. On the contrary, feudalism was individualism unrestrained; feudalism was the product of the Teutonic love of liberty and hatred of control. But this almost uncontrolled liberty was for the upper classes alone. Unfortunately, the primitive economic equality had been undermined by inequalities in the possession of land, which favored the growth of an aristocracy. The depression of multitudes to serfdom went on apace. These serfs were but the property of their lords. In England the primitive liberty of Teutonic times was soon restored by abolishing serfdom and extending to the lower classes the liberty which they had lost. A like development might have resulted on the Continent but for the revival of the Roman notion of the omnipotence of the State, or rather of the ruler of the State, which was a consequence of the revival of the Roman law, from whose influence England escaped. But even on the Continent the Teutonic individualistic spirit broke out with fresh fervor during the great religious Reformation of the sixteenth century, which was essentially a product of the Germanic spirit united with the spirit of primitive Christianity.[1]

[1] On the ancient Germans see Tacitus, *Germania*, esp. c. 7, 11, 12, 13, 16; Cæsar, *Commentarii de bello gallico*, IV; Gregory of

This brings us to the consideration of another factor of importance in the genesis and development of modern liberty; namely, Christianity.

Christianity plainly teaches the equality of all men before God, a notion which has again and again proved to be a levelling force to which no other can be compared. The words of Christ, " Render unto Cæsar the things which are Cæsar's, and unto God the things that are God's," [1] as well as the words of the apostles, " We ought to obey God rather than men," [2] are a declaration of war against the ancient view of the omnipotence of the State. Here is a sphere; namely, whatever concerns conscience, within which the interference of the State will not be tolerated. The individual is thereby enfranchised. The Roman emperors did not fail to recognize the meaning of this; therefore they adopted the policy of bitter persecution. To acknowledge freedom of conscience would have meant to consent to a limitation of sovereignty.

A third factor in the evolution of individual liberty, and one of great importance, is the influence of Natural Law, which passes from Roman jurisprudence into the literature of the Middle Ages, and from thence into modern thought. From Natural Law the creed of modern liberty and democracy develops.

Tours, *Historiae Francorum lib. X;* Fredegar, *Chronicon;* Beda Venerabilis, *Historia eclesiastica gentis Anglorum;* Grimm, *Deutsche Rechtsalterthuemer;* Eichhorn, *Deutsche Staats- u. Rechtsgeschichte;* Waitz, *Deutsche Verfassuungsgeschichte;* Sickel, *Der Deutsche Freistaat;* Stubbs, *Constitutional History of England;* Brunner, *Deutsche Rechtsgeschichte;* Thudichum, *Der altdeutsche Staat;* Roth, *Gesch. d. Benefizialwesens;* Laurent, *Études sur l'histoire de l'humanité,* t. V.; Laboulaye, *L'État et ses limites.*

[1] Matthew xxii. 21.

[2] Acts v. 29.

The Christian religion renders this conception more acceptable and plausible to the Middle Ages than it would otherwise have been, because it possesses a conception analogous to that of Natural Law. Thus Paul speaks of the Gentiles as doing by nature the things commanded by the law written in their hearts.[1]

Nor were the church fathers unfamiliar with this notion. Irenæus, in describing the divine plan of educating the human race, holds that God's purpose is to be carried out by means of the Natural Laws implanted in man's nature, to which he owes obedience. He believes that the patriarchs were already familiar with these laws. During the sojourn in Egypt they were forgotten. God, therefore, had them inscribed in the Decalogue. Christ did not abrogate the old law, but only expanded it, retaining all the Laws of Nature.[2] Tertullian aims to show that divine law is based upon reason and that rational laws only are worthy of regard. Custom is but the interpreter of reason. In God all things are alike natural and rational. As God did not foresee, dispose, or ordain anything without reason, so He wishes that nothing should be treated or understood without reason.[3] Ambrose speaks of the " true law, not engraved upon tablets or on stone, but impressed upon the mind and the senses; wherefore the wise man is not under the law, but is a law unto himself, inasmuch as the work of the law is written on his heart by a natural stylus and with a certain inscription." [4] Chrysostom says: " From the beginning of things, when God created

[1] Romans ii. 14, 15.

[2] Irenæus, *Adv. haer.*, IV. 13, 1; 14, 3; 15, 1; 16, 5.

[3] Tertullian, *De corona mil.*, 4; 10; *Apologia*, 4; *Adv. Marc.*, I. 23.

[4] Ambrosius, *Enarr. in Ps. civ.*

man, He implanted within him the natural law. And what is this natural law? Conscience has revealed it to us and has given us the notion of right and wrong." [1] St. Augustine holds that law, which is supreme reason, must by every thinking person be seen to be eternal and immutable. [2]

The *Decretum* of Gratian, which appeared in 1150 and was one of the chief works on Canon Law throughout the Middle Ages, begins with a consideration of Natural Law. It declares divine law to rest upon human nature, while human laws rest upon custom.

" Natural Right is common to all nations because it rests upon the instinct of nature, not upon ordinance, as the union of male and female; the succession and education of children; the common possession of all things and the equal liberty of all men; the acquisition of whatever is taken in the sky, on land or sea; the restitution of everything given in trust, or of money committed to charge; the repulsion of force by force. For these and similar things were never held to be unjust, but to be natural and equal." [3]   Natural Right differs from custom and ordinance. While by the former all things are common to all, by the latter this is mine, that another's. By its dignity Natural Right prevails over custom and ordinance. Whatever is contrary to it in custom or ordinance should be regarded as null and void. [4]

From the *Decretum* of Gratian the conception of Natural Law passes into the literature of scholasticism. We find this theory fully explained by Thomas Aquinas

[1] Chrysostom, *Oratio ad pop. Antiochenum*, xii. 9.

[2] *De libero arbitrio*, Ch. 6.

[3] *Decretum Gratiani*, Ed. Friedberg, I. 1.

[4] *Decretum Gratiani*, I. 8.

(1225–1274), the greatest teacher of the Middle Ages. Aquinas distinguishes four kinds of laws: 1. The eternal law,[1] constituting the plan according to which God created the universe and governs it; 2. Natural Law,[2] which is a derivation from the eternal law, being the impression of the divine light in man; 3. Human laws,[3] which are deductions from the precepts of Natural Law, designed to regulate certain affairs more particularly; 4. The divine law,[4] which is revealed in the Scriptures.[5]

Aquinas teaches that though there exists no universal earthly state, nor universal human law, there is a universal divine law, which is the highest reason, existing in God, and which is the source of all other laws. Natural Law is not in its essence different from the divine law, but is simply that part of the latter which is known to rational beings. Implanted in man at his creation, it has ever since survived in the human conscience. Man learns this Natural Law directly through the light of Natural Reason. But while man knows the divine law only in part, God knows it in its entirety. Natural Law existing in the nature of things, is not instituted by any human authority, and is unchangeable. According to this law things occur by necessity, while those actions with which human laws deal are performed because commanded. Whoever obeys the dictates of Natural Law is a virtuous man, for virtuous actions are agreeable to nature, while criminal or vicious actions are contrary to nature and reason.[6] The sum and sub-

---

[1] Thomas Aquinas, *Summa* 1a, 2 ae, xci. 1, 2, 3, *lex aeterna.*

[2] *Lex naturalis.*

[3] *Leges humanae.*

[4] *Lex divina.*

[5] *Summa* 1a, 2 ae, xci.

[6] *Ibid.,* xciv.

stance of Natural Law is to do right and avoid doing wrong.

Aquinas distinguishes three branches of Natural Law, according as it applies to all substances, to all animals, or to mankind only.   " First," says Aquinas, " there is in man an inclination toward that which is good by nature, which he shares with all substances, and according to which each substance strives after self-preservation.   As a result of this inclination those things pertain to Natural Law by which the life of man is preserved and injuries warded off.   Then there is in man an inclination toward other things more especially according to Nature, which he shares with other animals; in accordance with which tendency those things are according to the Law of Nature, which Nature teaches to all animals, of which class are the conjunction of male and female, the education of offspring, and the like.   Finally, there dwells in man an inclination toward that which is good according to the nature of reason, which tendency is confined to man; thus, man has a desire to know the truth concerning God, and a longing to live in society; wherefore those things pertain to Natural Law which apply to this inclination, to which class belong the injunction that man should shun ignorance, that he should not offend his associates, and other matters of like nature." [1]

Aquinas maintains that no government can command what is contrary to Natural Law without becoming tyrannical.   This amounts to an acknowledgment of the limitation of sovereignty.   He regards it as the duty of the ruler to secure the common welfare.[2]   But there is little in his system of political philosophy that

[1] *Summa*, 1a, 2 ae, xciv. 2.
[2] *De Regimine Principum*, I. 2, 3.

savors of individual freedom. Though he opposes the tyranny of temporal rulers, he maintains the infallibility and absolute power of the pope—a despotism which is worse, if anything, than that of temporal princes.

CHAPTER II

THE tyranny of the Church, as well as of the feudal lords, prevented the development of individual liberty during the Middle Ages, except so far as the privileged classes were concerned.

As a result of the intimate union between Church and State which had been brought about by Constantine, the temptation to employ the power which had now been placed at her disposal became too great for the Church to withstand. The Christian faith, which had hitherto spread by virtue of its inherent strength, was now extended by the employment of force. Heresy was suppressed as the worst of crimes. Freedom of thought was extinguished. The religion which had at its origin been so remarkable a factor in promoting the enfranchisement of the individual, became, during the Middle Ages, an instrument of his enslavement. There is but one qualification which must be made to this statement: the Church, though inimical to liberty, did endeavor to secure as large a degree of equality as possible, by working for the abolition of serfdom.

Not only had the influence of Christianity as a factor in the evolution of individual liberty been diminished, but the other factor in this process, namely, the individualism of the Teutonic peoples, had likewise failed to accomplish what it might have, had not the growth of feudalism weakened its force. Feudalism

34

divided mediæval society into sharply separated classes. The individual was rated as a member of this or that caste, not as a man. While the lords enjoyed a freedom which was almost unrestrained, the serfs were bound to the soil, being deprived completely of freedom. In England the effects of feudalism were gradually obliterated. The privileged classes joined hands with the lower classes against the king. As a result of this union not only was the king's power restricted, but liberty was extended to the common people. The process of elevating the lower classes went on without interruption in England. Magna Charta, as early as 1215, enumerated and guaranteed the liberties of the English people. Parliament, especially after the establishment of the House of Commons in 1265, acted as a check upon the royal power. Upon the Continent a different development took place. In France, the kings eventually succeeded in curbing the nobles with the assistance of the common people, especially of the cities. But only limited powers were conferred upon the municipalities, while little was done to emancipate the serfs. While the political power of the great nobles was at last broken, their feudal privileges were left almost untouched. Not until the Revolution was feudalism finally abolished in France. The French kings had succeeded in building up a despotic power. Undoubtedly they were aided in this by the victory of the Roman spirit of centralization and sovereignty over the Germanic spirit of individualism and liberty. The revival of Roman Law and the insistence of the legists upon the doctrine, "What the king wills has the force of law," [1] operated strongly

[1] Quod principi placuit, legis habet vigorem, Justinian, *Institutes*, I. 2, 6.

as a force in building up a royal despotism. In Italy the establishment of tyrannies in the cities, which had enjoyed a brilliant, but short-lived, existence as republics, likewise rendered individual liberty nugatory. In Germany the growth of a strong central power, such as in France, did not take place. The nobles of Germany succeeded in appropriating the powers of government in their domains, and, except in case of the cities, many of which were practically republics with a free and prosperous population, the lower classes in Germany were kept in complete thraldom.

However, both the individualism of Christianity and of the German nature experienced a revival during the great religious Reformation of the sixteenth century. The great reformers aimed to return to primitive Christianity and revive its spirit. This movement was in its effects a revolution of the most far-reaching consequences. The fact that it was a product of the Germanic spirit is evinced plainly enough by its having taken hold of the Germanic peoples of northern Europe alone. These are also the nations whose inhabitants possess the widest degree of liberty to-day. Although the political consequences of the Reformation did not manifest themselves at once, although Luther, Calvin, and others preached the doctrine of passive obedience to the powers that be, and had but little sympathy for political questions or for civil liberty, the results of this movement upon the enfranchisement of the individual could not but show themselves sooner or later. For what the reformers demanded for themselves was freedom of conscience. They attacked the principle of authority. It is true they put the authority of the Bible in the place of that of the pope, but this altered the case materially. The Bible is a book that must be interpreted. Each individual is likely to form his own opinion of its teachings. Toleration must follow as a result of the principle of Protestantism. This did not result until experience demonstrated the impossibility of controlling the consciences of men. With the acknowledgment of freedom of conscience the individual is practically enfranchised. The sovereignty of the State once limited in this respect, will still further be limited by the granting of other personal rights with which the State must not interfere.

But what of the theory of Natural Law, which is the theoretical side of this process? With the advance of education the influence of theories is intensified. Natural Law furnishes the programme of the individual rights for which the people of the civilized countries of western Europe contend. To follow its development becomes, therefore, a task of great importance.

Melanchthon, the friend and helpmate of Luther, the "preceptor of Germany," deserves the credit of having introduced the conception of Natural Law into modern thought. He said that in civil affairs he looked to Cicero rather than to the Scriptures. It is likely that he adopted his views concerning the Law of Nature from Cicero. Melanchthon divides laws into natural and positive. The former are rays of divine light in the human soul and are unchangeable, while the latter, founded upon possible, not upon necessary, grounds, are variable.[1] Natural Law forms the standard of justice among men, though not sufficient to the justice of God. Since man has no perfect knowledge of it, and it does not reveal the nature of God, it is best to return to faith. It is more convenient to extract the Laws of Nature from the Decalogue, where

[1] *Epitome philosophiae moralis*, p. 97.

God has announced them with perfect clearness, than to rely upon man's reason.

Melanchthon failed to deduce positive law from Natural Law, though he asserted the priority of the latter. This was done by Oldendorp, a syndic and professor at Rostock. Oldendorp discriminates clearly between Natural Law, the law of nations, and civil law, and attempts to construct a complete system of Natural Law.[1] But, like Melanchthon, he shrinks from using reason alone, and therefore falls back on the Decalogue as the clearest exposition of Natural Law.

The attempt to deduce Natural Law methodically from human nature, without recurring to the Scriptures, was first made by Hemming, a professor at Copenhagen.[2] Winkler, a professor at Leipzig, likewise wrote an extensive treatise on Natural Law.[3]

Albericus Gentilis, professor of Law at Oxford University, wrote a treatise *On the Right of War*,[4] which in many respects anticipated the celebrated book of Grotius. Grotius had a great admiration for Gentilis, and repeatedly acknowledged his indebtedness to him. Gentilis regards the Law of Nature as being concealed in the recesses of nature and as forming a part of divine law. Though darkened in many particulars, it may nevertheless become known to man. According to Gentilis, Natural Law is discovered spontaneously and is more powerful than any other law.

---

[1] Oldendorp, *Juris naturalis, gentium et civilis eisagoge*, 1539.

[2] Hemming, *De lege naturae apodictica methodus*, 1562.

[3] Winkler, *Principiorum juris libri quinque*, 1615.

[4] Gentilis, *De jure belli libri III.*, 1612. Extracts from the works of the five last mentioned writers are given in Kaltenborn, *Die Vorlaeufer des Hugo Grotius*, and also in Hinrichs, *Geschichte der Rechts- und Staatsprincipien*, Vol. I.

It is an instinct of Nature and immutable. All men, he maintained, are members of the same world and related to each other. Nature made men sociable and implanted in them a mutual love for each other. By nature there is no war. An eternal law, born with man, induces him to defend himself and what belongs to him.[1]

In 1594 appeared the first four books of Hooker's *Ecclesiastical Polity*, the first of which contains his exposition of Natural Law. Hooker defines a law in general as a rule to goodness of operation. There are various kinds of laws: the divine law which God has set down to follow in His works; the law of natural agents that work either by simple necessity or of their own accord; the law which the angels obey; the law guiding voluntary agents, dictated by reason; the positive laws for multitudes and political societies; the laws of each nation; those concerning the fellowship of them all, and finally the law which God has revealed.[2] The Law of Nature is the law which men have by natural reason discovered as a guide in their actions. Its principles are, and always have been, known to all men without divine revelation. Every person may not be able to formulate each particular law of Nature, but when once proposed he will recognize it as such. Natural Laws are eternal. What all men have at all times believed Nature herself must have taught. Nature's voice is God's instrument. The general and perpetual voice of men is the sentence of God Himself. The general persuasion of mankind is therefore the proof of right. Having a natural knowledge of the Laws of

[1] *De jure belli libri III.*, lib. I; Hinrichs, *Gesch. d. Staats- u. Rechtsprinc.*, Vol. I. pp. 53–60.
[2] Ch. 8, 16.

Nature men consider themselves as having originated these laws, but they have only discovered them.[1]   From these self-evident principles the moral duties we owe to God and man can be deduced without great difficulty. The Laws of Nature bind men absolutely, as men, even though they have no settled fellowship nor have ever agreed as to what to do and not what not to do.[2]   The observance of the Law of Nature results in great good. So long as each thing performs the work that is natural to itself, it preserves itself and other things.   Great injury must inevitably result, if man, the noblest creature in the world, yes, himself a world, transgresses the Law of Nature.[3]   Natural Laws are either mandatory, showing what must be done; permissory, declaring what may be done; or admonitory, stipulating what is most convenient to be done.[4]   The various mandates which Natural Reason teaches apply to our duty toward God and man.   Natural Reason teaches the main precepts of religion and morality.   It teaches men to love one another.   The desire of man to be loved by those who are naturally his equals imposes upon each person the duty of treating others as he wishes to be treated himself.   From the natural equality of men other principles of Natural Law result of which no man is ignorant, viz.: "Because we would take no harm we must do none"; "Since we would not in anything be extremely dealt with, we must avoid all extremity in our dealings"; "We are to abstain from all violence and wrong."[5]

[1] *Eccles. Pol.,* Bk. I. Ch. 8.
[2] *Ibid.,* Ch. 10.
[3] *Ibid.,* Ch. 9.
[4] *Ibid.,* Ch. 8.
[5] *Ibid.*

Because of the corruption of human nature, says Hooker, the Law of Nature requires some form of government. To take away all forms of public government in the world would be apparently to overthrow the whole world. While obedience to Natural Law is demanded by conscience, positive human laws constrain men by force and punish transgression. Natural Laws are valid in their very nature, while positive laws become obligatory only after public approbation has made them so.[1]

Hooker gave a complete exposition of Natural Law thirty-one years before Grotius, the great Dutch writer, who is by many given the credit which belongs to Melanchthon, Gentilis, and especially Hooker. The famous work of Grotius, *On the Right of Peace and War*, was not published until 1625.

Hooker's *Ecclesiastical Polity* is one of the few really great books in the world's literature. It contains, either explicitly or in germ, all the leading ideas of the eighteenth century.

By declaring the doctrines of religion to be founded in nature Hooker prepared the way for English deism. By stating that the principles of human conduct are likewise founded in nature he became the forerunner of the brilliant English school of writers on ethics.[2] This rationalistic spirit is applied by Hooker to every line of human thought. Hooker does not rely upon tradition to prove his assertions. He does not quote the fathers or the schoolmen. He establishes his points by argument, by the use of reason. That signifies a rupture with scholasticism. It means that for the first time the principle upon which modern learning rests is used fearlessly.

[1] *Ecclesiastical Polity*, I. 10.   [2] *Ibid.*

It was only natural that this rationalistic spirit should be applied by Hooker to politics and law as well. Reason, not tradition, is made the test which is applied to political institutions.   The laws founded in reason are the Laws of Nature.

Joined with this theory of Natural Law in Hooker's work, we find the doctrine of the sovereign power of the community, the contract theory, the doctrine of the separation of powers, which is often supposed to have been first announced by Montesquieu, and other ideas which were subsequently put forth by Sidney, Locke, and other writers of the seventeenth and eighteenth centuries.

It was only incidentally, as it were, that Hooker had expressed his views on questions of Natural Law and politics, his chief object being to vindicate the ecclesiastical polity of England. A writer to whom these questions were of prime importance was the famous Dutch scholar Hugo Grotius, whose monumental work *On the Right of Peace and War* [1] exerted a wonderful influence over his time, since it laid the foundations of a new science, modern international law. It is also the first complete and systematic treatise on Natural Law. Grotius was a man of the same stamp as Hooker. Though quoting extensively from ancient and mediæval authors, he employed reason in constructing his system, using tradition simply for the purpose of illustrating his arguments. It was he who first separated politics from theology. His great reputation secured a general predominance of his views. From his time on, down to the nineteenth century, almost every writer on government uses the conception of Natural Law. There was a rupture with custom and tradition. Reason was now applied to law and politics.

[1] *De Jure Belli ac Pacis*, Paris, 1625.

Grotius distinguishes between natural and voluntary laws. The latter have their origin in a will which may be human or divine. Human voluntary law is of three classes: civil law, which proceeds from the civil power ruling the commonwealth; the law of less extent, that does not issue from the civil power, though dependent upon it, and that contains the precepts of fathers, masters, and such like; finally, the law of larger extent, which is the law of nations.[1] Voluntary divine law has its rise from the will of God. It was thrice given to mankind: after the creation of man, after the Flood, and in the teachings of Christ. Natural Law is the dictate of right reason showing moral turpitude or moral necessity to be in an act, by its agreeing or not agreeing with rational nature, and therefore with the precepts of the Author of nature, God. Natural Law commands or forbids what is by itself, or in its own nature, due or unlawful; while divine law makes any act lawful or unlawful simply because it is commanded or prohibited by God. Natural Law is immutable. God Himself could not change it. It would exist even if God did not exist.[2]

Grotius adopts the division of law into voluntary and natural from Aristotle. He quotes also the Roman jurists, Cicero, the fathers, and Aquinas. But Grotius introduces a new principle into Natural Law, namely, the social principle. He considers it to be natural for man to seek a life spent in community with his fellow men, and considers this social instinct (*appetitus socialis*) as the source of Natural Law.[3] "This . . . concern for society in conformity with human reason is the source of that law which is properly called by such a name: to which pertains the abstinence from another's

[1] *De Jure Belli ac Pacis*, I. 1.   [2] *Ibid.*, I. 1.   [3] *Ibid.*, Proleg.

property and restitution thereof if any person possesses anything belonging to another; the obligation of fulfilling promises; the reparation of injury done by our fault, and the infliction of punishment according to desert." [1] But Grotius is not consistent in the use of the social principle as the source of Natural Law. He declares Natural Law also to be the dictate of right reason. He considers reason to be the true nature of man. Man has an inclination to search for reason in all things, so also in law. Reason discerns what agrees with human nature and what does not; what is in accord with the social relations of men and what is not.

Natural Law, according to Grotius, can be proved *a priori* and *a posteriori*. The former method is more subtle, the latter more popular. The former demonstrates the agreement or disagreement of a thing with the rational and social nature of man, the latter shows what is common to all nations. A universal effect requires a universal cause. Beliefs prevailing among all nations must have a common origin. [2]

In opposition to Carneades and others who declared that there is no universal standard of justice and that the only test of law is its utility, Grotius maintained that there is an essential justice and morality, founded in the nature of things. He affirmed that justice and right should rule among nations and direct both peace and war.

Grotius defines the State as the perfect union of free men for the purpose of enjoying the protection of the Law and promoting the common utility. [3] He does not say as explicitly as do his successors that the State is formed by compact; but inasmuch as he deduces all civil law from compact, he may well be regarded as hav-

[1] *De Jure Belli ac Pacis*, I. 8.   [2] *Ibid.*, I. 1.   [3] *Ibid.*, I. 1, 14.

ing introduced the compact theory into modern thought. He regards private property as having arisen from compact. If any individual has acquired property or any right in a lawful manner, it is contrary to Natural Right to deprive him of it. If a ruler does so, nevertheless, he should make restitution, for he has acted contrary to the true right of the subject. Grotius treats in one of the chapters of his book [1] of those things belonging to all men and distinguishes between what is ours according to the common right of men (*communi hominum jure*) and what belongs to us by our special right. This distinction later became that between inherent, or fundamental rights, and acquired rights, and anticipated the term " Rights of Man " of the eighteenth century.

Like all who believe in the compact theory of government, Grotius regards the State as an aggregation of individuals, not as a unit, or organism, or State in the true sense. He emphasizes the individual rather than the State. Grotius was a life-long champion of individual liberty. While the fierce religious conflict was raging in Holland between the Arminians and Gomarists, he advocated religious toleration and throughout his life endeavored to conciliate religious factions. A born republican, he believed in equality. He asserted that the life, limbs, and freedom of each individual belong to himself alone. [2] He was untrue to his own principles, however, when he said that an individual might alienate his liberty and even deliver himself into slavery. [3]

John Selden (1584–1654), one of the most learned

----

[1] *De Jure Belli ac Pacis*, II. 2.   [2] *Ibid.*, I. 2, 1.

[3] *Ibid.* On Grotius, see Hinrichs, *Gesch. d. Rechts- u. Staatsprinc.*, pp. 60–107; Bluntschli, *Gesch. d. neueren Staatswiss.*, 1881, pp. 88–100.

and celebrated jurists and antiquarians of his time, called by Grotius the "glory of England," endeavored to prove that reason is not the source of Natural Law. According to him reason is too uncertain and inconstant and lacks sufficient authority to make the precepts of Natural Law obligatory.[1] He believes in the existence of Natural Laws, however, and regards them as universal laws, the laws of the world, as God's way, word, mandate, and footprint. He says they will always remain firm and immutable. While denying that they were originally written in the conscience of men and discoverable by reason alone, he asserts that they were supernaturally revealed to the first generation of men; namely, the Noachids, and were then spread among the Greeks, Romans, and other peoples of antiquity. These primitive laws revealed to the sons of Noah he regards as a complete and wonderful résumé of all the laws and duties of society. What makes Selden's views still more strange is that he finds these laws in a book so little known as the Talmud. These prime Laws of Nature prohibit the worship of idols and of other gods, save the one Supreme Being; blasphemy; the spilling of human blood; cruelty to animals; and enjoin respect of marriage and the ties of blood, of property, and of justice, as well as the laws of one's country.[2]

In opposition to Salmasius, a countryman of Grotius, who had written a defence of Charles I. and endeavored to prove that kings have absolute power by divine and Natural Right, John Milton affirmed that the punish-

---

[1] *De Jure Naturali et Gentium juxta disciplinam Ebraeorum*, 1640, Lib. I. cap. 7.

[2] Hinrichs, I. pp. 107–114; Franck, *Réformateurs et publicistes de l'Europe, 17e siècle*, pp. 86–113.

ment of tyrants is according to the Law of Nature, and that by the same Law the right of the people is superior to that of princes. He says that by the Law of Nature the people instituted government for the preservation of their liberty, peace, and safety. By appealing to the Law of Nature he considered things according to their nature as discovered by reason.[1] Milton says " that all men were naturally born free, being the image and resemblance of God Himself." [2] In his *Areopagitica* Milton demands liberty of the press as the foundation of popular and personal liberty and the development of human thought. He was an ardent advocate of liberty of conscience, " which above all other things ought to be to all men dearest and most precious." [3] Individual liberty never had a more devoted champion than John Milton. He advocated the separation of Church and State. His principles were thoroughly republican. He was the forerunner of American ideas of government and personal freedom.

With Hobbes Natural Law assumes quite a different character. It becomes intimately associated with a state of nature. While Grotius believed man to be a social creature, Hobbes declared man to be naturally selfish and anti-social. He says that by nature men are equal as regards qualities of soul and body,[4] and that inequality was introduced by civil law. On account of this natural equality each person hopes to obtain that which he desires. When several desire the same thing one becomes the enemy of the other and seeks to subdue or remove the other. Though all are

[1] *Defence of the People of England*, 1651.

[2] *Tenure of Kings and Magistrates*, 1649.

[3] *The Ready and Easy Way to Establish a Free Commonwealth.*

[4] *De Cive*, I. 3; *Leviathan*, cap. 13.

equal, each thinks himself greater than the other and seeks to obtain preeminence.[1] Each desires his own good and seeks to avoid what is harmful to him. It is a right of Nature that every man protect his life and limbs to the extent of his ability.[2] This right of self-protection gives the right to employ all means necessary to attain the end desired. Nature gives the right to all things, the bodies of men not excepted. The natural state is therefore a state of war of all against all.[3] So long as this state continues there is no security. The reasons for desiring peace are fear, especially of a violent death, the desire for the objects necessary to live well, and the hope of obtaining these by industry. Peace is suggested by certain articles called Natural Laws which are derived from reason. These laws are precepts by which each person is prohibited from doing that which tends to his injury. They are eternal and immutable. What they forbid can never be commanded, and what they enjoin can never be forbidden. They are one with the moral law.[4] They are theorems, not the commands of a ruler. Hobbes deduces them from one another mathematically.

The first Law of Nature, says Hobbes, enjoins that peace be sought and enjoins upon each individual that he divest himself of his right to all things and content himself with the same liberty others have. Otherwise strife would continue endlessly.[5] Rights are ceded by simple renunciation, or by transfer to another. Rights are transferred in return for benefits received.

---

[1] *De Cive*, I. 3–7.
[2] *De Cive*, I. 7.
[3] *De Cive*, I. 12; *Lev.*, cap. 13.
[4] *De Cive*, III. 31; *Lev.*, cap. 17.
[5] *De Cive*, I. 2.

The transfer is mutual; it is a contract. A second Law of Nature commands that contracts must stand and faith be kept.[1] Where no contract is formed there is no transfer of right, consequently there is no injustice. The observance of contracts is the essence of justice.[2]

Hobbes formulates about a score of what he calls Laws of Nature, all of them principles of morality or practical wisdom, such as the following: That each person should be useful to others; that no man should despise another; that in inflicting punishment the future good, rather than the magnitude of the past offence, is to be considered; that all men are by nature equal; that such things as cannot be divided should be used in common; that messengers of peace should be safe; that in every controversy decision should be made by arbiters; that each person should do unto others as he would have them do unto him.[3]

Hobbes considers these laws binding upon conscience, the internal judge. The violation of them is a mistake, rather than a crime. Whoever observes them is a just person.[4]

It is evident that these laws contain little that savors of personal liberty. The principle of equality is emphasized, but it must be remembered that equality and liberty are by no means inseparable: liberty may exist without equality, while equality may prevail in a despotism. Far from limiting the interference of the State with the liberty of the individual, the Laws of Nature, according to the view of Hobbes, recommend that the state of nature, which is a state of unrestricted freedom,

---

[1] *De Cive*, III. 1; *Leviathan*, cap. 15.

[2] *De Cive*, III. 7.

[3] These laws are enumerated in his *De Cive*, III. 8–25

[4] *De Cive*, III. 30.

be exchanged for the political State, because there exists no force which can prevent the violation of contracts and the occurrence of war in the state of nature. The State is formed by a contract, in which all individuals transfer their separate wills to a general will.[1] The person or body to whom this power is transferred has supreme and absolute power.[2] All have promised to obey him. He is bound to no one. Hobbes recognizes three forms of government: democracy, aristocracy, and monarchy, but regards the monarchy as the best. He constantly confuses the State with the ruler of the State. The State has unlimited control over the property, the opinions, and the religious beliefs of the citizens. It is true that Hobbes regards it as the duty of the ruler to secure the welfare of the people,[3] but he alone decides wherein this welfare consists. The citizen has but to obey the law. Hobbes defines Law as the command of that person whose will is the foundation of obedience. In such a state as this there exists no sphere of individual rights. The ideas of Natural Law, a state of Nature, and of the social compact, which were employed by the forerunners, as well as most successors, of Hobbes to demonstrate the rightfulness and necessity of individual liberty, have become instruments in his hand to enslave the individual and establish the despotism of the State. What, however, could be more illogical than to suppose that men would voluntarily exchange their natural freedom for serfdom of the worst sort?

Spinoza (1632–1677), the great Dutch philosopher, was influenced by the theories of Hobbes, though differ-

[1] *De Cive*, V. 8; *Leviathan*, 17.
[2] *De Cive*, VI. 13; *Leviathan*, 18.
[3] *De Cive*, XIII. 2; *Leviathan*, 30.

ing from him in many particulars. He does not preach absolutism, as does Hobbes, but is an ardent champion of liberty of thought and expression.

Spinoza regards Natural Laws as rules of Nature determining the existence and actions of things in a specific manner.[1] Thus fishes occupy the water by Natural Right. By the same right the powerful prey upon the weak. Natural Right lies in the nature of things. The right of Nature as a whole, and of each individual, extends as far as his power. From this standpoint might is right. The power of natural things, by which they exist and act, is the power of God. Every man has as great a right to Nature as he has power to hold it.[2] The supreme Law of Nature is self-preservation—continuance in an appropriate condition. Whatever any person, under the empire of Nature only, deems useful, whether by reason or appetite, he desires by the supreme Law of Nature and may rightfully obtain, whether by force, cunning or entreaty, regarding him as an enemy who opposes him in the satisfaction of his desire.[3] Spinoza assumes a state of Nature. In this state the forces of Nature prevail, or, as he says, might makes right. Unlike Hobbes, Spinoza is a pantheist. The distinction between good and bad does not exist for him. It is lost in the unity of the divine Nature. Things seem wrong to us because of our limited understanding, while in reality there is harmony everywhere. According to Spinoza men are by nature enemies.[4] They are inclined to revenge rather than to sympathy. Since each strives after

[1] *Tractatus theologico-politicus*, cap. 16.
[2] *Tractatus politicus*, cap. 2.
[3] *Tract. theolog.-pol.*, cap. 16.
[4] *Tract. pol.*, cap. 2.

superiority conflict ensues. The victor glories rather
in having harmed his opponent than in having bene-
fited himself.[1] Though all may be persuaded that
such action is condemned by religion, which enjoins the
love of one's neighbor (that is, that each shall defend
the right of his neighbor as if it were his own), this persuasion has but little influence over their passions.
But each desires to live in peace and safety, and to be
free from fear. This is impossible so long as every one
does what passion dictates. To live in security men
must combine, each surrendering his individual rights
to the community. A compact is therefore formed
which is obligatory because of its usefulness, and is null
and void as soon as its promises are violated. It was
made to avoid a greater evil or to attain a greater good.
Rulers possess the right to rule only so long as they
have the power to enforce obedience. He who is
mightier than the ruler does not need to obey. Subjects must obey the commands of the chief authority,
for now that has become Right which supreme authority
declares to be so. But the duty to obey ceases as soon
as the supreme authority has lost the power to enforce
its commands.[2] This conception differs materially
from that of Hobbes. Its logical consequence is the
right of resistance to the supreme authority. In the
last instance the sovereignty is with the people. Spinoza
prefers the democratic form of government. It seems
to him to be the most natural form, inasmuch as it
accords best with the liberty each individual possesses by
nature. The abridgment of natural liberty is least and
still the disadvantages of the natural state are avoided.
In a democracy, as in the natural state, all men are

[1] *Tract. polit.*, cap. 1.
[2] *Tract. theolog.-polit.*, cap. 16.

equal. No one transfers his natural rights to another to such an extent that he has nothing at all to do or say in regard to public matters.[1] The end and aim of the State Spinoza considers to be liberty.[2] Individual right is never entirely abandoned to the supreme authority.[3] No one can be forced to transfer to another his Natural Right or faculty of reasoning freely.[4] Freedom of thought is the natural and inalienable right of all. All governments should guarantee the right to existence and to the fruits of one's industry.[5]

Among Frenchmen, Montaigne, in his Essays, denies the existence of firm, perpetual, and immutable Laws of Nature, which are said to be imprinted in human nature by their own essence. He says there is not one of these Natural Laws which is not contradicted by one nation or by several and that there is nothing in which the world differs so much as in laws and customs.[6]

Bossuet, Archbishop of Meaux, considers all laws to be founded on the first of all laws, which is that of Nature; that is, on right, reason, and natural equity, which cannot be broken without shaking the foundations of the earth, after which nothing remains but the fall of empires.[7] But with Bossuet Natural Law is of no further consequence as regards the development of individual liberty, for he tries to prove that a king has absolute power over his subjects. According to him the royal authority is holy, paternal, and absolute. Kings

[1] *Tract. theolog.-polit.*, cap. 16.

[2] *Ibid.*, cap. 20.

[3] *Ibid.*, cap. 17.

[4] *Ibid.*, cap. 20.

[5] *Ibid.*, cap. 20. On Spinoza's Political Philosophy see Pollock's *Spinoza;* London, 1880.

[6] *Essais* (1580), II. 12.

[7] *Politique tirée de l'Écriture sainte*, I. 4.

are gods on earth. Though the royal authority is regarded as subject to reason, there is little left to the subject of a state such as Bossuet describes but to obey and to serve.

Fénelon (1651–1717), the rival of Bossuet, and Archbishop of Cambray, defines law in general as the rule which each being ought to follow in order to act according to its nature. The most perfect law for finite wills is that of the Infinite Will, which is Natural Law. This law is common to all beings and is eternal and immutable. The Supreme Law is to love everything according to the dignity of its nature. From this flows respect and love of God; respect for, and good-will toward, all particular beings created by God; patriotism; and all other civil and political virtues. The general welfare should, according to this law, be preferred to any particular interest. Disobedience and lack of attention to it do not destroy the force and justice of Natural Law. It is not founded upon the accord of nations and legislators, but upon the immutable relations of our being with all that surrounds it.[1]

In Germany Samuel Pufendorf (1632–1694) attempted to harmonize the views of Grotius and Hobbes. He was the first professor of Natural Law and occupied a chair at Heidelberg specially created for him. He taught Natural Law as a science and applied to it the geometrical method which Descartes had applied to metaphysics and Spinoza to ethics. He enjoyed a great reputation in his day and deserves to be better known in our own.

Pufendorf accepts two principles as leading to the formation of the State: The social nature of man and the fear of injury. According to him the necessity and

[1] *Essai philosophique sur le gouvernement civil*, Ch. 2.

truth of Natural Law flow from the constitution of human nature, from which it can be deduced by reason. But inasmuch as it does not determine who shall command and who obey, and puts no penalties on disobedience, it is insufficient to preserve society; therefore men must determine by compact who shall prescribe positive laws and punish disobedience. Pufendorf defines law as the command of a superior to his inferiors to act in a prescribed manner. Laws should accord with reason, but must be obeyed because they are commanded, even if the reason for them be not obvious. Though founded in reason, Natural Laws presuppose the existence of God in order to have binding power. They are obligatory because of divine injunction. Like all living creatures, man strives to preserve himself. Every man is part of a greater entity. He must be concerned for the welfare of this greater whole, which is society. The Law of Nature enjoins all actions which conduce to mutual sociableness.[1] The two fundamental laws of Nature are: (1) that each individual preserve his body, his members, and all belonging to him; and (2) do not disturb, but benefit, society. The obligation to cultivate social life is equally obligatory upon all.[2] Every person should regard every other as equal to himself.[3] He calls it absurd to believe as did Aristotle that some men are slaves by nature. According to Pufendorf all men are naturally, and antecedently to any human deed, born free. Either their own consent or some act done by them causes an abridgment of their liberty. Antecedent to any deed or compact among men, no one has power over another, but each is master over his own

---

[1] *De Jure Naturae et Gentium*, II. 3, 15.
[2] *Ibid.*
[3] *Ibid.*, III. 2, 1.

actions and abilities. But when men enter society
this natural equality ceases and there arises an inequality between sovereign and subject. When subjects
passed into a public state they made over to their common sovereign as much of the power which they before
possessed as was necessary to support this new constitution.[1]

The work of Grotius and Pufendorf was continued
by Thomasius, one of the most enlightened men of all
times, an ardent and unwearied advocate of political,
intellectual, and religious liberty, and one of the founders
of the University of Halle. It is his merit to have separated the sciences of law and morals. He regards
morals as pertaining to the inner life, which is beyond
outward control. The province of law, on the other
hand, he regarded as being the regulation of outward
affairs. The principle of morals he declared to be virtue; that of law, justice. He distinguishes between
Natural and Positive Law. Natural Laws spring from
the nature of things. They are written in the heart of
man by God and enjoin the performance of those actions
which are in accordance with man's rational nature.
Positive laws must be published before they can be
known, while Natural Laws are discovered by reason.

Thomasius regards the fundamental precept of Natural Law to be to prolong and render happy the life of
men and to avoid that which renders life unhappy and
hastens death.[2] He considers the happiness of society

[1] *De Jure Nat. et Gent.*, III. 3, 9.   Pufendorf's chief work
was published in 1672. It was translated into French by
Barbeyrac. There were several English editions. (Second
Engl. ed. pub. 1710.) Pufendorf also published an abstract of
his larger work in 1673, bearing the title, *On the Duty of Man
and the Citizen.*

[2] *Fundamenta juris naturae et gentium*, 1705, I. 6, §§ 19, 21.

impossible without that of the individual.   Likewise, individual happiness is inseparable from that of society. Every individual should labor for the welfare of others as for his own.   Reasonable self-love demands that reason rule over sense and that the will of the individual be subordinated to the will of all.   Thomasius distinguishes three spheres of action: decency, virtue, and justice (*decorum, honestum, justum*).   The principle of decency is: Do unto thyself what thou wouldst have others do to thee; of virtue: Do unto others what thou wouldst have others do to thee; of justice: Refrain from doing unto another that which thou wouldst not have done unto thee.[1]

Thomasius makes a distinction between Natural Rights, which are derived from Nature and are inherent in man (*connatum jus*), and acquired rights (*acquisitum jus*), which arise from human laws.   Freedom, the common ownership of Nature's gifts, and the right to one's thoughts, life, and members are inherent rights, while the right to property and the exercise of authority are acquired rights.[2]

By separating law and ethics Thomasius established the sphere of inner life, which should be free from outward control.   He regards Law as the science of compulsory duties.   During his time certain principles had come to be generally accepted by jurists; such as the existence of a state of nature and the rights and duties existing in the same, the deduction of Natural

[1] *Fund. jur. nat. et gent.*, 1705, I. 6, §§ 40–43.

[2] *Ibid.*, I. 5, §§ 11, 12. On Thomasius, see Stahl, *Philos. des Rechts*, 2 ed., pp. 179–180; Rossbach, *Die Perioden der Rechtsphilos.*, 1840, pp. 140–145; Hinrichs, Vol. III.; Bluntschli, 215–246; Hettner, *Litteraturgesch. des 18. Jahrhdts.*, III. pp. 90–115.

Law from the nature of things by use of reason, the limitation of the province of law to *compulsory* duties, as against *moral* duties belonging to the inner life of man.[1]

In England, Richard Cumberland (1632–1719) attacked the materialistic theories of Hobbes. He maintained[2] that just as there are fixed principles which govern the physical world, so immutable and universal laws exist which govern the moral world. These he called Natural Laws. They demand that each individual seek his own good, as well as that of society. While Hobbes asserted the selfishness of man, Cumberland maintained the benevolence of human nature (*amor universalis*), which he regarded as the sum of Natural Law. The common good is, according to him, the supreme law. According to right reason men are benevolent toward each other and love peace, not war, as Hobbes had affirmed. The fundamental Law of Nature is: Seek the common happiness of rational men.[3] The Law of Nature is the rule impressed upon the mind by a First Cause, prescribing such action of rational agents as best promotes the general welfare and by the observance of which alone the undisturbed happiness of every individual can be procured.[4]

It would be difficult to name any other writer whose influence upon modern thought has been greater than that of John Locke. His influence on political thought was no less marked than that on philosophy. He popularized political theories. His doctrines spread

[1] Warnkönig, *Rechtsphilosophie*, 1854, p. 60.

[2] In his famous work, *De Legibus Naturae*.

[3] *Ibid.*, 5, § 57.

[4] Franck, *Réformateurs et publicistes, 17e siècle*, p. 354 *et seq.;* Hinrichs, I. 241 *et seq.*

among the masses. They became the program of the Whigs. They were the theories of the American and the French revolutions. Locke cannot be called the originator of these ideas, for they had been put forth repeatedly before his day, especially by Hooker, Grotius, and Milton. But they came to be associated with Locke's name, and it was he who secured for them their wide acceptance.

Like several of his predecessors, Locke presupposes a state of nature, which he conceives as a state of perfect freedom and equality, in which each person is independent of every other. But this does not imply the reign of license. The state of nature is governed by the Law of Nature, which is binding upon all. "Reason, which is that law," says Locke, "teaches all mankind who will but consult it, that, being all equal and independent, no one ought to harm another in his life, health, liberty, or possessions." [1] Every one is bound to preserve himself and the rest of mankind. The life, liberty, health, limbs, and goods of another must not be interfered with. The Law of Nature wills the peace and preservation of mankind. In the natural state the execution of the Law of Nature is, according to Locke, put into the hands of every man. Transgressors of the Law of Nature may be punished in order to prevent its violation. All men are naturally in the state of nature and remain so till by their own consent they become members of political society.[2] Locke distinguishes, not very successfully, however, between the state of nature and that of war. "Want of a common judge with authority," he says, "puts all men in a state of nature; force without right upon a man's person

<hr>

[1] *Of Civil Government,* Ch. 2.
[2] *Ibid.*

makes a state of war." The man who makes war upon another is a wolf or lion, and may be killed as such.[1]

Against Grotius, Hobbes, and Pufendorf, Locke asserted that man could not by free consent or compact enslave himself or give to another absolute and arbitrary power over himself. This inalienability of freedom was later insisted upon by the Massachusetts patriots, Otis, and John and Samuel Adams, and by the American Bills of Rights. "No man can, by agreement," says Locke, "pass over to another that which he hath not in himself, a power over his own life." Preservation of property is the chief purpose of leaving the natural state and forming government. Though men are free in the state of nature, the enjoyment of their rights is uncertain, inasmuch as the Law of Nature, though plain and intelligible to all rational creatures, is not of sufficient compulsory authority. Known and indifferent judges are also lacking, as is the power to execute sentence. On joining political society men give up the power to execute the Laws of Nature. But though they give up to society their natural equality, liberty, and executive power, it is only to secure life, liberty, and property more effectively. It would be irrational to change one's condition in order to render it worse. The power of society over its members does not extend any further than the common good requires.[2]

Locke asserts that the earth was originally given by God to all men in common. Every man, he says, has a property in his own person. "The labor of his body and the work of his hands, we may say, are properly his." By labor man removes things from the state of

---

[1] *Of Civil Government*, Ch. 3.
[2] *Ibid.*, Ch. 9.

nature and acquires property in them. As the labor belongs to each man alone, so that becomes his to which he has joined his labor.[1] Each man has free disposition over his property according to his own will, within the compass of law.[2] The preservation of property is, according to Locke, one of the chief ends of government. No person, not even the supreme ruler in the State, can take away from any man a portion of his property without his own consent.

It was of great importance that Locke, unlike Hobbes and afterward Rousseau, maintained that the Laws of Nature do not lose their force after men enter society. These laws do not only apply in the state of nature. Indeed, after the formation of political society, the force of these laws has increased, for now penalties are attached to breaking them. The Laws of Nature are eternal rules, forming the standard according to which legislators shall frame the positive laws of the State.[3] Neither do men lose their natural freedom and equality. There is only such a sacrifice of this natural liberty made as is absolutely necessary to the formation of the State and the establishment of government. Men do not relinquish their natural freedom in order to become slaves. They seek security for their natural rights. It is this view from which the idea arises of setting forth the Rights of Man in a solemn declaration, as was done by the Americans in their Bills of Rights, and subsequently by the French in their Declaration of the Rights of Man and of the Citizen.

[1] *Of Civil Government,* Ch. 5.
[2] *Ibid.,* Ch. 6.
[3] *Ibid.,* Ch. 11.

CHAPTER III

THE EIGHTEENTH CENTURY

WE have seen how the conception of the Law of Nature, which originated in early Greek philosophy, has steadily increased in dignity and importance, having been finally worked up into a system by such writers as Grotius, Pufendorf, and Locke.

The basis of Natural Law was the idea that there exists an essential justice, which is the same for all men of whatever race or State they might be members. The Laws of Nature were considered as being independent of tradition; as being given with the constitution of man; as being founded in reason, and as being unchangeable by any human, or even divine, power. These Laws of Nature were of course not legally binding upon men, since there was no authority to impose a penalty upon their infraction. But they were regarded as morally binding upon all men. It was a question of *ought*. The positive laws of every State *ought* to conform to the Laws of Nature. The citizens of every land *ought* to enjoy their natural rights; their rights as men; the rights to which the constitution and needs of human nature entitle them. These rights might be denied them in any State; but the denial meant that the government exceeded its just powers and had become tyrannical. Of course, *de facto* the sovereignty of the State is unlimited. Should it be *de jure*? Should there be a sphere within which the State must not interfere; namely, the sphere of the rights each citizen *ought* to possess as an individual, as a man? These questions were by the writers on Natural Law answered in the affirmative. They often forgot, however, that these so-called Laws of Nature are only morally, not legally, binding.

It is evident that the theory of Natural Law is admirably adapted to become the theory of revolutions, whereby the ordinary course of custom and tradition is interrupted and new standards are sought. When men are dissatisfied with things as they are, they will inquire, How ought conditions be? At such times they will ask for the reason back of customs and institutions.

It was but natural that the doctrines of Natural Law should be employed during the American, and more especially during the French, Revolution to attack abuses which had accumulated for centuries. Natural Law taught that men were naturally free and equal; that such rights as freedom of conscience, of religious worship, of speech, of the press, of public meeting, followed from the very constitution of human nature; that, given the personality of man, these rights are absolutely necessary to secure its development. The actual condition of affairs was far from agreeing with these demands of Natural Law in the Europe of the eighteenth century.

Not only did the disparity between theory and actual conditions render the doctrines of Natural Law dangerous to the order of things prevailing during the eighteenth century, but the danger had become particularly great, because of the general spread of these views, which was a consequence of the advance and wide dissemination of education.

Natural Law had a peculiar attraction for the people who lived at this period. It was a period during which men were singularly devoid of reverence for the past. The historical spirit was lacking. There was a general longing to be freed from the thraldom of antiquated customs and institutions. The foundations of things were examined. The fact that privileges had existed for ages was no longer regarded as a sufficient title why they should exist forever.[1] Reason was regarded as the panacea for all human ills. No other age had such a faith in the perfectibility of things. It was believed that the Golden Age could be realized by enthroning Reason. The application of reason to science resulted in a wonderful advance of human knowledge at this time. It was held that laws and political institutions must also conform to reason. The simple and perfect Laws of Nature were regarded as immeasurably preferable to the multitudinous and conflicting laws of the existing type.

Another reason for the popularity of Natural Law was the universal desire for individual liberty which marks this epoch. To the people of this period the constant meddling of the government in private affairs, carried on to a ridiculous extent, had grown almost intolerable. They sighed for liberty, for the free disposition of themselves and their property. They longed to be rid of the shackles of custom. As a reaction against paternalism and overcentralization the desire arose to restrict the interference of the State to a minimum. This movement culminated in the writings of Kant, Fichte, W. von Humboldt, John Stuart Mill, and Herbert Spencer.

[1] See Chapter 13 of De Tocqueville, *L'ancien régime et la révolution.*

It is interesting to note that the conception of Natural Law found expression in the *Antimachiavelli* of the young Prussian Crown Prince Frederick, later known as Frederick the Great. The book was written as a refutation of the political principles of Machiavelli, during Frederick's happy Rheinsberg days, between 1736–1740. Frederick thinks that before considering the different forms of states, the great Florentine should have examined the origin of princes and discussed the reasons which induced free men to submit to masters. He thinks it might not have been convenient to mention what should remove crime and tyranny, in a book which proposed to defend these. Machiavelli was perhaps unwilling to say that the people found it necessary for their repose and preservation to have judges to regulate their differences; protectors, to shield them from their enemies in the possession of their property; sovereigns, to unite all various interests in a single common interest. He was reluctant to acknowledge that the people had chosen those whom they believed the wisest, the most just, the least biassed, the most humane, and the most watchful, to govern them. "Justice ought to be the chief object of the sovereign. He should prefer the welfare of the people he governs to every other interest. What becomes, then, of those ideas of interest, of grandeur, of ambition, and of despotism? It will be found that the sovereign, far from being absolute master of the people which are under his domination, is but their first servant." [1]

It was from this point of view that Frederick II. regarded his position as king of Prussia. At a time when rulers had adopted the phrase of Louis XIV., "*L'état c'est moi*," and held their subjects to exist but

[1] Ch. 1. The first rendering has it *premier domestique d'État.*

for their sake, Frederick, influenced by Natural Law and the compact theory, labored for the good of his subjects and conceived himself to be, not the lord, but the first servant, of the State.[1]   Though wielding despotic power, he was influenced by considerations of justice and morality and did not use his vast power for personal ends, but to promote the welfare of Prussia. The influence of Natural Law upon the work of the great king can be seen from the following extract taken from his famous Code of Laws: "The good of the State, and of its inhabitants in particular, is the end of the civil association and the universal object of the laws. The head of the State, whose duty it is to further the public welfare, is entitled to guide and determine the external actions of all the inhabitants in conformity with this object.   The laws and ordinances of the State may not limit the natural liberty and rights of the citizen any further than the above-mentioned object requires." [2]

An enthusiastic disciple of Frederick, and likewise a representative of the system of "enlightened despotism," was Joseph II. of Austria.   He reformed the judicial system of his States, abolished serfdom and all unjust privileges, promoted education, strove in every way to elevate his people, and favored toleration and humanitarianism.   He desired a complete regeneration of conditions.   He had a passion for reforming.   He was animated by the noblest motives of justice, equity, and love of humanity.   But Joseph's great weakness was his lack of reverence for historical development.   He

[1] See Treitschke, *Das politische Königtum des Anti-Machiavell. Festrede, Preuss. Jahrb.*, Vol. 59, p. 341 *et seq.*

[2] Tocqueville, *Ancien régime*, Appendix; Philippson, *Geschichte des Preussischen Staatswesens*, I. Ch. 4.

respected nothing which did not conform to his ideals. He had been schooled in the principles of Natural Law as contained in Martini's work. These principles he applied to existing institutions. He said that since he had ascended the throne he had made philosophy the lawgiver in his realm.[1] Despite his want of historical understanding, a fault which caused general opposition to his well-meant plans on the part of those he sought to benefit, and which eventually caused the failure of wellnigh all his reforms, Joseph deserves honor and credit for his noble spirit and his devotion to the welfare of his subjects.

The representative philosopher of the eighteenth century was Christian von Wolff, the famous professor at Halle, who, though his works are now seldom read, in his day enjoyed an almost incredible reputation. Even in France his popularity was so great that for a time it seemed as if his works were destined to supplant those of the English writers. Driven from Halle by the pietistical Frederick William I., he was recalled by Frederick the Great. His return to Halle was regarded as an event of national importance. Wolff's influence declined during his later years, but only because his theories had become the common property of his contemporaries. Wolff usually entitles his books *Sensible Thoughts*. Perfectibility is the corner-stone of his system. He declares it to be the duty of the human race to strive for perfection. He deducts Natural Law from the moral nature of man. The Rights of Man flow from his duties. The former are inherent because they arise from innate duties. Rights and duties are equal for all men because they flow from human nature. All men are naturally equal. Acquired rights alone cause

[1] Haeusser, *Deutsche Geschichte*, I. 174 *sq.*

differences among individuals. No prerogative comes
from human nature. No one has any power over
another by nature. From the duty to perfect personality, which is incumbent upon every person, Wolff
deduces personal rights, such as the right to self-culture,
to the preservation of one's body, to labor. He declares
the purpose of the State to be the realization of the
common safety and welfare. Each individual sacrifices
only so much of his natural liberty as is necessary to
secure the common welfare.[1]

The views of Wolff on Natural Law are practically
the same as those of Locke and others. But Wolff contributed greatly to their dissemination. He had a host
of followers and disciples. Among them was Vattel,
whose *Law of Nations*, which accords entirely with
Wolff's teachings, enjoyed great celebrity in both
Europe and America and is frequently quoted by
John Adams, Samuel Adams, Otis, Jefferson, and Hamilton.

Let us now inquire what the views of the leading
French writers were in regard to Natural Law, and
what effect their ideas had in preparing the way for the
French Revolution.

The despotism of Louis XIV. had exerted a blighting
influence upon French literature. The recovery from
this condition was due to the fact that the French sought
for a new stimulus in a different country. This country
was England. In science, ethics, rational theology,
and political philosophy the English had at this time

---

[1] On Wolff's system see his *Institutiones juris naturae et gentium*, 1, 754; Bluntschli, *Geschichte der neueren Staatswissenschaft*, p. 248 *et seq.;* Hettner, *Litteraturgeschichte des 18.
Jahrhunderts*, III. 212–248; Janet, *Histoire de la science politique*, Liv. IV. Ch. 3 and 8.

made a most remarkable progress. The people on the Continent were wholly unfamiliar with the ideas of Hobbes, Locke, Berkeley, Newton, and other brilliant English thinkers until after the first quarter of the eighteenth century. After that time English philosophy, science, and principles of government began to spread to France and Germany, and to exert a most salutary influence. It was in England that Montesquieu, Voltaire, and a host of other Frenchmen received their inspiration and many of their ideas. Buckle has carefully collected a list of Frenchmen who visited England, or were familiar with the English language. This list is a very large one.[1] It was especially the English system of government, and the liberty of the people of England, which filled the French with admiration.

During the first half of the eighteenth century it was the Church which the French writers attacked. After 1750 the opposition turns against the State. It is after this date that the chief French books which deal with Natural Law or politics were written. Montesquieu's *Spirit of the Laws* is an exception to this statement, having been published in 1748.

It is with Montesquieu that we must first concern ourselves. He is not really a member of the school of writers on Natural Law, but rather a forerunner of the historical school. He does not believe in abstract justice, neither does he attempt to establish a system of perfect laws or to enumerate the Rights of Man. Montesquieu's method is based upon the relativity of politics. He concerns himself with all forms of government, endeavoring to discover the principles underlying each

[1] *Civilization in England*, I. 518 *et seq.*

form, rather than to determine the best system of government.

Yet Montesquieu is familiar with the theory of Natural Law. This conception is, however, of subordinate importance with him. He defines Law in general as human reason, inasmuch as it governs all the peoples of the earth; and considers the political and civil laws of each nation as the particular cases to which this human reason ought to apply.[1] He speaks of Laws of Nature which flow from the constitution of our being,[2] regarding these laws as those which man received before the establishment of society.[3] "Individual beings possessing intelligence," he says, "may have laws of their own making; but they likewise have those they have not made. These laws of the latter sort were possible before intelligent beings existed. There were relations possible, and consequently laws possible.—To say that there is no justice or injustice, except as the laws ordain or prohibit, is to say that before one had drawn a circle the radii were not equal."[4] And yet he defines liberty as the right to do that which the laws permit.[5] Writers of the Natural Law school would qualify this definition by adding *as long as the laws are just*. Montesquieu is not entirely logical. He seems to believe in essential justice, yet this belief is of no further consequence.

But even though Montesquieu makes no attempt to lay down laws of Natural Justice or enumerate the Rights of Man, he must be regarded as one of the greatest champions of liberty France ever produced. It is well known that Voltaire bestowed upon him the very much exaggerated praise that he had conferred upon the

[1] *Esprit des Lois*, I. 3.   [2] *Ibid.*, I. 2.   [3] *Ibid.*, I. 2.
[4] *Ibid.*, I. 1.   [5] *Ibid*, XI. 3.

human race the rights it had almost everywhere lost.[1]

Montesquieu distinguishes between political liberty in relation to the constitution and in relation to the citizen. He avoids the error which the ancients committed, and which has so often been made since, of confusing liberty with democracy. This mistake was also made during the French Revolution. It might have been avoided if the views of Montesquieu, rather than those of Rousseau, had been followed. Montesquieu also discriminates between liberty and equality. He regards equality as the principle of the democratic form of government, taking honor to be the principle of the monarchical form and moderation of the aristocratic form. He holds that each form degenerates from an excess or deficiency of its principle; thus a lack or an excess of equality would prove alike destructive to a democracy.[2] Montesquieu points out the diverse meanings which have been attached to the word *liberty*. Some regard the power to depose a tyrant as equivalent to the possession of liberty, while some identify liberty with the right of electing the ruler. Liberty is sometimes confounded with the right of bearing arms, or of exercising violence, or of being governed by a ruler belonging to one's own nation; or even, as was the case in Russia, with the right of wearing a long beard. Often liberty has been put in the existence of a particular form of government, such as a democracy, and the power of the people is confused with the liberty of the people.[3] Even though in democracies the people may seem to be able to do what they please, democracies and aristocracies are not free by their nature, for liberty

[1] *Idées républicaines, Œuvres*, V. 403.
[2] *Esprit des Lois*, II. and III.
[3] *Ibid.*, XI. 2.

does not consist in doing what one pleases, and real liberty exists only in moderated governments.[1] While philosophical liberty consists in the exercise of one's own will, political liberty consists in security.[2] To Montesquieu the indispensable safeguard against tyranny and guarantee of liberty lies in the separation of the executive, legislative, and judicial powers of government, which he believes exists in England.[3] This doctrine of the separation of powers, though based upon a misconception of the English constitution, had great fascination for the Americans. They carried it out in the constitution of both federal and state governments. It is expressed in most of the Bills of Rights of the states. It was likewise put into the Declaration of the Rights of Man drawn up by the Constituent Assembly. Concerning the doctrines of natural liberty and equality and Natural Rights or Rights of Man there is little or nothing in Montesquieu's book.

Worthy of a place beside Montesquieu as a champion of liberty in France is Voltaire, the famous poet, philosopher, and wit. Voltaire can hardly be called an individualist. Though a bitter opponent of the existing order of things, he favored such reforming sovereigns as Louis XIV., Frederick II., and Catherine II. of Russia. He cared very little for the English system of self-government. As Sorel says: "He expected everything from the State, and, at bottom, worked for the State alone. . . . His political ideal is an enlightened despotism tempered by tolerance and reason."[4] "To whatever side we turn our eyes," says

---

[1] *Esprit des Lois*, XI. 2, 3.   [2] *Ibid.*, XII. 2.

[3] *Ibid.*, XI. 6.

[4] *L'Europe et la Révolution Francaise*, I. 101; Michel, H., *L'Idée d'État*, p. 13.

Voltaire, " we find contrariety, harshness, uncertainty, and arbitrariness. We endeavor in this century to improve everything; let us seek, then, to perfect the laws upon which depend our lives and fortunes." [1] In theory, however, republican sentiments gain the upper hand. He holds that a perfect government never existed, because men have passions, and if they were without passions, government would not be needed. Notwithstanding, he considers the republican form the most tolerable, because it preserves the natural equality of men more nearly than any other. He maintains that every father of a family should be master of his house alone, and not of his neighbor's, and that, since society is composed of many houses and lands, it is contradictory that a single person be the master of these houses and adjoining lands; and in the nature of things that each master have a voice in the securing of the welfare of society.[2] Again, he believes that a republic, being governed in common, should be richer and more populous than if governed by a master, because each citizen, enjoying security of property and person, toils for his own welfare with confidence, and, by bettering his own condition, improves that of the entire society as well.[3] According to him, it is because a community of persons lack the courage, or else the ability, of governing themselves, if they are under the rule of one or more masters.[4] He defines civil government as the will of all, executed by one or more persons, by virtue of laws which all have made.[5]

---

[1] *Des délits et des peines, Œuvres* (Didot), V. **420.**
[2] *Idées républicaines, Œuvres,* V. **401, 402.**
[3] *Ibid.,* V. 402.
[4] *Ibid.,* V. 396.
[5] *Ibid.,* V. 397.

Voltaire often speaks of Natural Right and the Laws of Nature, regarding Natural Right as that which Nature teaches all men. Human laws must be founded upon Natural Right. The grand principle, the universal rule binding all, is: Refrain from doing that which you would not have done unto yourself.[1]

Voltaire believes in equality, but not in the absolute sense. He holds that all are equally men, having the same needs and desires, but all are not equal as members of society.[2] All men have an equal right to liberty, to the possession of their property, and to the protection of the laws, but all are not equal in talents; therefore public dignities, that is, public burdens, should be bestowed upon those best able to bear them.[3]

As sensible as Voltaire's views on equality, are his ideas concerning liberty. Liberty is not absolute, but is dependence upon the laws alone.[4] Enlightenment and liberty go hand in hand. The more eagerly men search for the truth, the more they will love liberty. " The same force of mind which leads to truth makes us also good citizens. What does it mean, in fact, to be free? It is reasoning justly and knowing the Rights of Man; and being known, they will be defended." [5] The defence of the rights of human reason is to him equivalent to the defence of liberty. The more enlightened men become the greater will be their freedom. For this reason, freedom of speech and of the press are Natural Rights, and the basis of all other liberties. They are the means of mutual enlightenment. They

---

[1] *Traité sur la Tolérance*, V. 519.

[2] *Œuvres*, V. 351.

[3] *Idées républicaines*, *Œuvres*, V. 397.

[4] *Pensées sur l'administration*, *Œuvres*, V. 351.

[5] *Questions sur les miracles*, *Lettre* xi.

are denied only in tyrannies of the worst sort.[1] "It is because of this that the English nation has become a nation truly free. It would not be free were it not enlightened. It would not be enlightened if each citizen had not the right of publishing what he wished."[2] Of course, this liberty may be abused. But it would be as foolish to deny men these rights on pretexts such as this, as it would be to prohibit them from drinking because some men get drunk.[3] The import of Voltaire's contention for freedom of speech and of the press can be fully understood only when one remembers the fact that most of his own books, as well as those of all other leading thinkers of his time, had to be printed in foreign countries because of the iron censorship prevailing in France.

The greatest opponents of freedom of thought and of expression were undoubtedly the French clergy. This is one of the reasons why Voltaire assailed the Church with such bitter animosity. The Church seemed to him the chief antagonist of the reforms he longed for so intensely. It was this conviction which inspired the bitter invective he hurled against the Church as a political institution. "The most absurd of all despotisms," he said, "the most humiliating to human nature, the most repugnant, the most fatal, is that of the priests."[4] Voltaire pleaded for the abolition of serfdom, which still prevailed upon some of the lands of the Church, branding this institution as a crime against humanity.[5] He took up the case of the unfortunate Jean Calas, who

[1] *Questions sur les miracles, Lettre* xiii.
[2] *Ibid.*
[3] *Ibid.*
[4] *Idées républicaines, Œuvres*, V. 396.
[5] *Œuvres*, V. 463, 478–492.

was executed at Toulouse, a victim of clerical bigotry, and in his treatise on Toleration spoke of intolerance as absurd and barbarous; as the right of tigers; yes, as even more horrible, since tigers destroy only to eat, while in France the people mutually exterminate themselves for love of paragraphs.[1]

In other ways, also, Voltaire evinced his love of personal freedom. Thus he demands freedom from arbitrary arrest, regarding it as tolerable, perhaps, to imprison a citizen in time of trouble and of war, without giving previous information, or allowing judicial trial, but maintaining that such treatment in time of peace is tyrannical in the extreme.[2]   Again, he opposes sumptuary laws of all sorts, not only on economic grounds, but also because they deprive those who possess property of their natural right of enjoying it, and because they interfere with the liberty of the citizen to clothe, nourish, or lodge himself as he pleases.[3] Finally, Voltaire opposed feudal dues of all sorts, and thinks there is no possible reason for the distinction between the nobles and the commons, which was in its origin a distinction between lords and slaves. It seems idiotic to him that the larger part of the nation should be degraded for the advantage of a few.[4]

There is nothing incendiary about these ideas.   In fact, it is remarkable that enlightened men of the stamp of Voltaire and Montesquieu, who had seen and suffered so much under the evils of the old order of things, should be so moderate in their views of liberty and equality.   They did not intend to prepare men for a

[1] *Traité sur la Tolérance, Œuvres*, V. 520.
[2] *Idées républicaines, Œuvres*, V. 398.
[3] *Ibid.*
[4] *Ibid.*

revolution, but expected reforms to be carried out by the rulers themselves.

Of essentially the same nature were the doctrines of the writers of the great *Encyclopédie*, men like Diderot, D'Alembert, Holbach, yes, even of Turgot, Condorcet, and of the physiocrats in general.[1] Natural Liberty is defined in the *Encyclopédie* as the right Nature gives all men to dispose of their person and property as they judge best, being subject to Natural Laws alone. In the state of nature men are independent of each other, but are not independent of Natural Law. By nature men cannot sell, exchange, or destroy themselves; for, naturally, all men are equal, inasmuch as they are not subject to the power of a master and no one has the right of property over them. After entering political society men are entitled to civil liberty, which consists in dependence upon the laws only, and is simply Natural Liberty curtailed by the absence of individual independence and community of property. Most of these ideas are based upon the doctrines of Locke.[2]

Holbach, the noted materialist and atheist, truly remarks that the Greeks and Romans did not possess civil liberty because they confused liberty with sovereignty. The day when liberty shall rule lies in the future. Holbach holds that it is the duty of the State to secure the happiness of the citizens. This end can be attained only by allowing the just liberty, whereby each may work for his own interest and well-being providing he does not injure the well-being of his fellow citizens. Freedom exists only in a State whose members are subject, not to the will of man, which is likely

[1] See Ch. 15 of De Tocqueville's *L'ancien régime et la révolution*.

[2] See article on *Liberté naturelle et civile* in the *Encyclopédie*.

to change, but to that justice which is invariable.[1]
Security of person and property seems to him one of the
greatest advantages of liberty.[2] He demands freedom
of thought, because the tyranny over thought is the
most cruel, revolting, and useless of all violations of
the liberty of man.   Freedom of the press is a consequence of liberty of thought.   Men have not abrogated their Natural Rights upon entering society, but
seek a more assured satisfaction of the needs of nature.[3]
Every law depriving man of his liberty, security, and
property is unjust.

Turgot, the famous writer on political economy,
maintains that true morality regards all men with the
same eye, recognizing in all an equal right to happiness,
which is founded upon the destination of man's nature.
Whoever oppresses another opposes the divine order
and abuses his power.   Might and right are not identical.   The strong have no right over the weak.   " Every
convention contrary to these natural rights has no
other authority than the right of the stronger: it is real
tyranny." [4]   Turgot does not believe in the equality
of men.   He believes that inequality of conditions is
necessary to the progress of society.   But liberty seems
to him to be a priceless possession, which cannot be
guarded too carefully.   It is for this reason that he
holds the principle that nothing ought to limit individual liberty except the greater good of society, as
false and dangerous.   He thinks there is too much of
a tendency to sacrifice the happiness of individuals to
the presumed rights of society.   Every man is born

---

[1] *La politique naturelle*, I. 75; *Le système social*, II. 3.

[2] *La politique naturelle*, II. 73.

[3] *Le système social*, 2d part, Ch. 1.

[4] *Lettres sur la Tolérance, Œuvres*, II. 680–687.

free. The natural liberty of man can be interfered with only when it degenerates into license; that is, when it ceases to be liberty and becomes usurpation. It is only the liberty to destroy which ought to be prohibited. There can be no doubt that Turgot here indicates one of the greatest dangers threatening liberty—that, namely, of sacrificing the principle of liberty to the principle of the public welfare, by which both are generally surrendered. Turgot perceived and cautioned against a tendency to which France was particularly inclined and which was destined to prove fatal to personal liberty in that country. " We forget that society is made for individuals," writes Turgot, " that it is instituted only to protect the rights of all in assuring the accomplishment of all mutual duties." [1]

When Turgot was appointed minister by Louis XVI. it was universally believed that these ideas would be carried into effect and that the day of liberty had at length dawned. It seems that Turgot was less sanguine. The words he had written before his rise to power seem prophetic: " Liberty! I say it with a sigh, men are perhaps not worthy of thee! Equality! they desire thee, but they cannot attain thee." [2] Turgot was removed; reform failed. But the ideas Turgot represented did not perish; the Revolution attempted to apply them to society and government. Doctrines that had hitherto been living in the brains of a few thinkers now became the common property of a great nation—yes, of the entire civilized world. To what was the rapid dissemination of these principles due? It was due to their having been put forth as Rights of Man in a solemn Declaration by the Constituent Assembly. Of such a plan mention had nowhere been made in the

[1] *Lettres sur la Tolérance, Œuvres,* II. 686, 687. [2] *Ibid.,* II. 786.

writings of any political philosopher, even though the specific principles had long been known. The notion we are speaking of was an American idea. It came to France from the New World, where the Rights of Man were not only proclaimed, but also observed by the government.

Nor had the Americans originally imported these ideas from France. They had learned them from English authors, such as Milton, Locke, Harrington, and others, primarily. It must be remembered that these English authors had exerted a wonderful influence upon such French writers as Voltaire, Montesquieu, Holbach, and Turgot.

Another English writer must be mentioned whose work was widely read in America and England, and who represents, as it were, the views on Natural Right and individual liberty, which had come to prevail at the outbreak of the American Revolution. This writer is Blackstone, whose famous Commentaries on the Laws of England first appeared in 1765. Burke says that as many copies of this work were sold in America as in England. An American edition was published in 1771, and of this edition 1400 copies were sold in advance, the name of John Adams heading the list of subscribers.[1]

Blackstone divides individual rights into absolute and relative rights, regarding the former as rights belonging to men in a state of nature, " which every man is entitled to enjoy, whether out of society or in it." [2] The chief aim of society is the protection of individuals " in the enjoyment of those absolute rights which were vested in them by the immutable Laws of Nature, but which could not be preserved in peace

[1] See Hammond's Edition of Blackstone, Preface, viii.

[2] Blackstone's *Commentaries*, I. Ch. 1, 124.

without that mutual assistance and intercourse which is gained by the institution of friendly and social communities. Hence it follows that the first and primary end of human laws is to maintain and regulate these absolute rights of individuals. Such rights as are social and relative result from, and are posterior to, the formation of States and societies." [1] Blackstone regards the absolute Rights of Man as being summed up in the general term Natural Liberty. "This Natural Liberty consists properly in a power of acting as one thinks fit, without any restraint or control, unless by the Law of Nature; being a right inherent in us by birth, and one of the gifts of God to man at his creation, when He endued him with the faculty of free will. But every man, when he enters into society, gives up a part of his Natural Liberty, as the price of so valuable a purchase; and, in consideration of receiving the advantages of mutual commerce, obliges himself to conform to those laws which the community has thought proper to establish." [2] "This species of legal obedience and conformity," Blackstone proceeds, "is infinitely more desirable than that wild and savage liberty which is sacrificed to obtain it. For no man that considers a moment would wish to retain the absolute and uncontrolled power of doing whatever he pleases; the consequence of which is that every other man would also have the same power; and then there would be no security to individuals in any of the enjoyments of life." [3] Blackstone considers the absolute rights of every Englishman to be founded in nature and reason, and regards them as coeval with the English form of government. According to him English rights consist in a number

[1] Blackstone's *Commentaries*, I. Ch. 1, 124.   [2] *Ibid.*, 125.
[3] *Ibid.*, 126.

of private immunities which are either the residuum of Natural Liberty left to individuals, or the civil privileges granted by the State in place of the natural liberties given up by individuals. These liberties he considers to have once been the rights of all mankind. They have been debased in other parts of the world, he thinks, and at his time were in a peculiar and emphatical manner the rights of the English people. These absolute rights he considers to be the right of personal security, the right of personal liberty, and the right of private property.[1] The right of personal security consists in the enjoyment of life, limbs, body, health, and reputation. Life, being the immediate gift of God, is a right inherent by nature in every individual.[2] Likewise man has a natural inherent right to his limbs.[3] Personal liberty consists in the right of changing one's situation or habitation according to will.[4] The right of property, inherent in every Englishman, consists in the free use, enjoyment, and disposal of all acquisitions, without control or diminution, save by the laws of the land.[5] The right of private property is sacred and inviolable. " No subject of England can be constrained to pay any aids or taxes, even for the defence of the realm or the support of government, but such as are imposed by his own consent, or that of his representatives in Parliament." [6]

Blackstone gives as subordinate rights, which protect and maintain inviolate the great and primary rights: 1. The constitution, powers, and privileges of Parliament; 2. The limitation of the king's prerogative by bounds so certain and notorious that it is impossible he should exceed them without the consent of the people;

[1] Blackstone's *Commentaries*, I. Ch. 1, 129.   [2] *Ibid.*, 129.
[3] *Ibid.*, 131.   [4] *Ibid.*, 135.   [5] *Ibid.*, 138.   [6] *Ibid.*, 140.

3. The right to apply to the courts of justice for redress of injuries; 4. The right of petition for redress of grievances; 5. The right of bearing arms.[1] These subordinate rights constitute the check upon the government by which individual liberty is rendered secure.

[1] Blackstone's *Commentaries*, I. Ch. 1, 141, 143.

PART II

HISTORY OF THE DOCTRINE OF THE SOVEREIGNTY OF THE PEOPLE

HISTORY OF THE DOCTRINE OF THE SOVEREIGNTY OF THE PEOPLE

CHAPTER IV

ANTIQUITY AND THE MIDDLE AGES

In nearly all the Greek city-states the form of government passed through four stages: monarchy, oligarchy, tyranny, and democracy. Sparta was the chief exception to this rule. In the other Greek cities the tyrants had been expelled and republics established before the Persian wars. Rome, too, was a republic from 509 B.C. to 31 B.C. In both Greece and Rome, government was originally theocratic in its nature. The rulers were regarded as a sacerdotal class. Magistrates exercised religious functions. The laws were religious traditions. Custom, sanctioned by religion, reigned supreme. With the progress of civilization custom gradually lost its hold and was supplanted by reason. Laws were no longer regarded as being externally imposed by the gods or some great lawgiver, but as the creation of the popular consciousness. The rulers were now no longer regarded as priests, but as magistrates.[1] When Demos

[1] Fustel de Coulanges, *The Ancient City*, Am. ed., pp. 411, 426 *et seq.;* Madvig, *Verfass. u. Verw. des röm. Staats*, I. p. 213.

conquered, the will of the people became the source of law, the consent of the majority its foundation. Public interest became the principle of government. The suffrage of the people, by creating both law and magistrates, was regarded as the true sovereign. " What the votes of the people have ordained," the Twelve Tables say, " in the last instance is the law." [1] " No one has power," says Cicero, " except from the people." [2] The people made the laws and decided concerning peace and war.[3] " This is the condition of a free people," Cicero affirms in another oration, " and especially of this chief people, the lord and conqueror of all nations, to be able to give or to take away by their votes whatever they see fit." [4] Even Augustus issued the laws in the name of the people. The doctrine of the sovereignty of the people was put forth by jurists during the time of Hadrian. Ulpian, as late as the time of the Emperor Severus, declared the validity of the imperial constitutions to derive from the fact that the people had delegated their sovereign power to the emperor.[5] The autocratic Emperor Justinian declares " that to be a law which the Roman people constituted so." " But likewise that which pleases the ruler has the force of law," he says, " because the people have, by the *Lex regia*, conceded to him their *imperium* and power." [6]

---

[1] Livy, VII. 17; IX. 33, 34; Hildenbrand, *Rechts- und Staatsphilos.*, I.pp. 23–25; Fustel de Coulanges, *Ancient City* (Am. ed.), pp. 411, 426, 428, 429.

[2] Cic., *De Lege Agr.*, II. 11.

[3] Polyb., VI. 14.

[4] *Pro Plancio*, IV.

[5] Bruns, in Holtzendorff, *Encykl. der Rechtswiss.*, p. 103.

[6] Justinian's *Institutes*, I. 2, §§ 4, 6.

The theory of the Roman jurists, that the Roman people conferred their sovereignty upon the emperors by means of the *Lex regia*, gave rise to the compact theory of government which plays so important a part in the political philosophy of mediæval and modern times. The idea of a compact, however, was already familiar to the Sophists and to Aristotle.[1]

With the appearance of Christianity and of the Germans on the scene of history, ancient history closes and a new period begins. These two factors produced an entirely new civilization. Both favored individualism and democracy.

Christianity taught that God is no respecter of persons; that in His sight all men are equal; that every individual is accountable to a personal God for all his actions; that there is no human mediator between God and man. Christ is the Saviour of mankind, not of any particular race or people. The God of Christianity does not prefer particular places or peoples. Christianity tore down the barriers between Greeks, Romans, and barbarians, and created a feeling of human brotherhood which supplanted and exceeded in strength the patriotism of the old nations. Christ aimed to break down the barriers not only between the nations, but also between the classes, by endeavoring to elevate the lower classes and so obviate the inequality which ages had hallowed. Christianity contained the germs of a new social and political order. Whenever there is a revival of primitive Christianity, a renewal of the democratic spirit is observable.[2]

The individualistic and democratic spirit is also a

[1] Aristotle, *Rhetoric*, I. 13; Plato, *Republic*, II.

[2] Laurent, *Études sur l'histoire de l'humanité*, IV. Ch. 3; Ritter, *Geschichte der christl. Philosophie*, I. pp. 7, 8.

striking characteristic of the ancient Teutons. The Teuton demanded free disposition of himself and was passionately devoted to his liberty. He would submit to no corporal punishment, except when inflicted by a priest, who was regarded as representing the gods. His relation to the constituted authorities was one of fidelity rather than of obedience.[1]

The government of the ancient Germans was thoroughly democratic. The people were the real source of power. The freemen formed the kernel of the people. Slaves were not numerous. Though a nobility existed, the nobles formed no political caste, but only enjoyed a somewhat higher social consideration than the ordinary freemen. Moreover, kings were chosen from noble families only.[2]

The popular assemblies, whether those of the hundred or of the tribe, were the centres of political life and power. All freemen were members of these assemblies and participated in their deliberations. While the meeting of the hundred seems to have been mainly for judicial purposes, the tribal assembly dealt with the weightiest questions, for it decided concerning peace or war, elected the chiefs, and had control over all matters too important to be left to the chiefs.[3]

The royal authority was not unlimited, but was a creation of the will of the people.[4] Kings were chosen from noble families. There was no fixed order of succession. The people elected the king from a definite family. When the old family had died out or when

[1] Tacitus, *Germania*, c. 7.

[2] Waitz, *Deutsche Verfassungsgeschichte*, I. 151, 190.

[3] *Germania*, c. 11; Waitz, I. 338 *sq.;* Eichhorn, *Deutsche Staats- und Rechtsgeschichte*, I. 60.

[4] *Germania*, c. 7.

royalty was first to be established, the decision rested entirely with the people.[1]

The chiefs or dukes were likewise chosen by the people in their assemblies to lead in time of war.[2] Likewise did the election of princes (*principes*) rest with the assembly. They were chosen from noble families, probably for life, and had charge of minor affairs, besides being judges in the ordinary courts.[3] Thus the people were the source of all power. In the tribes where there were no kings, the assembly of all the freemen of the tribe exercised chief control over affairs. Where there were kings the royal power was limited by the assembly.[4] Before Pippin deposed the Merovingian family he conferred with the people. From them, also, he obtained his crown in 751, just as Chlodovech had before him.[5] Pippin submitted to the people an agreement he had made with the pope regarding the Lombards.[6] With the consent of all the Franks, Charles, at the death of his brother Karlmann, became king, to the exclusion of the sons of his brother.[7] Even during the early Merovingian period the king had but little power as against the entire people assembled in the army.[8] But as the State gradually went beyond the limits of a single tribe a change set in as regards its constitution. Great conquests had increased the power òf the Frankish

[1] Waitz, I. 320–321.

[2] *Germania*, c. 7.

[3] *Germania*, c. 12; Waitz, I. 244, 250.

[4] Schulte, *Lehrb. d. deut. Reichs- u. Rechtsgesch.*, p. 40; Waitz, I. 356.

[5] Fredegar, *Chron.*, 117; *Mon. Germ.*, SS. XV. 1; Gregory of Tours, *Hist. Francor.*, II. 40.

[6] Ranke, *Weltgesch.*, V. 2, p. 35.

[7] Mühlbacher, *Deut. Gesch. im Zeitalter der Karolinger*, 139a.

[8] Greg. Tour., IV. 51.

king. He had become master over an immense domain which was at his disposal. A large part of these lands were distributed among his faithful followers, especially among the servants of his household, whose power was thereby greatly increased,[1] especially after they succeeded in making their office hereditary. Thus a new nobility arose.[2] While on the one hand the royal power and prestige had increased immensely, having also been hallowed by religious consecration, and while a nobility had arisen which was fitted out with the means to make its pretensions felt, the number of freemen was steadily and rapidly diminishing, while that of the dependent class was increasing. Both the Church and the great families were intent upon increasing their possessions and the number of their dependents.[3] The Frankish king no longer ruled over a free people who were in general equal. Classes had arisen. Social changes had produced political changes. A powerful aristocracy now stood over against the king. The power of the old assembly of the tribe had become evanescent and was no longer adapted to the new circumstances. A meeting of the tribe had become impossible as the size of the State had increased. Only the army could check the royal authority. There were no representative institutions to succeed the old popular assembly and arrest the disintegrating progress. The administration passed into the hands of the royal officers—the counts and missi. Commendation and the custom of granting benefices produced the feudal constitution of society and disintegrated the State. The ruler was no longer a popular king, but the head of a feudal oli-

[1] Inama-Sternegg, *Deutsche Wirtschaftsgeschichte*, I. 281 *et seq.*

[2] Waitz, IV. 182 *et seq.*

[3] Inama-Sternegg, I. 287 *et seq.*

garchy. He was now a feudal overlord rather than the sovereign of the nation.

Yet the traditions of the Roman republic and of early German freedom lingered on throughout the Middle Ages. The names *respublica* and *populus Romanus* had not lost their significance, especially to the city of Rome. The Roman law had never fallen into complete forgetfulness, at least not in Italy. A large part of Roman law, including the sections of Justinian's *Institutes* which relate to the transfer of sovereignty or *imperium* from the people to the emperor, was incorporated in the *Collectio Anselmo dedicata*, which arose between 883-897. This collection, which brought the Roman law into connection with the Canon law, was for a long time in general use.[1] Ivo, Bishop of Chartres, who died in 1115, likewise embodied the section of Justinian treating of the *Lex regia* into his two collections, the *Pannormia* and the *Decretum*.[2]

During the struggle between Hildebrand and Henry IV. in the last quarter of the eleventh century, the doctrine of the sovereignty of the people was used by the adherents of the pope to prove that the emperor did not rule by divine right. The German monk, Manegold von Lautenbach, denied that royalty is founded in nature and claimed that it was an office. He believed that a compact had been made between the people and their king. If the king broke this contract and became a tyrant he might be driven away, as one would drive away a swine-herd. The same ideas, which were derived from Justinian's *Institutes*, are expressed in a document issued by several cardinals who opposed Gregory. But

[1] Savigny, *Römisches Recht im Mittelalter*, II. 2. Ausg. 289–291, 506; Eichhorn, *Staats- u. Rechtsgeschichte*, II. 238.

[2] Savigny, II. p. 303 *et seq.*, 506.

whereas Manegold maintains that the people have a right to revoke the sovereignty they have once conferred on their ruler, the cardinals contend that the will of the people becomes binding and cannot be changed. We have here the views of Hobbes and Locke put forth at this early date.[1]

The influence of the ideas and traditions of antiquity during the Middle Ages is strikingly exemplified by the movement that took place in Italy during the middle of the twelfth century, which was chiefly brought about by the fiery eloquence of Arnold of Brescia, a man who was, as regards several of his ideas, many centuries in advance of his time. Half priest, half political reformer, he preached that Church and State should be separated; that the simplicity of the apostolic times should be introduced, the corruption of the Church, the pride and worldliness of the clergy be done away with; and that a republic, with Roman laws and institutions, should replace the feudal State. He declared serfdom to be contrary to the teachings of Christianity and the temporal power of the Church to be a violation of the Scriptures. The Romans, stirred into activity by his eloquence, renounced their fidelity to the pope and restored the Roman senate and republic. The letter written by the Romans to the Emperor Conrad III. contains the following words: "To the most distinguished and famous lord of the city and of the whole world, Conrad, by the grace of God ever august Roman king, the senate and Roman people send greeting and their hopes for the happy and glorious government of the Roman

[1] F. v. Bezold, *Die Lehre von der Volkssouv. im Mittelalter*, in Sybel's *Hist. Zeitschr.*, XXXVI. p. 322; *Monumenta Germaniae Historica, Libelli de Lite*, I. p. 365 *et seq.;* Gierke, *Political Theories of the Middle Age*, trans. by Maitland, 1900, p. 42 *sq.*

empire." [1] It is their desire to restore the Roman kingdom and empire to the condition "in which it was in the time of Constantine and Justinian, who ruled the world through the power of the senate and the Roman people." They wish that Rome, the head of the world, might become the capital of the empire as it had been in the days of Justinian.[2] A partisan of Arnold, in a letter to Frederick Barbarossa, the successor of Conrad, expresses identical views. He holds that the imperial dignity, like every government, is an emanation from the majesty of the Roman people, who alone can create emperors. He advised Frederick to receive the imperial dignity according to the law of Justinian and thereby avoid a revolution.[3] The republicans had driven Pope Hadrian from the city. The assistance of Frederick was sought by both parties. The German king decided for the pope. Before reaching Rome he was met by deputies of the republican party. "We," these messengers said, "the delegates of the city, and not of a small part of it, O best king, are sent to your presence by the senate and Roman people. Hear serenely and kindly what is despatched to you by the gracious city, the mistress of the world, whose chief emperor and lord you will, by the grace of God, soon be. . . . You seek dominion over the world. I arise gladly and meet you joyfully, to offer you the crown. . . . You were a guest; I have made you a citizen. You were a stranger from the land beyond the Alps; I have made you a prince. What was lawfully mine I have given to you." [4] It is needless to say

---

[1] Otto v. Freising, *Gesta Friderici*, I. 28.

[2] *Ibid.*

[3] Gregorovius, *Geschichte d. Stadt Rom im Mittelalter*, IV. 483 *sq.*

[4] Otto v. Freising, *Gesta Frid.*, II. 21.

that the proud Hohenstaufen did not accede to the Roman demands, but insisted on his divine right. He put down the rebellion. Arnold was burned. The attempt to found a State based on the sovereignty of the people did not succeed.

While the above ideas are derived from Justinian's Institutes, Aquinas was influenced by Aristotle and by the conception of Natural Law of Cicero. Like Aristotle, he declared the common welfare to be the purpose of government and considered that government to be unjust which neglected the general good and sought only that of the ruler.[1] Though he prefers monarchy as a form of government, he declares that the constitution of any kingdom should be such that the royal power is moderated. The king must not command anything that is contrary to Natural Law. This law stands above him. Aquinas does not sanction the murder of tyrants by private persons, but he maintains that they may be proceeded against by public authority. As it belongs of right to a society to select a king, so it is not unjust for society to depose him or limit his powers. Faith is not broken thereby even if the society surrendered itself forever, for if the king has not fulfilled his duty, he himself has merited his fate and caused the compact to be broken.[2]

The doctrine of the sovereignty of the people was most fully developed during the Middle Ages by Marsilius of Padua, elected rector of the University of Paris in 1312, who espoused the cause of the German Emperor Ludwig the Bavarian, in his struggle with

[1] *De Regimine Principum*, I. c. 3.

[2] *Ibid.*, I. 6; Baumann, *Die Staatslehre des heil. T. v. Aquino;* Dunning, *Polit. Theories*, p. 189 *seq.*

Pope John XXII. The great work of Marsilius, the *Defensor Pacis*, which appeared in 1325, not only vindicated the right of the State against the pretensions of the papacy, but also asserted the sovereignty of the State to rest in the people. He regards the power to make laws as belonging to the people, or to the majority of their representatives, manifesting their will in a general assembly. He considers no other laws obligatory except those passed by the people, for they alone know the interests of the whole body. He calls it the height of injustice that a single person or a few have the power to control all, as if all men were not equal, but the slaves of another. In obeying the laws which issue from the body of the people each citizen obeys but himself. The rulers in the State derive their authority from the people, whose agents and executives they are. They must act in accordance with the wishes and the consent of their subjects. As the legislative power creates the executive, so it may correct or depose it. In reading Marsilius, Ockam, and other publicists of the first half of the fourteenth century, one is struck by the originality and modernness of their thoughts. They seem to us like men of our own day. Marsilius in many respects anticipated the ideas of the *Contrat Social*. He applies his democratic principles not only to the State, but also to the structure of the Church. He demands that congregations elect their priests. The State shall summon ecclesiastical councils whose members are to be chosen by popular suffrage of the congregations. For a while it seemed as if Ludwig were bent upon realizing the doctrines of his friend and coadjutor, whose influence over him was very great. But though, as it is almost needless to say,

Marsilius's democratic ideals were not carried out, his book was not forgotten.[1]

Lupold of Bebenburg, Bishop of Bamberg, who died in 1362, believes that the Roman people, meaning thereby the citizens of the Holy Roman Empire, have the power of making laws and of transferring the empire from one dynasty to another, if they see fit to do so, since the people are greater than the prince.[2]   In Germany the Kurfürsten were by some publicists held to have taken the place of the senate and the Roman people regarding the right to choose the emperor.[3]

It was in France that liberal principles throve best. The great French poem, the *Roman de la Rose*, which appeared in the early part of the fourteenth century, introduced among the people ideas of a natural state, in which the people lived in freedom and equality, without property, without strife or fear of each other.

In 1380, during the stormy times that characterized the beginning of the reign of Charles VI., the king's chancellor, yielding to the demands made by the people, said in a discourse to them, that, though kings deny it a hundred times, they rule by the consent of the people (*reges regnant suffragio populorum*), and that the royal splendor flows from the sweat of the subjects.   The vigilance of the king should procure the people's welfare and allow them to enjoy the charms of repose and ease.

[1] See Franck, *Réformateurs et publicistes;* Sullivan, in *Amer. Hist. Review*, II. pp. 409, 593; Janet, *Histoire de la Science Politique*, I. p. 457 *et seq.;* Riezler, *Die litterarischen Widersacher der Paepste;* Gierke, *Political Theories of the Middle Age*, p. 46 *seq.*

[2] *De Juribus regni et imperii Romani*, c. 12; Eichhorn, *Deut. Staats- u. Rechtsgeschichte*, III. 32.

[3] Gierke, *Althusius*, pp. 125–126; *Political Theories of the Middle Age*, p. 42.

The king ought never to abuse his power, but to govern his subjects clemently and mildly.[1]

The theory of the sovereignty of the people exerted an influence upon ecclesiastical affairs during the period of the great councils of the fifteenth century. The highest authority in church affairs was said by the advocates of the councils to rest, not with the pope, but with the entire church or its representatives. Paris took the greatest part in the movement. Its chief representative was John Gerson, the famous chancellor of the University of Paris. With Gerson the conception of Natural Law is fundamental. He enumerates a score of such Laws of Nature, among them that God must be obeyed before man; that God gave men power to build up, but not to destroy, the Church; that it is lawful to repel force by force; that the end gives a right to the means.[2] The Law of Nature is, according to him, the supreme law. Church councils may create, depose, yes, even kill, popes, but they cannot command what is contrary to Natural Law.[3] Gerson says that obedience is not due to a king who acts contrary to the interests of his people. In like manner a pope may be deposed if he does not fulfil his duties. The temporal ruler may call together a church council to deal with such a pope.[4]

Of like nature were the views of the German publicist, Nicolaus Cusanus, whose *De concordantia catholica* appeared in 1435. He regards every constitution as being based on Natural Law. Nothing con-

---

[1] *Chronique du religieux de St. Denys*, I. 50, in *Collect. de doc. inédits sur l'histoire de France;* Ranke, *Franz. Gesch.*, I. 41.

[2] Gerson, *Opera* II. 120.

[3] *Ibid.*, 117.

[4] See Gierke, *Althusius*, pp. 128–130.

trary to this law is valid. It is innate, but clearer in the consciousness of some than of others. Those who are most penetrated by it are the natural leaders and lords of men. Inasmuch as all men are by nature equally free and powerful, no authority can be established but by the agreement and the consent of the subjects, that is, by election. The laws, also, can be established only by agreement. There is a general compact of society to obey kings. In a well-regulated State the rulers hold their position by election alone. They are themselves subject to the laws.[1] Like Marsilius of Padua, Nicolaus of Cues holds that the laws must be passed by all who are to be bound by them, or by the representatives of all. Only on this condition can all citizens be obliged to obey the laws. To society belongs, likewise, the interpretation of the laws.[2] He believes that the German electors elect the emperor in the name of the Roman people. According to him, all authority and all subjection arise voluntarily. The right of election is implanted by the Divinity through common necessity and Natural Law. All power being, like man himself, originally from God, is even then divine when originating in the consent of the subjects. The ruler elected becomes a public person and the father of the people. While he regards himself as the creature of the whole body of subjects, he is in reality the father of the citizens.[3] Nicolaus considers it to be the duty of every ruler to promote the general good.[4] Like Gerson, he applies his democratic ideas to the

---

[1] *De conc. cathol.*, II. 14; Scharpff, *Nic. v. Cusa*, Tüb., 1871, p. 22.

[2] Scharpff, *Nic. v. Cusa*, Tüb., 1871, p. 22.

[3] *De conc. cathol.*, III. 4.

[4] *Ibid.*, III. 7.

structure of the Church. He holds that a general council is without doubt superior to the pope.[1]

Like doctrines were put forth by Æneas Silvius Piccolomini, afterwards Pope Pius II. (1458–1464). He believes in a state of nature in which men originally lived after the expulsion from Paradise, in the manner of wild beasts. Discovering that the society of their fellow men contributed to good living, they assembled to form society, built homes, surrounded cities with walls and discovered the arts which heighten the value of life. Civil life suited them wonderfully well. But as there are many favors conferred upon man by his fellows, so there is no injury which does not originate with man. Soon society began to be violated, faith to be broken, peace to be disturbed, injuries to be inflicted upon neighbors—in short, all rights were violated. It was cupidity that did not permit the laws of society to be observed. Oppressed by the more powerful among their number, men betook themselves to one who possessed overtowering strength and virtue, that he might shield the weak and deal out justice to all alike. Thus kingship arose. This dignity was conferred upon an individual for the promotion of public utility and the ministration of justice.[2] That king is a tyrant who seeks his own private advantage instead of the welfare of the people.[3] Applying

---

[1] Scharpff, pp. 34, 41; Stumpf, *Die politischen Ideen d. Nik. v. Cues*, Köln, 1865; Bezold, in *Sybel's Hist. Zeitschr.*, XXXVI. pp. 356, 357; Gierke, *Althusius*, p. 126; Dunning, p. 270.

[2] Æn. Silv. Picc., *De ortu et autoritate imperii Romani*, lib. I. 1.

[3] *De concilio Basilensi*, in Flacius Illyricus, *Catalogus testium veritatis*, p. 14.

these ideas to ecclesiastical affairs, Æneas Silvius says:
"The pope holds the same position in the Church as
the king does in his realm. Just as kings who rule
badly and become tyrants are at times driven from the
kingdom, so the Roman pontiff can likewise be deposed
by the Church, that is, by a general council. This no
one can deny." [1] The councils of Pisa (1409), Con-
stance (1414–1418), and Basel (1431–1443), were dominated by these ideas. The papal power had greatly
sunken. Papal infallibility came to be doubted, for
several popes alike claimed to be infallible. It was the
Schism which made the democratic movement possible.
Inasmuch as the right of the emperor to institute popes
at his pleasure was at this time denied, the quarrel
between rival popes could be settled only by the synods
of the entire Church. But the papacy recovered its
former power and superiority. Already in 1460 it was
forbidden to appeal from the pope to a council. Æneas
Silvius, in his youthful days the champion of the supremacy of church councils, after becoming pope, denounced the views he himself had once put forth. In
France, however, the democratic ideas of this movement survived. [2]

In 1484, during the minority of Charles VIII.,
political doctrines were uttered in the states-general
at Tours which are strikingly modern. "Originally,
the sovereign people created kings by their votes,"
said La Roche, a deputy from Burgundy. Those were
chosen as kings, he asserted, who excelled in noble
qualities. The people chose rulers for their welfare.
It is the duty of princes not to despoil the people and

[1] *De conc. Bas.*, p. 14.

[2] Friedberg, *Kirchenrecht*, 3d ed., pp. 43, 44; Geffken, *Church
and State*, Engl. ed., I. p. 262 *et seq.*; Gierke, *Althusius*.

enrich themselves, but to forget their own interest in enriching the State. If they act otherwise they are tyrants—wolves, and not true shepherds. The State is the people. Power was entrusted to kings by the people. Those who hold power by force or otherwise than by the consent of the people are tyrants and usurpers. The king cannot dispose of the State. He cannot relinquish his power to one or more. Power reverts to the people, who gave it originally. They resume it as their own.[1]

We have seen that the Middle Ages were by no means as barren in political thought as is generally supposed. Marsilius of Padua, Manegold of Lautenbach, Ockam, Gerson, Nicolaus of Cues, and others were the forerunners of the Monarchomachists, of Milton, Sidney, Locke, and Rousseau, and put forth nearly all the political principles of the eighteenth century. There is surprisingly little novelty in political thought. Mediæval political ideas were themselves but a reproduction and development of the theories of antiquity—of the Roman jurists, of Cicero, Aristotle, Plato, and other writers.

These doctrines exerted but little lasting influence during the Middle Ages. Marsilius's plans were not realized; the restoration of the Roman republic attempted by Arnold of Brescia and Rienzi proved abortive; the Italian republics of the Renaissance fell into the hands of tyrants; the power for a time exercised by the great church councils of the fifteenth century reverted to the papacy.

The Middle Ages did not favor individualism. Custom and tradition had too strong a power. Men had little standing as individuals: they were members of a

[1] *Journal des États generaux de France en 1484, Documents inédits sur l'Histoire de France*, pp. 146–148.

caste, of a guild, or some other association, primarily. Men occupied a status: they stood in a definite relation to something or somebody. The Renaissance and the Reformation discovered the individual. They recognized man as man—as being something in himself. Men must become self-conscious before they can become free.

CHAPTER V

THE REFORMATION AND THE MONARCHOMACHISTS

THE great religious reformers themselves did little to enrich political thought or promote political freedom. Melanchthon declared that rulers have their power from the people and must not act contrary to their will, but this had no further results so far as his political philosophy is concerned. Luther, himself the originator of a revolutionary movement, though demanding freedom of thought and belief, advocated paternalism in political affairs, and turned away from the peasants who applied his principles to temporal matters. The demands of the peasants, as expressed in the famous Twelve Articles, would have changed the entire subsequent development of German history, and would, in many respects, have forestalled the reforms effected by the French Revolution. At times during the Peasants' War really modern thoughts were put forth. The "prophets" of Zwickau preached the equality and fraternity of all men.[1] The view was expressed during the war by some, that since all are children of one father and redeemed by the blood of Christ, there should no longer be an inequality of wealth or condition among men.[2] That part of the uprising known as "Poor Conrad"

[1] Zimmermann, *Gesch. d. Bauernkriegs*, I. p. 237.
[2] Ranke, *Deutsche Gesch. im Zeitalter der Reformation*, 6. Aufl., II. p. 128.

demanded entire freedom and general equality.[1] The most radical views of all were uttered by Thomas Münzer. He aimed at a complete transformation of the existing order of things. In many of his views he was centuries in advance of his contemporaries and anticipated the ideas later put forth by the Puritans, by Penn, Rousseau, and others.[2] The third of the articles of Heilbronn demands that all cities and communes be reformed according to divine and natural law, agreeably to Christian freedom. The sixth article stipulates that all worldly laws hitherto in force are invalid and superseded by divine and natural law, and that the poor man should have equal right with the highest and wealthiest (1525).[3] In the beginning Luther counselled peace and moderation to both princes and peasants. He condemned rebellion and considered it contrary to divine law.[4] He believed that the gospel freed the souls of men, but not their bodies and property.[5] When the peasants fell into extremes and committed excesses, Luther with harsh words urged the princes to proceed against them. This they did, taking a fearful vengeance. Luther later gave up his views on passive obedience, though reluctantly. Manly love of freedom and respect for justice supplanted the belief that blind submission was due to the demands of authority. He was forced to this position by circumstances. He had asserted his religious opinions in opposition to the powers that existed. They found many adherents. Favor-

---

[1] Zimmermann, *Gesch. d. Bauernkriegs*, I. p. 84.

[2] Ranke, II. 144 *et seq.;* Zimmermann, I. 182.

[3] Zimmermann, II. p. 374.

[4] *Ermahnung zum Friede auff die 12 Artikel der Bauerschaft in Schwaben.*

[5] Ranke, II. 149.

able circumstances contributed to make the new faith a force. But at length the Emperor Charles V. intended to proceed against the Protestant heretics. Their destruction seemed imminent. Should they submit or resist? This was the question agitated by the Protestant theologians, jurists, and princes. Luther, Jonas, Bucer, and Melanchthon drew up an opinion in January, 1539, to the effect that subjects may defend themselves, yes, owe it to God as a duty incumbent upon them, to protect themselves in case the government or any person undertakes to compel them to accept idolatry and forbidden worship. The attempt of a ruler to exercise unjust power over his subjects is to be resisted. As the gospel confirms government, so it also confirms natural and divine rights. Every father is bound to protect wife and children against public murder. There is no difference between a private murderer and the emperor if the latter exercises unlawful power, for public violence puts an end to all duties of the subject to his lord by the right of nature.[1] The Protestant princes waged the war of Schmalkalden against the emperor, their lawful sovereign, which shows that they gave up the idea of non-resistance.

While Lutheranism cannot be said to have exerted a great direct influence upon political thought and development, the case was very different with Calvinism. Calvin's ideal was a republic in which aristocratic and democratic elements were blended. He distinguished theoretically between State and Church, but was under the influence of the theocratic views of the Old Testament. He wished Christ and the Bible to reign in both Church and State. His State has a religious

[1] Quoted in the art. on Luther in Bluntschli's *Deut. Staatswörterbuch.*

mission. We see this theocratic character of the Calvinistic church manifest itself subsequently in the congregations of the Puritans. The early settlers in New Haven and Massachusetts declare the laws of God to be binding upon them and to be the supreme laws of the colony and hold that the State realizes its purpose only by the intimate union with the Church.

Calvin does not teach the sovereignty of the people. He regards civil government as ordained of God, the source of all power. He does not acknowledge the right of subjects to rise up against authority, even against arbitrary power. It is true he makes an exception in case temporal rulers command what is contrary to the obedience due to God, but, as if he wished to excuse himself for doing so, insists upon obedience to government in all other respects.[1]

It is more probable that Junius Brutus, Hotman, Poynet, and other writers known as the Monarchomachists were influenced by the works of John Gerson, Pierre d'Ailly, and the other writers on the conciliar movement than by Calvin's political ideas, as is generally assumed. In France the remembrance of that period and of those famous publicists must still have been fresh at the time the Calvinistic writers put forth their views concerning the murder of tyrants. We shall see presently how the opinions of the great writers on church councils found their way to Scotland and became known to Knox and Buchanan.

Of greater influence than Calvin's political ideas was his system of church government. From it grew the Presbyterian and Congregational systems. Of the influence of Congregationalism on the growth of democ-

---

[1] *Institutio*, IV., c. 20, s. 32; Kampschulte, *Johann Calvin, seine Kirche u. sein Staat*, I. pp. 272, 273.

racy we shall treat later. Luther often spoke and wrote concerning the priesthood of all Christians, but the Lutheran system of church polity was not influenced by democratic principles. Calvin made the laity the vital part of his system, theoretically at least. He permitted the congregation of the faithful to choose their ministers, after these had been examined as to their faith, motives, and ability, and had been accepted as candidates by the body of ministers and by the council.[1] Calvin says that it is in nowise to be conceded that the Church consists of the assembly of ministers alone. The pastors may not even excommunicate without the knowledge and approbation of the congregation.[2] The concentration of his system lies in the consistory or presbytery. This body consists of clergy and laymen. The latter outnumber the former. The consistory represents the union of Church and State. Calvin's spirit dominated this body and exercised through it that censorship over the citizens of Geneva which transformed the character of that people and left its impress upon them for many generations.

The democratic ideas which manifested themselves at various times during Antiquity and the Middle Ages do not reappear in the writings of the great reformers. Their views were theocratic. They did not apply to temporal affairs the principles which underlay the great movement they inaugurated. But the consequences of these principles did not fail to make their appearance. The Reformation asserted the right of the individual to think for himself. It was a protest against the

[1] *Ordonnances ecclesiastiques, Opera* X. 17. On the democratic tendencies of Calvinism, see Buckle, *Civilization in England*, I. 611.

[2] *Inst.*, IV., c. 12, s. 7; Kampschulte, pp. 268–270.

enslavement of mind and soul. It was an investigation into the claims of spiritual authorities to control the beliefs of men. The demand for freedom to investigate religious truth led of necessity to the demand to inquire into political truth. The inquiry into the title of spiritual authorities could not but result in an examination of the foundations of temporal power.

During the latter half of the sixteenth century a group of writers in Scotland and France of the reformed faith give expression to similar political views. They belong to the class commonly called "Monarchomachists," because of their views concerning the murder of tyrants. John Knox and George Buchanan in Scotland, Junius Brutus, generally thought to have been Hubert Languet, and Francis Hotman in France, are the most famous of these publicists.[1]   The teacher of both Knox and Buchanan was John Mair or Major. He had been educated in France, had taught at the University of Paris, and had become an advocate of the views of Gerson, Pierre d'Ailly, and other authors who asserted the authority of church councils to be superior to that of the pope, adopting also their political doctrines. "He taught that the authority of kings and princes was originally derived from the people; that the former are not superior to the latter collectively considered; that if rulers become tyrannical or employ their power for the destruction of their subjects, they may lawfully be controlled by them, and proving incorrigible may be deposed by the community as the

---

[1] I have never seen the word "Monarchomachists" used by English writers, though it is frequently employed by German authors. It is derived from $\mu o \eta \acute{a} \rho \chi \eta s$, monarch, and $\mu a \chi \acute{\eta}$, battle, and is a very convenient name for a group of publicists whose views are much alike.

superior power, and that tyrants may be judicially proceeded against, even to capital punishment." [1]   Knox,
the great Scotch reformer, preached these doctrines to
Mary Stuart. He spoke to her of the contract between
herself and her subjects. Her subjects owed her obedience, he said, but only in God. While she craved service of them, they craved of her protection and defence
against evil-doers. If she denied her duty to them,
she could not demand full obedience on their part. [2]

The book of John Poynet, Bishop of Winchester,
entitled *A Short Treatise of Political Power*, which
appeared in 1558, declared that kings derive their
authority from the people. It affirmed that they who
have delegated certain functions as a trust may withdraw what they have given on just motives, especially
if the power they have transferred is misused. [3]

Buchanan, in his *De jure regni apud Scotos* (1579),
expresses related views in form of a dialogue. He
believes in a contract between people and prince. When
this is broken all power reverts to the people. War
against tyrants, that is, against kings whose acts tend
to the dissolution of society, whereas they have been
instituted for its conservation, he considers the most
just of wars. A tyrannical prince may, says Buchanan,
be deposed, exiled, or put to death. [4]

The religious wars in France gave rise to a number
of works written by Protestants which in general express
the same opinions and of which the *Vindiciae contra*

[1] M'Crie, *Life of John Knox*, pp. 4–6, and Appendix, note D,
pp. 384, 385.

[2] *History of the Reformation*, p. 327; M'Crie, pp. 30, 187, 435–
437.

[3] Baudrillart, *Bodin et son temps*, Paris, 1853, p. 44.

[4] Baudrillart, p. 45; Janet, II. 46–48.

Tyrannos of Junius Brutus may be regarded as characteristic. This book appeared in 1579, seven years after the Night of St. Bartholomew. The author declares that subjects must not obey kings who command what is forbidden by the law of God. Submission in such a case would be rebellion against Christ. He legitimizes tyrannicide, asserting that in certain cases it becomes a duty. He asks whether that shepherd is clement who allows the wolf to remain in the fold, and whether he is merciful who permits a host of innocent persons to be slaughtered out of respect for the life of a single individual. This is the Huguenot reply to the massacre of St. Bartholomew. With these writers of the reformed faith the practical object of legitimizing resistance to oppression predominates over mere theoretical interest.

The views of Junius Brutus are associated with the theory of Natural Law. It is the prime Law of Nature, he declares, to preserve life and liberty against violence and injury. Nature implanted this law not only in dogs, to be asserted against wolves, but also, and more especially, in man against him who has become a wolf to his fellows.[1] According to him there is a mutual obligation between a king and his people which, whether civil or natural, tacit or express, can be invalidated by no agreement, violated by no right, rescinded by no force. If the prince violates it contumaciously he becomes a tyrant. If the people break it voluntarily they may truly be called seditious.[2] It is the people who create kings and give them their realms.[3] The individual subject is inferior to the prince, but the people as a whole, and those who represent them, are supe-

---

[1] *Vindiciae contra Tyrannos*, q. iii. p. 183.

[2] *Ibid.*, q. iii. p. 170.

[3] *Ibid.*, q. iii. p. 76.

rior to him. He holds it to be plain that "men are by
nature free, impatient of servitude, and born to command rather than to obey, and that they have voluntarily chosen foreign rule only because of the great
utility to result." For no other reason have they
renounced the law of their nature, as it were, to obey
another. Kings were not elected to convert to their
own use the property which was collected by the sweat
of many, for each individual seeks his own advantage
and loves his own possessions.[1] Junius Brutus likens
the State to a ship. The king is only the pilot; the
people are the real owners. A king who is concerned
for the public good will be obeyed. He is but the servant of the State. He does not differ from a judge or
tribune except in that his burdens are greater.[2] "To
rule is but to counsel; the sole end of empire is the public welfare. The only duty of emperors and kings is to
advise the people. Royal dignity is not property or
one's own glory, but a burden; not an immunity, but
a charge; not a remission, but a commission; not
license, but public servitude."[3] No one would care to
bear the burdens incident to royalty unless they were
seasoned with the honor that attaches to the office.

The work of Junius Brutus had been preceded by
the *Franco-Gallia* of Hotman, which was written at
Geneva in 1573 by one of the most famous French lawyers of the time. The author investigates the nature of
royal power and collects statements from early his-
torians to prove that the people had a share in government, maintaining that the early kings of France held
their position by suffrage rather than by heredity.

---

[1] *Vindiciae contra Tyrannos*, q. iii. p. 107.

[2] *Ibid.*, p. 86.

[3] *Ibid.*, p. 109.

The right of electing kings, he holds, implies the right of deposing them.[1] If royalty can be revoked, it is not absolute. "Under some form or other, whether field of March or May, parliaments of barons or states-general, the sovereignty has in last resort always belonged of right and fact to the suffrage of all, or at least to that of the most illustrious of the nation."[2] When Henry of Navarre became a candidate for the throne of France, Hotman forgot the views he had put forth in favor of election and maintained that nothing was more conducive to the stability of the State than the right of heredity. The accession of Henry IV. put an end to the warfare between the League, and, by removing the cause, to further political productions of the Calvinists.

A number of Jesuits arrived at the same views as the French Protestants, but their purpose in publishing them was a different one. While the latter employed the idea of the sovereignty of the people in a war of self-defence, the Jesuits used it to debase the State, in contrasting it with the divinely instituted Church. Their purpose was the same as that of Hildebrand had been when he declared the State the work of Satan. They wished to show that what men have instituted must *eo ipso* be inferior to what God has instituted— that is, that the Church, which is of divine origin, is superior to the State. Lainez had contrasted State and Church at the Council of Trent in 1562, setting the Church of God, which did not create itself or its institutions, but was given its laws by Christ, over against human States which freely institute their own government. Originally all power is in the community by whom it is delegated to the rulers. By this transfer,

[1] Ch. 10.   [2] Ch. 13.

Lainez holds, the community does not divest itself of its power.

Bellarmine, another famous Jesuit, asserted that no ruler reigns by divine right as does the pope. Power belongs to the entire multitude, who may transfer it by Natural Right to one or more, as they choose. It depends upon the multitude to select a king, consuls, or other magistrates. If there is a legitimate cause the multitude may change a kingdom to an aristocracy or to a democracy.[1]

Mariana, a Spanish Jesuit of great learning, born in 1537, wrote a book, *De Rege et regis Institutione*, which he dedicated to Philip III., even though his object was to debase the State. He desires a State torn by internal dissensions. He wishes, however, an immutable, independent, and all-powerful Church.

He believes in a state of nature. In the beginning, he holds, men wandered about from place to place after the manner of wild animals, bound by no law, subject to no authority. Their number increasing, they seemed to represent the rude form of a people. They selected father or grandfather as leader. They lived in happiness and simplicity. There was no fraud, no falsehood, no inequality. But rabid avarice soon brought robbery, deception, and slaughter into this state. Crime went unpunished. To escape violence and discord men agreed to bind themselves mutually by a compact, and began to look to an individual of superior qualities for justice and faith. He was chosen to prevent domestic and foreign injuries, to institute equity, and to bind all by equal right. Thus arose the State and royal majesty.[2] But the citizens did not

[1] *De membris ecclesiae militantis*, III. VI.

[2] *De Rege*, 1599, cap. I.

wish to deprive themselves of all authority. They kept for themselves the greater part of their power.[1] Nothing is better, according to the views of Mariana, than authority limited by laws; nothing worse than absolute power. The people are more powerful than the prince. Ought the offspring be more powerful than the parent, the brook better than its source?[2] The king cannot change the laws without the consent of the people. He is himself subject to the laws. Absolute power is a usurpation. A usurper may be slain by the first comer without process of law. If a legitimate king persists in ruling arbitrarily and disregarding the popular will, he becomes a public enemy and should be treated as such.[3]

The same views were expressed by Suarez in his *Tractatus de Legibus ac Deo Legislatore.*

Richard Hooker believes "that every independent multitude" has, before a particular form of government is established, "full dominion over itself." God has endued mankind naturally with the power to choose whatever kind of society it wishes. " That power which naturally whole societies have may be derived into many, few, or one, under whom the rest shall live in subjection." Kings hold their right in dependence "upon the whole body politic over which they have rule as kings." Hooker speaks of the "first original conveyance when power was derived from the whole into one," that is, of the contract between king and

[1] *De Rege*, pp. 17, 57.

[2] *Ibid.*, p. 71.

[3] Franck, *Réformateurs et publicistes*, pp. 71–85; Ranke, *Werke*, Vol. 24, pp. 228–230; Art. *Mariana* by Prantl in *Deut. Staatswörterbuch* of Bluntschli; Ranke, *Die römischen Päpste*, Bk. VI.

people. When there is no one to inherit dominion it reverts to the people. Power resides in both body politic and ruler; in the one "fundamentally and radically," in the other "derivatively." [1]

A Frenchman, Jean Bodin, is the first person in Modern Times who undertook to define and inquire into the nature of sovereignty.[2] The word itself is of French origin. Bodin considers sovereignty to be one of the characteristics of the State. He regards sovereignty as the unity of political power. It is absolute power and is irrevocable. He alone is sovereign who possesses the supreme power in the State.[3] But Bodin commits the mistake of confounding the power of the State with that of the supreme organ in the State.[4]

Unlike Bodin, Althusius ascribes sovereignty to the people, not to the ruler. Althusius was a German professor, born in 1557, syndic of the free city of Emden, and a man of great learning and ability. He had studied at Geneva and was imbued with the Calvinistic spirit. His work on politics appeared in 1603 and has the avowed purpose of applying the doctrine of the sovereignty of the people to all parts of the social body. Sovereignty is, according to his view, the necessary attribute of the social body, without which it has no right to the name of State. The property and use of the sovereign rights are inalienably associated with the people in their entirety. Even if the people wished to renounce them and transfer sovereignty to another, they cannot do so any more than an individual can transfer

---

[1] Hooker, *Ecclesiastical Polity*, Bk. VIII.

[2] His famous *De la Republique* first appeared in 1576.

[3] Liv. I.

[4] Bluntschli, *Geschichte der neueren Staatswiss.*, p. 26; Gierke, *Althusius*, p. 151; Baudrillart; Janet, II. 214 *et seq.*

his life to another.[1] " The people," says Althusius, "are by nature and in time prior and superior to their governors and more powerful than they." [2] He enters into a consideration of the various social groups or associations (*consociationes*); namely, family, corporation, community, province, and State. He holds that historically the higher forms of association have developed from the lower. The State is the result of development. Necessity impels men to unite. Each association is formed by a compact. It rests upon the consent of its members and has for its end the common good.[3] He defines the State as "the universal public association by which cities and provinces bind themselves, by mutual communication of things and services, to hold, constitute, exercise, and defend the rights and powers of a kingdom by mutual strength." [4]   He conceived the State to be formed by the contract of cities and provinces, not of individuals. His view of the State is federal. The sovereign power of the State he holds to be "the preeminent power and universal sum of powers giving control over those things which pertain to the welfare and care of both body and soul of the members of the kingdom or republic." [5]   " That is a just, legitimate, and beneficial administration," says Althusius, "which seeks and procures the things that are salutary and appropriate to the members of the kingdom singly and collectively, averts all evils and inconveniences, defends the State from injury and violence, and regulates the actions of the administration according to the laws." [6] Magistrates are divided by Althusius into two classes: the ephors and the chief magistrates. The former administer the rights of the people against the

[1] Preface to *Politica*.   [2] c. 18.   [3] c. 1.
[4] c. 9, § 1.   [5] c. 9, § 19 *et seq.*   [6] c. 18.

latter. The ephors form a college, which is the representative body of the people. They elect the chief magistrate in the name of the people. They give him advice and correction. When he cannot perform his duties they appoint a regent. They may offer resistance to tyrannical power and in case of utmost necessity depose the tyrant. The chief magistrate is at the head of the State. There is a compact between him and the people by which he binds himself to administer the kingdom according to the laws of God, of right reason, and of the State, while the people swear obedience to him.[1] This contract is binding until broken by one of the parties. If the people break it, the ruler is relieved of his duties. If the chief magistrate violates it, the people may depose him and select a new ruler or form of government.[2]

Grotius defines sovereignty, which he calls *summa potestas* or *summum imperium*, as the power which is not subject to any other authority, and which cannot be overridden by the judgment of any other human will. This power, he says, belongs to the State in general, and to the person or persons who form the supreme authority in the State, in particular.[3] "The imperium, which is in the king as in the head," says Grotius, "remains also in the people, as in the body, of which the head is a member." [4] He denies that sovereignty is always actually with the people, so that they may correct and punish kings who misuse their power. As any man may sell himself and become a slave, so a people may prefer to relinquish all power to the ruler.[5] But

[1] c. 19.

[2] c. 20. See Gierke, *Johannes Althusius*, Breslau, 1880.

[3] *De Jure Belli ac Pacis*, 1624, I. 3, 7.

[4] *Ibid.*, II. 9, 8.

[5] *Ibid.*, I. 3, 8.

this amounts to saying that the power is originally in the people. The people, Grotius holds, may select any form of government they please.[1] When an elected king dies or the royal family becomes extinct, sovereignty reverts to the people.[2] Grotius developed the theory of contract in his *Prolegomena*. Though he himself does not say explicitly that the State arose from compact, he was instrumental in bringing about the predominance of the contract theory in political philosophy.

[1] *De Jure Belli ac Pacis*, I. 3, 8.
[2] *Ibid.*, II. 9, 8.

CHAPTER VI

INDEPENDENTS, LEVELLERS, AND WHIGS

THE ideas whose development we have been tracing—of natural rights, sovereignty of the people, *salus populi*, resistance to oppression, and others—manifested themselves in England during the Puritan Revolution. They were no longer the thoughts of a few scholars only, but had become the common property of an entire religious sect—the Independents. It was only after being popularized in this manner that these theories became of great practical importance. With the victory of Cromwell's army, in which the Independents predominated, it seemed as if the victory of these ideas had been assured, and as if they were to lead to the permanent establishment of a republic. But republicanism was contrary to the temper of the English people. It was, after all, not in England, but in America, that the principles of the Independents were destined to exert their greatest influence. There they gave rise to modern republicanism. From America they spread to France. The French Revolution disseminated them throughout Europe.

It was in English Independency or Congregationalism that the individualism of the Reformation found its most complete expression.

Luther delivered the church into the hands of temporal princes because he believed the people to be inca-

121

pable of managing their own church affairs. Calvin admitted the people to a share in his ecclesiastical system, though his church polity was still largely aristocratic. The church system of the English Independents was entirely democratic in its nature.

The Independents believed in the autonomy of each congregation. They opposed the union of Church and State and all external control. A number of Independents who were accused of denying the royal supremacy, declared in the House of Lords, January 19, 1640, "that they could acknowledge no other head of the Church but Christ; that they apprehended no prince on earth had power to make laws to bind the conscience; that such laws as were contrary to the laws of God ought not to be obeyed; but that they disowned all foreign power and jurisdiction." [1] The Congregational system was likewise based on the idea that each member of the Church had a right to participate in its administration. Robinson, one of the fathers of Congregationalism, speaking of the "proper subject of the power of Christ," says: "The papists plant it in the pope; the Protestants in the bishops, the Puritans, as you term the reformed churches and those of their mind, in the presbytery; we, whom you name Brownists, put it in the body of the congregation, the multitude called the Church." [2]

Thus each congregation was a miniature republic. The usual form of constituting a church was by covenant. Robert Browne, who first formulated the Congregational polity, defines a church as "a company or number of Christians or believers, which, by a willing covenant made with their God, are under the govern-

[1] Neal, *History of the Puritans*, II. p. 394.
[2] *Justification of Separation.*

ment of God and Christ, and keep His laws in one holy communion; because Christ hath redeemed them unto holiness and happiness forever, from which they were fallen by the sin of Adam." [1] John Robinson, one of the earliest Congregationalist ministers, wrote: "The elders, in ruling and governing the Church, must represent the People and occupy their place. It should seem, then, that it appertains unto the People—unto the People primarily and originally, under Christ—to rule and govern the Church, that is, themselves." [2]

Browne describes the formation of his church at Norwich as follows: "A covenant was made and their mutual consent was given to hold together. There were certain points proved to them by the Scriptures, all of which, being particularly rehearsed unto them with exhortation, they agreed upon them . . . saying: To this we give our consent." [3] Browne believed in the separation of Church and State. Half a century before Roger Williams, he taught that magistrates "have no ecclesiastical authority at all, but only as any other Christians, if so they be Christians." [4] There can be no doubt that the Calvinistic doctrine of predestination not only influenced the formation of the Congregational system, but also intensified the growth of a democratic spirit. The members of each congregation were the elect. Every member alike had a divine call and might speak before the congregation when moved by the Spirit. " If the excellency of this calling were

---

[1] Browne, *Booke which Sheweth*, Def. 35; Dexter, *Congregationalism of the Last Three Hundred Years*, p. 105.

[2] John Robinson, *A Just and Necessary Apology*, 1625; Hanbury, *Memorials of the Independents*, I. 379.

[3] *True and Short Declaration*, 19; Dexter, pp. 105, 106.

[4] *Treatise of Reformation*, Def. 4.

well weighed and rightly prized," wrote Robinson,[1] " no man honored therewith should be thought worthy to be despised for any other meanness; nor without it, to be envied for any other excellency, how glorious soever in the world's eye." Under such circumstances there could be no spiritual prerogative, no caste distinction between clergy and laity, no external control.[2]

A religious democracy of this sort, based on the freedom and equality of all individuals, could not but give rise to democratic political principles. The covenant by which the individual congregation is formed, applied to the State, is the contract theory of government. It was not difficult to conclude that, since any number of individuals could of their own free consent form a congregation, so they could also voluntarily contract to form a State; as the authority rested in the entire congregation, so in the body of the people; as Church members are equal, so are the citizens of the State.

The bitterness with which James I. and Charles I. attacked the Independents was due in no small degree to their realization of the fact that the heretical religious opinions of the Separatists would eventually breed liberal political views. Peter Heylyn, a creature of Laud, attacked the "puritan tenet" "that kings are but the ministers of the commonwealth; and that they have no more authority than what is given them by the people." He regards the Puritan religion as "rebellion" and their faith as "faction." [3]

The Independents not only opposed the episcopal system of church government, to which the Stuarts had committed themselves by their adage "no bishop,

---

[1] *Essays or Observations Divine and Moral*, 1625, Obs. 27.

[2] Weingarten, H., *Die Revolutionskirchen Englands*, 1868, p. 28.

[3] Hanbury, *Memorials of the Independents*, II. 15, 16.

no king," but also denied that kings ruled by divine right and that subjects must render passive obedience.

The doctrine of the divine right of kings found a blasphemous expression in the speech of James I. from the throne delivered in 1609, which contained the words: "God hath power to create or destroy, to make or unmake at His pleasure, to give life or send death; and to God both body and soul are due. And the like power have kings: they make and unmake their subjects; they have the power of raising and casting down, of life and of death—judges over all their subjects, and in all causes, and yet accountable to none but God only. They have power to exalt low things, and abuse high things, and make their subjects like men of chess: a power to take a bishop or a knight, and to cry up or down any of their subjects as they do their money." [1]

The Anglican Church preached these doctrines from the pulpit. The clergy bitterly attacked the doctrine that "all civil power, jurisdiction, and authority were first derived from the people and disordered multitude, or either is originally still in them, or else is deduced by their consent naturally from them; and is not God's ordinance originally descending from Him and depending upon Him." [2]

The Canons of June 30, 1640, affirmed that the most high and sacred order of kings is of divine right, being the ordinance of God Himself, founded in the prime laws of nature and revelation, by which the

[1] Neal, *History of the Puritans*, London, 1732, II. 76; Rapin, *History of England*, II. 178.

[2] Bishop Overall's *Convocation Book of 1606*; Gardiner, *Hist. of England*, 1603–42, I. 289, 290; Green, *Short History*, Ch. 8, sec. 2.

supreme power over all persons, civil and ecclesiastical, is given to them.[1]

Against such assertions made by autocratic royalty and servile episcopacy, the Independents declared with Junius Brutus that they would obey the king if he obeyed the law; that sovereignty, the *majestas realis*, lay not in the king, but in the people, and that magistrates had no power over the consciences of men. Their ideas found a classical expression in the works of Milton.

It was during the Civil War that the Independents came into prominence in England. The "Brownists," as the earliest Congregationalists were called, who made their appearance during the reign of Elizabeth, had almost entirely disappeared by the close of her reign. Most of them had emigrated to Holland. Thus a congregation driven from Scrooby had, together with their pastor, John Robinson, sought refuge first at Amsterdam, then at Leyden. Upon this congregation the fate of Congregationalism may be said to have rested, not only because Robinson changed "Brownism" to Congregationalism, but for the reason that this congregation migrated to America and founded Plymouth in 1620. In America Congregationalism found a home and became the prevalent church polity of New England. In England it was known as the "New England way." American Independents, Thomas Hooker, Roger Williams, and Sir Henry Vane, were the first democrats among the Congregationalists. Roger Williams' *Bloudy Tenent*, in which the sovereignty of the people is expressed, was sent to the English Parliament in 1644. Vane, the boy governor of Massachusetts Bay, returned

[1] Laud's Works, V. 607 *sq.* Gardiner, *Hist. of England*, IX. 144, 145.

to England and played a prominent part during the Civil War and Commonwealth.[1]

After the meeting of the Long Parliament and the execution of Strafford, Nonconformists from all parts of Europe and from the colonies returned to England. Among them were many Independents. For a while they joined with the Presbyterians in opposing episcopacy.[2] The two denominations worked together in harmony until Laud was imprisoned and the Episcopal Church vanquished. Then dissensions arose between them. Soon the two parties became mortal enemies.

In Cromwell's army the Independents played a very important part. After the victory at Naseby their number and power increased rapidly. Nearly the whole of Fairfax's army of twenty-two thousand men consisted of Independents.[3] During the Civil War the prevailing appellation of the Independents was the "Saints." [4] Baxter, the famous preacher, who entered the army to convert the sectaries, tells us that many of the soldiers were vehement advocates of democracy both in Church and State, and that they denounced all government except a popular one, and opposed the interference of magistrates in Church affairs. He classes Sir Henry Vane and Arthur Haselrigg among fanatical democrats and advocates of universal liberty of conscience.[5]

[1] On New England Independency see Cotton Mather's *Magnalia;* Dexter, *Congregationalism of the Last Three Hundred Years; Life of Vane,* by Hosmer; Weingarten, *Die Revolutionskirchen Englands;* Masson's *Life of Milton,* Vol. III.; Gardiner, *History of England;* Osgood, in *Polit. Science Quarterly,* 1891.

[2] Baillie, *Letters and Journals,* I. 311.

[3] Godwin, *History of the Commonwealth,* II. pp. 64, 152.

[4] Weingarten, p. 83.

[5] Abridgment of *Baxter's Life and Times,* by Calamy, I. pp. 90, 91, 100.

Among the Independents there were those to whom political questions were of prime interest. Of them Bastwick says: "I myself have heard many of them say that it is unlawful to fight for religion, and they professed that when they went out with the sword in their hands they fought only for the liberty of their consciences and for a toleration of religion, which is a part and branch, as they said, of the subject's birthright." [1]

They were known as Levellers and falsely accused of being communists by many of their contemporaries. The theory of Natural Law was at the foundation of their political ideas. They claimed that no laws were valid that conflicted with the Laws of Nature. They held that the people had rights which were "due to them by God's Law of Nature." [2] "It is equal, necessary, and of natural right," the Levellers said, "that the people, by their own deputies, should choose their own laws." [3] They demanded that laws be grounded upon equity and reason, giving universal freedom to all.[4] Their religious beliefs were theistic. They looked to the law of righteousness in men, rather than to the Scriptures,[5] for guidance and instruction. They demanded a reformation of social and political affairs according to the light of nature and right reason.

The Levellers used the expression "birthright" frequently, meaning thereby the rights to which every free-born Englishman was naturally entitled by abstract right. Before the Norman Conquest the common peo-

---

[1] *The Utter Routing of the Whole Army of the Independents and Sectaries.* Lond., 1646.

[2] The Leveller, in *Harleian Miscellany*, IV. p. 547.

[3] *Ibid.*, p. 545.

[4] Letter to Lord Fairfax, *Harl. Misc.*, VIII. p. 590.

[5] *Ibid.*, VIII. 591; Edwards, *Gangraena*, III. p. 20.

ple were in possession of their rights, they said, but
William the Conqueror "turned the English out of
their birthrights," [1] and compelled them to be servants
to him and his Norman soldiers.   To the Norman Conquest some of the Levellers, commonly known as Dig-
gers, held the enslavement of the common people to be
due.   According to them, Charles was the successor to
the English crown from William the Conqueror, and all
the laws that had been made in every king's reign had
but confirmed and strengthened the power of the Norman Conquest, and still held the commons of England
under slavery to the kingly power, his gentry, and
clergy.[2]   They declared that the lords of manor were
the successors of the chief officers of the Conqueror
and held their land by the power of the sword.   They
asked whether lords of manor had not lost their royalty
to the common land, since the common people of England had "conquered King Charles and recovered themselves from under the Norman Conquest." [3]   The Norman conqueror "took freedom from every one," some
of the Levellers said, "and became the disposer both
of inclosures and commons;   therefore all persons, upon
the recovery of the Conquest, ought to return into freedom again without respecting persons," and ought "to
have the land of their nativity for their livelihood." [4]
The Levellers demanded that all laws "not grounded
upon equity and reason, not giving an universal freedom to all, but respecting persons . . . be cut off
with the king's head." [5]   They held that "every man,
of what quality or condition, place or office whatsoever, ought to be equally subject to the laws." [6]

---

[1] *Harleian Miscellany*, VIII. p. 589.   [3] *Ibid.*   [5] *Ibid.*
[2] *Ibid.*   [4] *Ibid.*, p. 590.
[6] *Ibid.*   See also Edwards, *Gangraena*, III. p. 194.

The Levellers wished the government of England to be by laws and not by men. The laws should be the preservers and protectors of the people's persons and estates. "They ought to decide all controversies and repair every man's injuries." "The rod of the people's supreme judicature ought to be over the magistrates to prevent their corruption or turning aside from the laws." "No man should be subject to the crooked will or corrupt affections of any man." [1] "All the laws, levies of moneys, war, and peace," they asserted, "ought to be made by the people's deputies in Parliament, to be chosen by them successively at certain periods of time, and that no council table, orders, ordinances, or court proclamations ought to bind the people's persons or estates." "It is the first principle of a people's liberty," they said, "that they shall not be bound but by their own consent; and this our ancestors left to England as its undoubted right, that no laws to bind our persons or estates could be imposed upon us against our wills, and they challenged it as their native right not to be controlled in making such laws as concerned their common right and interests." The laws should be for "the common and equal good of the whole nation." [2] They demanded the abolition of the House of Lords as not representative of the people and universal suffrage based on natural right. [3]

Edwards sums up the arguments of the Levellers as follows: "Seeing all men are by nature the sons of Adam and from him have legitimately derived a natural property, right, and freedom, therefore England and all other nations, and all particular persons in every nation,

---

[1] The Leveller, *Harl. Miscellany*, IV. p. 543.
[2] *Ibid.*
[3] *The Clarke Papers*, Preface, pp. 61, 63.

notwithstanding the difference of laws and governments, ranks and degrees, ought to be alike free and estated in their natural liberties, and to enjoy the just rights and prerogative of mankind, whereunto they are heirs apparent; and thus the Commoners by right are equal with the Lords. For by natural birth all men are equally and alike born to like property, liberty, and freedom; and as we are delivered of God by the hand of nature into this world, every one with a natural innate freedom and property, even so are we to live, every one equally and alike to enjoy his birthright and privilege." [1]

Many of the soldiers in Fairfax's army adopted the principles of the Levellers. These doctrines were suited to the times. Having taken up arms against the king it was but natural that the members of the army should be favorable to republican ideas. In a time of upheaval when the whole constitution of the country was being changed, the theory of Natural Right was seasonable.

The chief Levellers were Lieut.-Col. John Lilburn, Col. Rainborow, Wildman, Ewer, Scot, Overton, and Walwyn. On the 9th of October, 1647, a paper called "The Case of the Army" had been drawn up and signed by the agents of five regiments, which had been composed as a protest against the conduct of the officers who were accused of betraying the soldiers by entering into combination with the House of Lords, the Presbyterians, and the king's friends. It protested also against disbanding the army and called on the soldiers not to disperse until their grievances had been redressed and certain conditions fulfilled. The paper demanded that a term be set to the present Parliament; that Par-

[1] Edwards, *Gangraena*, III. p. 16.

liaments called in future be biennial and chosen by
universal suffrage; that a period be set for their meeting and dissolving; that the supreme power rest in the
House of Commons; that monopolies and tithes be
abolished; and that the laws of England be abridged
and codified.[1]

The mutiny in the army had become serious. October 27, 1647, the "Case of the Army" was taken into
consideration by the General Council of the whole army.[2]

On the 1st of November a paper of proposals from
nine regiments of horse and seven of foot, known as the
"First Agreement of the People," was presented to the
Council. It gave expression to essentially the same
principles as the "Case of the Army." This paper
declared the power of the representatives of the nation
to be "inferior only to those who choose them," and
to include all powers not expressly reserved by the
people. The reserves were as follows:

"1. That matters of religion and the ways of God's
worship are not at all entrusted by us to any human
power, because therein we cannot admit or exceed a
tittle of what our consciences dictate to be the mind of
God without wilful sin; nevertheless the public way of
instructing the nation, so it be not compulsive, is
referred to their discretion.

"2. That matters of impressing and constraining
any of us to serve in the wars is against our freedom,
and therefore we do not allow it in our representatives;
the rather because money, the sinews of war, being
always at their disposal, they cannot want numbers of
men apt enough to engage in any just cause.

"3. That after the dissolution of this present Par-

[1] Godwin, *History of the Commonwealth*, II. pp. 445–447.

[2] Rushworth, VII. 849; Godwin, *Commonwealth*, II. 445–451.

liament no persons to be at any time questioned for anything said or done in reference to the late public differences, otherwise than in execution of the judgments of the present representatives or House of Commons.

"4. That in all laws made or to be made every person may be bound alike, and that tenure, estates, charter, degree, birth, or place do not confer any exception from the ordinary course of legal proceedings whereunto others are subjected.

"5. That as the laws ought to be equal, so they must be good, and not evidently destructive to the safety and well-being of the people."

These they declare to be their "native rights."[1]

We have here the idea of a constitution in the American sense—the idea of laying down certain principles of government and popular rights with which the government might not interfere. The same distrust of the representatives of the people influenced the Levellers as the American colonists of later days.[2]

In the debates that took place in the council of the army on these two papers, there seemed to be an agreement that government is founded on contract. Pettus said: "Every man is naturally free, and I judge the reason why men, when they were in so great numbers, chose representatives, was that every man could not give his voice, and therefore men agreed to come into some form of government that they who were chosen might preserve property."[3] Even Ireton, who was averse to manhood suffrage and abstract right, considers property to be founded on contract. He opposed

[1] Rushworth, VII. pp. 860, 861; Godwin, II. 449, 450.
[2] Borgeaud, *The Rise of Modern Democracy*, 1891, *passim.*
[3] *The Clarke Papers*, I. p. 312.

the natural rights theory because of the dangerous consequences that might result therefrom. He held that one person would have as much right to appropriate anything necessary for his sustenance and the satisfaction of his desires as another if it were not for the fact that men are under contract, by which each enjoys the undisturbed right to the property he receives from his ancestors, with submission to that general authority which is set up to preserve peace and support the law. This is considered "the foundation of all right any man has to anything but to his own person." [1] He opposed the belief of Wildman that unjust engagements might be broken. He said it made him tremble to think of the boundless and endless consequences that might result if men might observe or break engagements according as they deemed them just or unjust.[2]

The Levellers believed in manhood suffrage. "The poorest he that is in England," said Col. Rainborow, "has a life to live as the greatest he. . . . Every man that is to live under a government ought first by his own consent to put himself under that government. . . . The poorest man in England is not all bound in a strict sense to that government that he has not had a voice to put himself under." [3]

Ireton replied that the argument for universal suffrage must be based on absolute natural right—on what is just and due to all inhabitants and not on what is allowed them by the law. It was his opinion that no one had a right to a share in determining the affairs of a country who had no permanent interest in that country.

[1] *The Clarke Papers*, I. pp. 263, 264.
[2] *Ibid.*
[3] *Ibid.*, p. 301.

Rainborow held it must be either by the law of God or of man that the meanest person is prohibited from exercising his rights as well as the greatest. He said he could find nothing in the law of God, the law of nature, or that of nations, to the effect that a lord should choose twenty burgesses, a gentleman two, and a poor man none. All Englishmen, he maintained, must be subject to English laws, and no man would deny "that the foundation of all law lies in the people." [1] Pettus also holds that all "inhabitants that have not lost their birthright should have an equal voice in elections." [2]

Wildman asserted that the people had hitherto been enslaved. Their laws had been made by their conquerors. But the people were now engaged for their freedom. "Every person in England had as clear a right to elect his representative as the greatest person in England." Wildman conceived it to be "the undeniable maxim of government that all government is in the free consent of the people." "There is no person that is under a just government or has justly his own unless he, by his own free consent, be put under that government." [3]

Sexby said that the soldiers had ventured their lives in war to recover their birthrights. Every man, he held, had a birthright, even though he possessed no property. [4]

The principles of the Levellers are most completely expressed in Lilburn's "Third Agreement of the People," of May, 1649. These principles are: That men are naturally free and equal; that they have natural rights; that all powers emanate from the people; that government is founded in the consent of the governed. The

[1] *The Clarke Papers*, I. p. 304.   [3] *Ibid.*, p. 318.
[2] *Ibid.*, p. 300.   [4] *Ibid.*, pp. 322, 323.

Levellers demanded a reformation of the government of England according to republican principles. Their political programme was: No king, no House of Lords; the House of Commons to be the supreme authority, and to be truly representative of the people; periodical parliaments; universal suffrage; equality of all before the law; separation of Church and State; universal toleration to all except papists and exclusion of these only on political grounds; no test acts; no imprisonment for debt; conviction for life, liberty, etc., by jury alone; men's lives to be taken only for murder; freedom of trade and labor; self-government: cities, towns, and boroughs to elect their officers for a year; abolition of all privileges and exemptions; every parish to choose its own ministers.[1]   These ideal laws were to be eternally binding.

Cromwell, Ireton, and other Independents, though themselves inclining to republicanism, would not go as far as this. Of the first agreement as proposed by the Levellers, which was not even as radical as the third agreement, Cromwell said: "This paper does contain in it very great alterations of the very government of the kingdom, alteration from that government that it has been under, I believe I may almost say since it was a nation . . . and what the consequences of such an alteration as this would be, if there were nothing else to be considered, wise men and godly men ought to consider." [2]

The "Agreement of the People" (no longer Lilburn's paper, however) was approved by the Council of Officers January 15, 1649, and presented to Parliament. But neither the officers of the army nor Parliament

[1] See *résumé* in Whitelocke, *Memorials*, III. 25, 26.
[2] *The Clarke Papers*, I. pp. 236, 237.

purposed to carry it out. The House of Lords ceased to meet after February 5; monarchy was abolished February 7. The Commons now took all power into their own hands.[1] On the 4th of January, 1649, the Commons resolved: "That the people are, under God, the original of all just powers; that the Commons of England, in Parliament assembled, being chosen by and representing the people, have the supreme power in this nation; that whatsoever is enacted or declared for law by the Commons in Parliament assembled hath the force of law, and all the people of this nation are concluded thereby, although the consent and concurrence of king or House of Peers be not had thereunto."[2] But the Commons did not intend to sign their own death-warrant by accepting the "Agreement of the People" presented by the army, much less the more radical third agreement composed by Lilburn in May, 1649, whose main tenets we have given above. Parliament claimed to be representative of the people, but was far from resting on the idea of the sovereignty of the people.[3] The Levellers did not succeed in effecting the reforms they contemplated. Nor did their influence extend beyond their own day. It was the more moderate republicans—Sidney, Harrington, and Milton —whose influence continued beyond their own time. Milton gives the fullest expression to the views of the Independents. His *Tenure of Kings and Magistrates* appeared February 13, 1648–1649, soon after the establishment of the Commonwealth. It is entirely republi-

[1] Cobbett, *Parliamentary History*, III. p. 1284; Ranke, *History of England*, III. p. 8.

[2] Cobbett, *Parliamentary History*, III. 1275; Gardiner, *History of the Great Civil War*, III. p. 561.

[3] Ranke, *History of England*, III. p. 6.

can in its principles. He considers all men to have been born free, inasmuch as they are the image of God. They were born to command, not to obey. Sin brought violence and wrong into the world. To escape common destruction men agreed to bind each other from mutual injury. In this way cities, towns, and commonwealths arose. This is the unhistorical contract theory of the origin of society which was held since antiquity. The people then formed another contract, by which they deputed the power that was naturally and originally in them singly and collectively to kings and magistrates, intending them to be deputies and commissioners, not lords and masters. They were entrusted with power in order that they might execute that justice which each by nature and by covenant must have executed for himself. While magistrates are above the people, the law is above them. Milton considers it to be destructive of law and government to hold that kings are answerable to God alone. "Since the king or magistrate holds his authority of the people, both originally and naturally for their good in the first place, and not his own; then may the people, as oft as they shall judge it for the best, either choose or reject him, retain him or depose him though no tyrant, merely by the liberty and right of free-born men to be governed as seems to them best." [1]

Milton considers a tyrant to be a ruler who reigns for himself and not for the common good. Such a man may be proceeded against as a common pest. Here, as in other respects, Milton shares the views of the Calvinistic Monarchomachists. He proves from both Old and New Testament and from history that tyrannicide is lawful. He accuses the Presbyterians of hypocrisy

[1] *Tenure of Kings and Magistrates.*

and inconstancy because they began the Revolution and then denied that subjects had a right to punish their king. He employs all the resources of his learning to prove to them their errors. He draws his arguments from history, literature, and logic. A boundless love of freedom pervades this pamphlet. In reading it one feels the feverish agitation of the time. Though Milton defends tyrannicide, it is not from low or selfish motives he does so, but from the lofty consideration of public necessity.

In his *Defence of the People of England* Milton undertook to efface the impression the fate of Charles I. had made upon Europe. It was an answer to the *Defensio regia* of Salmasius, a famous French scholar who held a professorship in the University of Leyden, the rendezvous of English royalists. Salmasius was accused of having turned traitor to his former liberal views for love of gain, and of having become the tool of the Pretender. It is necessary to bear this in mind to understand the virulence of Milton's attack upon him. The contention between the two resembled that between Filmer and Locke at a later date, in regard to the principles contested.

Milton points out the difference between royal and paternal power, which Salmasius asserted to be identical. While fathers beget their children, he asserted, kings do not make their subjects, but are themselves made by them. A tyrant may be deposed and punished according to his deserts. This Milton endeavors to prove by illustrations from history, and by natural and divine law. The king is for the people. Since the people collectively are superior to him, he has no right to enslave or oppress them. Milton puts forth the theory that royal power is but deputed power. By natural right men formed governments and set up kings for the preservation of life, liberty, and safety. By natural right they may depose those very persons whom they advanced to the government. "Nature does not regard the good of one or of a few, but of all in general." The people did not exhaust themselves by transferring power to their rulers. This power still virtually resides in them. Power was not settled on the king absolutely as if it were his property, but committed to him as a trust, to be exercised for the public safety and liberty.

To the doctrine of divine right, Milton opposes that of the sovereignty of the people. He regards the common welfare as the supreme law and the end of government. Law shall rule in the State, not the pleasure of the prince. Whoever breaks the law must be punished, even though he be king. On every page of this book Milton's reverence for the law, hatred of tyranny, love of individual liberty, and moral earnestness manifest themselves and serve, in some measure at least, to counteract the unpleasant impression left upon the mind by reading the abusive language which the stern Puritan heaps upon his servile opponent.

In his *Defence* Milton declines to decide which form of government is the best. He says that though many eminent men have extolled monarchy, it was under the supposition that the prince excelled in noble qualities and was more competent than any other person to reign. If he is not such a person, no form of government is so likely to degenerate into a tyranny. He believes those persons extremely rare, if they can be found at all, who deserve to be clothed with a power on earth that resembles the power God exercises in heaven, for they must infinitely excel all other men, and both for wisdom and goodness in some measure resemble the Deity.

Milton's *Ready and Easy Way to Establish a Free Commonwealth*, written on the eve of the Restoration, echoes his own disappointment and that of the Independents, at the failure of their hopes for a free government. It is incomprehensible to him how a people calling themselves free, can allow any man to be hereditary lord over them, renounce their freedom, and become servants and vassals. How a people who have fought so gloriously for freedom can change their noble words and actions into the base necessity of court flatteries and prostrations, he declares to be lamentable to think upon. Milton cannot comprehend "how any man who hath the true principles of justice and religion in him can presume to take upon him to be king and lord over his brethren, whom he cannot but know, whether as men or Christians, to be for the most part every way equal or superior to himself; how he can display with such vanity and ostentation his royal splendor, so supereminently above other mortal men; or, being a Christian, can assume such extraordinary honor and worship to himself while the kingdom of Christ, our common king and lord, is hid to this world."

Milton believes that civil and religious liberty can exist only in a free commonwealth. He prizes toleration as a sacred right, and expresses the views of the Independents on the subject, who, since Roger Williams' visit in 1644, had made religious toleration part of their political platform.[1] "Who can be at rest," writes Milton, "who can enjoy anything in this world with contentment, who hath not liberty to serve God and to save his own soul according to the best light

[1] Masson's *Life of Milton*, III. p. 113 *et seq.*

which God hath planted in him to that purpose, by the reading of His revealed will and the guidance of His Holy Spirit?" "This liberty of conscience," he continues, "which above all other things ought to be to all men dearest and most precious, no government is more inclinable not to favor only, but to protect, than a free commonwealth, as being most magnanimous, most fearless, and confident of its own fair proceedings. Whereas kingship, though looking big, yet indeed most pusillanimous, full of fears, full of jealousies, starting at every umbrage, as it hath been observed of old to have ever suspected most and mistrusted them who were in most esteem for virtue and generosity of mind, so it is now known to have most in doubt and suspicion them who are most reputed to be religious."

But not only is religious freedom most certain in a free commonwealth, Milton holds, but also the enjoyment of civil rights and advancement of every person according to his merit.

It was in America that the ideas of Milton were most completely realized. One cannot fail to be struck with the similarity of his views to those of the fathers of the American republic. There is also hardly a single idea in Locke's political philosophy which is not already found in Milton's writings.[1]

James Harrington's writings exerted but little influence in his own country. This may be due to their fantastical style. Perhaps the republican principles contained in them were distasteful to his countrymen. But

[1] On Milton see Masson's *Life*, esp. III., IV.; Weber, in *Raumer's Hist. Taschenbuch*, Dritte Folge, 3, 4; Treitschke, *Histor. u. polit. Aufsätze*, I. p. 86 *et seq.*, and in the *Staatswörterbuch* of Bluntschli; Bluntschli, *Gesch. d. neuer. Staatswiss.*, pp. 105–119.

the American colonists were very fond of his books. Otis confesses himself greatly indebted to the "great and incomparable" Harrington.[1] John Adams and Jefferson were also familiar with his writings, as their works show.

The *Oceana* appeared in 1656. The first part of the book treats of the principles of government; the second, of the art of making a commonwealth; the third, of the effect of such art; the fourth, of the consequences of such a government. The principles contained in the book resemble those of the Levellers in many instances.

Harrington wishes government to be "the empire of laws, not of men."[2] "The liberty of a commonwealth," he says, "consists in the empire of her laws."[3] "There is a common right," he holds with Hooker,[4] " Law of Nature, or interest of the whole, which is more excellent . . . than the right or interest of the parts only."[5] As the interest of mankind is the right interest, so the reason of mankind must be right reason. The interest of popular government comes nearest to the interest of mankind. So the reason of popular government comes nearest to right reason, for reason is nothing but interest.[6]

Harrington believes that there is a natural aristocracy diffused by God throughout the whole body of mankind. The people have not only a natural but also a positive obligation to make use of these natural aristocrats of genius as guides. They are to form the senate in the commonwealth and to be, not the com-

---

[1] In his *Rights of the Colonies.*
[2] *Oceana*, p. 2.
[3] *Ibid.*, p. 11.
[4] *Eccles. Pol.*, Bk. I.
[5] *Oceana*, p. 12.
[6] *Ibid.*

manders of the people, but their counsellors and advisors.[1]

The interest of the commonwealth he declares to be in the whole body of the people.[2] The commonwealth consists of the senate proposing, the people resolving, and the magistracy executing.[3] The magistrate is answerable to the people that his administration be according to the law.[4] "This free-born nation," he says of the commonwealth, "liveth not upon the dole or bounty of one man, but, distributing her annual magistracies and honors with her own hand, is herself King People."[5]

The republican principles of Milton, Harrington, and the Independents were also shared by the noble Algernon Sidney. Of the early Britons and Germans Sidney says that liberty and a participation in the government was "their common right and inheritance unalienable," the common council being the basis and hinge of government however the administration rolled. He says that when Germany gave Britain a people it gave her a free people.[6]

Of the mediæval schoolmen Sidney holds that though they "were corrupt, they were neither stupid nor unlearned; they could not but see that which all men saw, nor lay more approved foundations than that man is naturally free; that he cannot justly be deprived

[1] *Oceana*, p. 14.

[2] *Ibid.*, p. 14.

[3] *Ibid.*, p. 15.

[4] *Ibid.*, p. 15.

[5] *Ibid.*, p. 83. See the article of T. W. Dwight, in the *Political Science Quarterly* for 1887, for the influence of Harrington on the American colonists.

[6] *A General View of Government in Europe*, p. 28; first printed in 1744, though written long before.

of that liberty without cause, and that he doth not resign it, or any part of it, unless it be in consideration of a greater good, which he proposes to himself." Sidney asserts that nations are left to the use of their own judgment in making provision for their own welfare, and that there is no lawful magistrate over any people but such as they have themselves set up. In creating their magistrates, he affirms, the people do not seek the advantage of these, but their own interest.[1] He names Hayward, Blackwood, and Barclay as admitting the natural liberty and equality of mankind.[2] His view of the origin of government is the following: "Every number of men, agreeing together and framing a society, became a complete body, having all power in themselves over themselves, subject to no other human law than their own. All those that compose the society, being equally free to enter into it or not, no man could have any prerogative over others unless it were granted by the consent of the whole. Nothing obliging them to enter into the society but the consideration of their own good, that good, or the opinion of it, must have been the rule, motive, and end of all that they did ordain. It is lawful, therefore, for any such bodies to set up one or a few men to govern them, or to retain the power in themselves. And he or they who are set up, having no other power but what is so conferred upon them by that multitude, whether great or small, are truly by them made what they are, and, by the law of their own creation, are to exercise those powers according to the proportion and to the ends for which they were given."[3]

[1] *Discourses concerning Government*, Ch. 2, sec. 3.
[2] *Ibid.*
[3] *Ibid.*, Ch. 2, sec. 5.

Sidney holds that men form civil society by their own free will. Their consent to resign that part of their liberty which the good of the whole demands, is the voice of Nature and the act of men, according to natural reason, seeking their own good.[1] It is from God and nature, not from kings, that the liberties of men spring.[2] No people can be obliged to suffer from their kings what these have no right to do. The contract between people and magistrates is real, solemn, and obligatory. It continues in force only so long as he with whom this compact is made performs its stipulations.[3] The mischiefs suffered from wicked kings are such as render it both reasonable and just for all nations that have virtue and power to exert both in repelling them.[4] Unjust commands are not to be obeyed.[5] The sanction of laws is derived, not from antiquity or from the dignity of the legislator, but from intrinsic equity and justice. Laws should be framed according to that universal reason to which all nations, at all times, owe an equal veneration and obedience. By this Law of Nature princes are obliged to preserve the lands, goods, lives, and liberties of their subjects. By this same law subjects have a right to their liberties, lands, and goods, and need not depend upon the will of any man. Such dependence would be the destruction of their liberties.[6]

The revolutionary tendency of such doctrines as these is apparent. Natural Law, which at its genesis seemed so harmless, had already shown its destructive tendencies. The doctrines latent in this conception

[1] *Discourses*, Ch. 2, sec. 20.
[2] Ch. 2, sec. 31.
[3] Ch. 3, sec. 4.
[4] Ch. 3, sec. 5.
[5] Ch. 3, sec. 20.
[6] Ch. 3, sec. 2, 16.

had all shown themselves during the Puritan Revolution—such ideas as the contract theory, government being based upon the consent of the governed, the right of resisting a ruler who has violated faith with his people, the natural liberty and equality of men, and other kindred theories which, during the French Revolution, were to upset the entire existing social and political order. Sidney is one of the most famous exponents of these ideas.

Most of these political doctrines were accepted by the Whigs, who are to be regarded as the descendants of the Independents. The Whigs brought about and justified the bloodless Revolution of 1688, which drove James II. from the English throne. The Convention affirms concerning the matter: "That King James the Second, having endeavoured to subvert the constitution of the Kingdom, by breaking the original Contract between King and People, and having, by the advice of Jesuits, and other wicked persons, violated the fundamental laws, and withdrawn himself out of this Kingdom, has abdicated the Government, and that the throne is thereby vacant."

The theories of the Independents and Whigs, especially as expressed in the works of Sidney, and of John Locke, the leading Whig political philosopher, also found many advocates in France. Bourdaloue, the famous preacher at the court of Louis XIV., preached them from the pulpit, even in the presence of royalty.[1] It was especially after the Revolution of 1688 that these doctrines spread on the Continent. Sidney's *Discourse on Civil Government* was translated into French in 1702 and was read by Rousseau. In 1750 d'Argenson wrote:

[1] Hettner, *Litteraturgeschichte des 18. Jahrhunderts*, II.

"The English ideas on politics and liberty have passed the sea and are being adopted here." [1]

Before we consider the influence of these doctrines on Rousseau we must show how they found an expression in the famous work of Locke on Civil Government. John Locke regards the legislative power as supreme in the State. To it all other parts of the government must be subordinate. But the legislative power is only fiduciary. There rests "in the people a supreme power to remove or alter the legislative." When the trust placed in it is violated the power devolves back to the people who gave it. Whenever the liberties and properties of the subjects are subverted, the community may use its supreme power. "No man, or society of men, having a power to deliver up their preservation, or consequently the means of it, to the absolute will and arbitrary dominion of another, whenever any one shall go about to bring them into such a slavish condition, they will always have a right to preserve what they have not a power to part with, and to rid themselves of those who invade this fundamental, sacred, and unalterable law of self-preservation, for which they entered into society. And thus the community may be said in this respect to be always the supreme power, but not as considered under any form of government, because this power of the people can never take place till the government be dissolved." [2]

If the executive power uses force against the legislative, there is no other remedy but to repel force by

---

[1] See J. Texte, *J. J. Rousseau et les origines du cosmopolitisme littéraire*, Paris, 1895, pp. 25, 26; Buckle, *History of Civilization in England*, I. Ch. 12, which contains a list of those Frenchmen who were familiar with English literature.

[2] *Of Civil Government*, Ch. 13, § 149.

force.[1] Should either executive or legislative attempt
to enslave or destroy the people, the people, having no
judge on earth, can appeal only to Heaven. For the
rulers have, by such attempts become tyrants, and
exercise a power never given to them.[2]

Tyranny is the exercise of power beyond right, says
Locke; the use of government, not for the good of the
citizens, but for private advantage. Any magistrate
who exceeds " his lawful power acts without authority
and may be opposed as any other man who by force
invades the rights of another." If "illegal acts have
extended to the majority of the people, or if the mis-
chief and oppression has lighted only on some few, but
in such cases, as the precedent and consequences seem
to threaten all, and they are persuaded in their consciences that their laws, and with them their estates,
liberties, and lives are in danger, and perhaps their
religion too, how they will be hindered from resisting
illegal force used against them I cannot tell." [3] From
this it will be seen that Locke is the theorist of revolutions. The foundation of his political system is the
sovereign power of the community. The end of all
government is the good of the people. Institutions can
be founded on the consent of the people alone.[4]

In America the principles of the Whigs fell upon a
more fruitful soil than in England. The Whig platform
became the platform of the colonists. Its doctrines
were embodied in the Declaration of Independence and
the American Bills of Rights.[5]

---

[1] *Of Civil Government*, Ch. 13, § 155.

[2] *Ibid.*, § 168.

[3] *Ibid.*, Ch. 18.

[4] *Ibid.*, Ch. 16.

[5] Hutchinson, *Hist. Mass.*, III. 103; Maine, *Ancient Law*, pp.
91, 92; Hallam, *Literature of Europe*, II. 362; Frothingham,
The Rise of the Republic of the U. S., p. 165.

CHAPTER VII

NOTHING could be more erroneous than to attribute to Rousseau's influence the formation of the French Declaration of the Rights of Man. As we shall endeavor to show, it was from America that the French learned of the idea of such a declaration. It was not from Rousseau the Americans derived their principles. In reality Rousseau's political philosophy, which aimed at securing freedom and equality, was destructive to individual rights. He has the individual surrender all his rights, without retaining a remnant of them, to the sovereign people or *volonté générale*. By this contract the individual exchanges "his natural liberty and an unlimited right to all he holds and is able to obtain" for the civil liberty which is limited by the general will.[1] Though Rousseau asserted liberty to be inalienable, though he believed that equality would be preserved by having all individuals alike sacrifice the sum total of their liberties to the sovereign of which each individual is a part, he nevertheless established a despot whose power is as autocratic as is that of the *Leviathan* of Hobbes. This tyrant is Demos. The views of Rousseau could not give rise to the Declaration of the Rights of Man because he holds that each individual, upon entering society, surrenders his natural rights completely, without retaining the least residuum. Rousseau's *volonté*

[1] *Du Contrat Social*, I. 8.

générale is almighty, and is not restricted by the rights of the individual. To lose sight of this is to oversee one of the cardinal points of his system. It was the English theorists, notably Milton and Locke, who had insisted upon the fact that the natural rights of the individual were inalienable. It was their view that gave rise to the Declaration of the Rights of Man, not Rousseau's. Again the latter maintains that upon the sovereign people no law of any kind can be binding. Neither is any guarantee necessary, for the sovereign can never intend his own injury. Whatever the sovereign wishes ought to be. Obviously this view militates against any reservations of individual rights.

Yet though we cannot give Rousseau the credit of having given rise to this declaration, we must regard him as the apostle of a new social and political era. Though his works are full of contradictions and visionary ideas, probably no writer ever exerted a greater influence than he. That is largely due to the fact that he was the true child of his time. He was oppressed by the abuses and evils of the old régime and longed for a more natural condition of affairs. It is this desire for freedom which characterizes him as it does his contemporaries. It was this desire for liberty, for naturalness, which appealed to them. Most of them did not see the real consequence of his political system until the Reign of Terror opened their eyes to the fact that sovereign Demos may become as great a tyrant as any king. It is therefore safe to say that though the *Contrat Social* did not beget the Declaration of the Rights of Man, the enthusiasm with which the idea of such a declaration met in France was due in no small part to the writings of Rousseau. A brief consideration of his doctrines will, therefore, not be out of place.

"Man is born free, and everywhere he is in chains. Many a person considers himself lord over his fellows, and yet is more of a slave than they. How has this change taken place? I know not. How can it be made legitimate? I believe I can answer that question." Thus Rousseau begins his *Contrat Social*. These words define the purpose of that work.

"The strongest is not strong enough to remain master if he does not change his might into right, obedience into duty." Might, says Rousseau, does not confer right. Since no man has a natural power over his fellows, there is no other foundation of lawful power among men except what arises from contract.[1]

He declares it to be absurd "to believe a man may give himself away gratuitously. Such an act is unlawful and void, because the person who performs it is devoid of good sense. To say a people may enslave themselves is to declare them to be insane; insanity does not give right."[2] "To renounce one's liberty is to renounce the quality of being a man, the rights of humanity, and even its duties. No adequate compensation can be made to any person who has relinquished all. Such a renunciation is incompatible with the nature of man. To take away freedom of will is to remove all morality from one's actions. It is a vain and contradictory agreement to stipulate absolute authority on the one hand and boundless obedience on the other. Is it not evident that one has not engaged in anything to any person from whom one has a right to exact anything?"[3] Even though in these words Rousseau declared that an individual could not relinquish his liberty, with even more emphasis than Milton, Locke, or any other political philosopher, yet

[1] I. 3, 4.   [2] I. 4.   [3] I. 4.

his attempt to preserve this freedom and equality intact was not successful because he confuses liberty with democracy.

When men have arrived at a point where the single efforts of individuals do not suffice to overcome the obstacles that are pernicious to men's preservation in the natural state, this original condition can last no longer without leading to the destruction of the human race. Since men cannot produce new forces they must combine existing forces and have them work as a whole. This combination can be formed only when a number combine their efforts. How can this be achieved without sacrificing the strength and freedom of each individual? How can a "form of association be found which defends and protects with the entire combined force the person and property of each individual associated, and by which each, uniting himself to all, obeys but himself and remains as free as before"?[1] The social contract is the solution of this problem.

The stipulations of this contract are so constituted that the least change makes them void and ineffective. Though not explicitly pronounced, they are everywhere accepted tacitly. If the contract is broken, each individual receives his original rights and natural liberty again, losing the freedom which rested upon contract, to obtain which he relinquished his natural rights.

All these stipulations may be reduced to a single one, namely, the alienation of each person with all his rights to the entire community. If each gives up himself entirely the condition is alike for all and equality is preserved. No one is interested in rendering the relation which is the same for all, onerous to any one in particular. Inasmuch as each gives himself to all, he

[1] *Contrat Social*, I. 6.

gives himself to no one in particular. Since each receives the same right over every other individual as he yields to him, he receives a compensation for what he loses, and more force to preserve what he possesses. "Each of us gives to the community his person and all his power under the supreme direction of the general will, and we receive each member as an indivisible part of the whole body." [1] The social contract, says Rousseau, produces a moral and collective body composed of as many members as the assembly has voices. The association gives to the body resulting therefrom its unity, its common self (*son moi commun*), its life, and will. This public person is called republic or body politic. When passive it is a State; when active, sovereign; when compared with other like bodies, power. In regard to those associated, the name people is employed. Each individual is a citizen when considered as a participant in the sovereign authority, and a subject when submitting to the laws of the State.[2]

This contract between the individual and the State being mutual, binds the individual as a member of the sovereign to the other members, as member of the State to the sovereign. The sovereign cannot be bound toward himself; he can impose no law which he could not break. Inasmuch as the sovereign can consider himself only in one and the same relation, he is in the same situation as a private person contracting with himself. There is no sort of fundamental obligation for the body of the people, not even the social contract.[3]

The sovereign owes his existence to the sanctity of the contract. He can therefore never bind himself to anything which would cause an alteration of this contract. He can never alienate any portion of himself.

[1] *Contrat Social*, I. 6.   [2] I. 6.   [3] I. 7.

He cannot submit to another sovereign. The violation of the fundamental compact by which he exists would be self-destruction.[1]

Rousseau regards freedom as unalienable because based on the equality of all. This equality itself results from the absolute reciprocity of the relinquishment each individual has made to the sovereign. Freedom is not given up even though natural rights are exchanged for civil rights. The association compels its members to be free, for if a single member of the body politic is harmed the whole body suffers. The sovereign's interests are identical with those of each individual. There is no necessity for any guarantee to the subjects, that is, for a declaration of their rights which the sovereign must not transgress, for the body can impossibly wish to harm its members. The sovereign is always what he ought to be.[2] "That which man loses by the social contract," says Rousseau, "is his natural liberty and the unlimited right to all he possesses and is able to obtain. What he gains is civil liberty and property in all he possesses. . . . It is necessary to distinguish natural liberty, which has no limits but the power of the individual, from civil liberty which is limited by the general will; and possession which is the result of force, or the right of first occupancy, from property, which can only be founded upon a positive title." [3]

Rousseau concludes his first book with the words which he declares to be the base of his system: "The fundamental compact does not destroy natural equality, but substitutes a moral and legitimate equality for the physical inequality nature may have put between men, so that though they be unequal in strength or intellect, they all become equal by convention and right." [4]

[1] *Contrat Social*, I. 7.   [2] I. 7.   [3] I. 8.   [4] I. 9.

In the second book of the *Contrat Social* Rousseau investigates the nature of sovereignty. He declares it to be the exercise of the general will. It can never be alienated. The sovereign, being a collective being, can only be represented by himself. The power may be transferred, but never the will.[1] Sovereignty is not only unalienable, but also indivisible. It is the general will, not a particular will; the will of the body of the people, not of a part. It is only the general will that possesses sovereignty and makes the law. The will of a particular person is at most a decree.

To divide sovereignty in its object, says Rousseau, that is, into force and will; legislative and executive powers; rights of taxation, of justice, and of war; is to make of the sovereignty a fantastic being formed of related parts. The error arises from considering as parts of this authority what are only emanations from it. The rights which are held to be parts of sovereignty are subordinated to it. They all presuppose a supreme will which is only executed by them.[2]

"The general will," Rousseau holds, "is always in the right and always tends to public utility. This is not saying that the decisions of the people are always equally right. Though any person always wishes for his best, it is not always possible to see what is best. The people cannot be corrupted, but they are often deceived. It is only then that they seem to wish what is evil."[3]

The general will (*volonté générale*) must be distinguished from the will of all (*volonté de tous*). While the former aims at the common welfare, the other looks only to private interest and is but the sum of particular wills. If the extremes be taken from the sums of the individual wills, there remains the general will.

[1] *Contrat Social*, II. 1.   [2] II. 2.   [3] II. 3.

Rousseau considers freedom and equality the greatest good. Every system of legislation should have their realization for its end. Liberty is necessary because the dependence of any individual reduces the force of the State. Equality is necessary because liberty cannot subsist without it. By equality it is not necessary to assume that degrees of power and wealth be absolutely the same. But power must never become violence, and must never be exercised except by virtue of office and the law. No citizen should be so rich as to be able to purchase another, nor so poor as to be compelled to sell himself.[1]

In the third book of the *Contrat Social* Rousseau enters upon a consideration of government. He declares every free action to result from a moral and a physical cause. The first determines upon the action, the second executes it. The body politic possesses both power and will. The latter constitutes the legislative, the former the executive, function. Without their cooperation nothing can happen in the State.[2]

The legislative power belongs to the people and can belong to them alone. The executive power cannot in the same way belong to the whole body. The executive power has to do only with private acts, which are not laws, and therefore not acts of sovereignty. "The public force requires an agent who unites it and puts it into action according to the directions of the general will, who connects State and sovereign and performs in some sort in the public person what the union of body and soul does in man. This is the government of the State, which is often confounded with the sovereign, whose servant it is."[3]

Government is "a body intermediate between the

<hr>

[1] *Contrat Social*, II. 2.   [2] III. 1.   [3] III. 1.

State and its subjects, established for their mutual correspondence, charged with the execution of the laws and the maintenance of civil and political liberty." [1] "The act by which a people submits to its chiefs is not a contract, but a commission by which, as simple officers of the sovereign, they exercise in his name the power whose depositors they are and which the sovereign may limit, modify, and resume whenever he pleases. The alienation of such a right being incompatible with the nature of the social body, is contrary to the purpose of the association." [2]

"Government or supreme administration is the legitimate exercise of the executive power, and the prince or magistrate is the man or body charged with the administration." [3]

Rousseau declares that as the sovereignty cannot be alienated, so it cannot be represented. It is the general will, and a will cannot be represented. "The deputies of the people are not their representatives; they are but agents (*commissaires*), and may not conclude anything definitely. Every law is void which the people do not ratify in person, and is no law. The English believe themselves to be free. They deceive themselves. They are free only during the time they elect members of Parliament. When these are elected they are slaves; they are nothing." [4]

He defines the law as the declaration of the general will. This definition found its way into the French Declaration of the Rights of Man.

Rousseau's ideal is a pure democracy. According to him it is not sufficient that a people assent to a code of laws or institute a special form of government. There must be regular and periodical assemblies of the people

[1] *Contrat Social*, III. 1.   [2] III. 1.   [3] III. 1.   [4] III. 15.

in which they take an active part in public affairs. These popular assemblies should be the more frequent if the government is very powerful.[1] When the people assemble as the sovereign authority, the executive power is suspended. The person of the meanest citizen is then of equal sanctity and inviolability with that of the highest officer. When the sovereign is present there are no longer representatives.[2]

The political doctrines of Rousseau were not new. His political philosophy was eclectic. From Locke he learned that men are free and equal. From Hobbes he borrowed his principle of absolutism, but while Hobbes ascribed absolute power to the prince, Rousseau puts it into the hands of the people. The doctrine of the sovereignty of the people had not been forgotten since put forth by the ancients. Rousseau's view of this doctrine resembles that of Althusius in many particulars. One cannot determine what Rousseau owes to Althusius, for while he mentions the names of persons whom he attacks, such as that of Grotius, he passes over in silence the names of those to whom he is indebted. The English political philosophers had declared the supreme authority to lie in the people. But they held the power of the people to be latent and to break forth only in case of tyranny. Rousseau regards the power of the people as being constantly in activity. They are the real sovereign.

While other writers had regarded the people as being only in passive possession of sovereignty, Rousseau considers them to be constantly exercising their sovereign power. Herein he differs from Milton, Sidney, Locke, and others.

In his *Considerations on the Government of Poland,*

[1] *Contrat Social,* III. 13.   III. 14.

written in 1772, Rousseau endeavors to carry his principles into practical effect. There is nothing in that pamphlet that concerns us here.

There is no suggestion of a Declaration of the Rights of Man and of the Citizen to be found in any of Rousseau's writings. Indeed, as we have seen, such a declaration is not in accord with his political philosophy. He does not believe that individuals reserve rights when they agree to form political society. On the contrary, they surrender all their natural rights to the sovereign *volonté générale*.

On the other hand, the enthusiasm with which Frenchmen hailed the American idea of a Declaration of the Rights of Man was in no small part due to the influence of Rousseau's writings. He had familiarized them with the doctrines of the sovereignty of the people, of liberty and equality. Though he conceived these ideas in a different sense from what the Americans did, the difference in conception probably escaped most Frenchmen.

The great mistake of Rousseau is the error committed by all writers who believed in the contract theory. Like them Rousseau proceeds from the individual to the State. His view is entirely unhistorical. He fails to see that the State is an organism; that a collection of individuals can never become a unity.[1]

[1] On Rousseau: Gierke, *Althusius*, pp. 201–5; Franck, *Ref. et Publ.*; Bluntschli, *Gesch. d. neueren Staatswiss.*, pp. 334–363; Fester, *Rousseau u. d. deut. Geschichtsphilosophie*, 1890; Höffding, *Rousseau*; John Morley, *Rousseau*; Janet, II. 415 *et seq.*

PART III

THE AMERICAN BILLS OF RIGHTS

THE AMERICAN BILLS OF RIGHTS

CHAPTER VIII

THE POLITICAL INSTITUTIONS AND DOCTRINES OF THE AMERICAN COLONISTS

The theory of natural rights was already known to the Greeks; that of the sovereignty of the people was put forth frequently during ancient and mediæval times, and yet in Europe neither of these theories had given rise to a Declaration of the Rights of Man. Not even during the seventeenth century, when both these theories were in England held by the Levellers, by Milton, Sidney, Locke, and others, did such a declaration result.

The question naturally arises, Why did the Declaration originate in America?

The answer must be sought in the character, history, and peculiar conditions of the American colonists. Most of the colonists had been driven from their native land by political or religious oppression. They were men to whom their liberties were dear. They were mainly Englishmen, than whom no other people was more devoted to freedom. Furthermore, the time when they had emigrated was one of great ferment in England; a time when the spirit of opposition to the assertions of royal prerogative and to the encroachments upon popular rights made by autocratic kings was at its height. They held the most liberal religious and political views of their time. Many were Independents who opposed the union of Church and State and demanded liberty of conscience as a sacred right.

Their democratic principles of church government gave rise to a democratic political spirit.

Each congregation was a miniature republic, electing its pastor and church officers and, while independent of all others, having absolute control over its own affairs.

There were many other dissenters besides the Independents scattered throughout the colonies—Baptists, Presbyterians, Quakers, and others. This was a fact of great importance for the subsequent history of America. Religious liberty and political freedom have ever gone hand in hand. There is but a step from religious dissent to political opposition.

Men who had suffered persecution for their beliefs, who had braved the dangers of the sea, and had undergone the privations and sufferings incident to the settlement of a new and uncultivated land, were not likely to submit to oppression and infringement of their political liberties.

The colonists tried to procure the most liberal charters possible, and a large part of their early history relates to the attempts made to obtain such charters and to compel the enforcement of their stipulations after they had been secured.

All the colonies possessed their own local legislatures,

although the early charters made no provision for such bodies.[1]

The colonists would not be subject to arbitrary power, but insisted upon having a share in making the laws by which they were governed. Without such participation in framing the laws there seemed to them to be no guarantee for political and civil liberty.

After the Restoration there was not a single colony in which the people were not represented in their colonial legislatures.[2]

While the right of the people to frame their laws was not questioned in the colonies having proprietary or charter government, this right was sometimes denied in the provincial governments by the Crown, which claimed the right to withdraw this privilege and to decide what number of representatives should be chosen and from what places. The Crown also claimed the right of dissolving the legislative body or continuing it indefinitely without a new election. To these claims of royal prerogative, except that of dissolving the legislature, the colonists opposed the most vehement resistance. Struggles took place repeatedly between them and the crown.[3]

The colonial legislatures claimed the exclusive right of regulating their own domestic and internal affairs, insisting especially upon voting their own taxes. A statute passed during the reign of George III. declared that the king, with the advice and consent of Parliament, "had, hath, and of right ought to have full power

[1] Douglas, *Summary*, I. pp. 213–215; Story, *Comm. on the Const.*, 5th ed., I. p. 117.

[2] Hutchinson, *Hist. of Mass.*, I. p. 94, note; Story, I. p. 118.

[3] Story, I. 119; Pitkin, *Political and Civil History of the U. S.*, I. 85–87; Chalmers, *Opinions*, I. 189, 268, 272.

and authority to make laws and statutes of sufficient force and validity to bind the colonies and people of America in all cases whatsoever." [1]

Since the colonies and the mother country were each determined to maintain the position taken, a conflict between them was inevitable.

While Parliament insisted upon its rights of making laws that were binding upon the colonies and of levying taxes upon them, the colonists stoutly resisted all such attempts as violations of their charter privileges and as infringements of their rights as Englishmen. Arbitrary taxation above all things was odious to them. As Burke said in his celebrated speech: "Here they felt the pulse of liberty, and as they found that beat they thought themselves sick or sound." [2]

Inasmuch as representation in Parliament was impracticable for them, the colonists demanded that the colonial legislatures have the power of regulating the internal affairs of the colony and of levying taxes. They acknowledged their allegiance to the Crown, but they would not admit the controlling power of Parliament.[3] They considered the colonial legislatures sovereign within their territory. They were composed of representatives of all the citizens of the colony.

The democratic nature of their political institution and the extent to which they enjoyed the right of self-government could not but breed in the colonists a love of freedom and of individual liberty.

The feeling of equality in the colonies was fostered

[1] 6 George III. Ch. 12; Pitkin's *Polit. and Civil Hist. of the U. S.*, I. 123.

[2] Burke's *Works*, II. 38–45

[3] *Declaration of Rights by the Congress of 1774*, Art. 4; Pref. to Bradford, *Hist. of Mass.*

by the general equality of economic and social conditions.   There was no native nobility.   There were no
feudal customs.   Land was held in fee simple.   Estates
were not entailed.   The custom of primogeniture did
not generally prevail.   There was no dependent peas-
antry, nor were there great estates, except in Virginia.
The feeling of caste was lacking.   Being absolute owners
of the soil and situated in independent and homoge-
neous circumstances, the colonists loved their liberties
and were determined to offer resistance to any infringement of them.[1]

The main reason why the liberal principles whose
development we have been tracing exerted so great an
influence upon the American colonists and were so generally accepted by them, was because they found a basis
in the institutions existing in the colonies and because
of the historical development of these colonies.

The compact theory had an especial meaning to the
colonists.   It was the Congregationalist Church covenant applied to civil society.   The congregation of
John Robinson had entered into a covenant before leaving England for Holland.[2]   Before disembarking from
the Mayflower those of that church who had come to
America, drew up and signed a compact whereby they
constituted a body politic.   "We whose names are
underwritten," runs this famous agreement, "covenant
and combine ourselves together into a civil body politic
for our better ordering and preservation and further-
ance of the ends aforesaid; and by virtue hereof to
enact, constitute, and frame just and equal laws, ordinances, acts, constitutions, and offices, from time to

[1] Story, I. 125, 126, 131; Doyle, *Engl. Colonies in America*,
II. 48 *et seq.*
[2] Mather's *Magnalia*, I. Ch. 2.

time, as shall be thought most meet and convenient for the general good of the colony, unto which we promise all due submission and obedience." [1] The colonists that settled at Salem in 1629 entered "into an holy covenant" whereby a Church-State was formed.[2] The platform of Church Discipline of 1649, which continued in use for many years, declares the covenant to be the form whereby men "give up themselves unto the Lord, to the observing of the ordinances of Christ together in the same society," and considers this the only way "how members can have church-power over one another." [3]

That Puritanism gave rise to democratic political doctrines is shown by the fact that the first republicans in America were Puritan ministers, namely, Roger Williams, Thomas Hooker, and John Wise.

That remarkable work of a most remarkable man, the *Bloudy Tenent of Persecution*, written by Roger Williams in 1644, and sent to England as a plea for religious toleration, contains these memorable statements: "The sovereign, original, and foundation of civil power lies in the people; whom they must needs mean by 'the civil power' distinct from the government set up; and if so, that a people may erect and establish what form of government seems to them most meet for their civil condition. It is evident that such governments as are by them erected and established have no more power, nor for no longer time, than the civil power, or people, consenting and agreeing shall betrust them with. That is clear, not only in reason but in the experience of all commonweals, where the people are not deprived

---

[1] Bradford's *History of Plymouth Plantation*, II. Book.

[2] Mather's *Magnalia*, Book I.

[3] *Ibid.*, Book V.

of their natural freedom by the power of tyrants." [1] Roger Williams says that "civil magistrates, whether kings or parliaments, states, and governors, can receive no more in justice than what the people give, and are, therefore, but the eyes and hands and instruments of the people." [2] He considers the object of government to be the commonweal or safety of the people in their bodies and goods. [3] He holds that the people cannot entrust magistrates with any spiritual power in matters of religion, but only with a civil power belonging to their goods and bodies, [4] and demands universal toleration and complete separation of Church and State. [5]

Even before this the doctrine of the sovereignty of the people had been put forth in the colonies by the Rev. Thomas Hooker, also a Congregationalist minister. In a sermon preached at Hartford, May 31, 1638, he had declared "that the choice of public magistrates belongs unto the people by God's own allowance," and that it is in the power of those who appoint officers and magistrates "to set bounds and limitations of the power and place unto which they call them." In the sermon Hooker had asserted the foundation of authority to lie in the free consent of the people. [6]

In a letter to Governor Winthrop, Hooker wrote: "Reserving smaller matters, which fall in occasionally in common course, to a lower counsel, in matters of greater consequence, which concern the common good, a general counsel chosen by all to transact business

---

[1] *Bloudy Tenent*, Hanserd Knollys Soc. Reprint, Ch. 92.

[2] *Ibid.*, Ch. 120.

[3] *Ibid.*

[4] *Ibid.*, Ch. 128.

[5] See also Baxter's *Life*, III. 11; Hanbury, *Memorials of the Independents*, III. 149; Baillie, *Letters and Journal*, II. 191.

[6] *Coll. Conn. Hist. Society*, I. p. 20.

which concerns all, I conceive . . . under favour most suitable to rule and most safe for relief of the whole." [1]

The democratic ideas of Hooker and of Roger Williams found expression in the constitutions of the colonies with whose foundation they were associated.

The constitution of the United Colonies of Windsor, Hartford, and Wethersfield, drawn up in 1639, was based upon the doctrine of the sovereignty of the people. It was the first democratic constitution ever formed. The supreme power of the commonwealth resided in the general court whose members were elected by the freemen of the several towns. All magistrates were chosen by the whole body of the freemen. These magistrates were sworn into their office. The governor was required to swear "to promote the public good and peace" of the commonwealth.[2]

The Providence Plantations declared in the preamble to their Code of Law, drawn up in 1647, "that the form of government established . . . is democratical, that is to say, a government held by the free and voluntary consent of all or the greater part of the free inhabitants." [3]

The democratic political principles of the Independents also found expression in the Constitution of Pennsylvania. Quakerism was but an offshoot of Independency. In America William Penn carried out his ideas of liberty of conscience and of political freedom. The humanitarian spirit of Quakerism is evident in the laws and institutions of the colony which Penn founded.

[1] *Coll. Conn. Hist. Society*, I. p. 12.

[2] *Conn. Col. Records*, I. pp. 20–25; Johnson, *Hist. of Conn.*, p. 72 *et seq.*; John Fiske, *Beginnings of New England*; G. L. Walker, *Life of Thomas Hooker*.

[3] *Records of Rhode Island Col.*, I. p. 156.

William Penn believed in Natural Law and in the sovereignty of the people. It was very probably from the Levellers that he adopted these theories. Lilburn, the head of the Levellers, spent much time with the Quakers during his last years.

Penn regards all laws as either fundamental and immutable, or superficial and alterable. By the first he understands such laws as enjoin men to be honest, just, virtuous; to do no wrong, to kill, rob, deceive, prejudice none, but to do as one would be done unto; to cherish good, and to terrify wicked men; in short, laws derived from Universal Reason. These laws he considers to be subject to no change. No emergency, time, or occasion can ever justify their suspension or abrogation. They "are as the corner-stone of human structure, the basis of reasonable societies, without which all would run into heaps and confusion." While superficial laws, being made for present occurrence, may be abrogated for the good of the kingdom, the fundamental laws continue in force "till houses stand without their foundations and Englishmen wholly cease to be." [1]

Apart from these fundamental natural laws, there are, according to Penn, three rights and privileges which form the birthright of Englishmen. These are: 1. An ownership and undisturbed possession. 2. A voting of every law that is made, whereby ownership or property is maintained. 3. An influence upon, and a real share in, that judiciary power that must apply every such law, which is the ancient, necessary, and laudable use of juries.[2] Concerning the people as the

[1] Penn, *The People's Ancient and Just Liberties Asserted, 1673*, Sel. Works, p. 376.
[2] *Ibid.*

source of power, Penn says: "The estate goes before the steward; the foundation before the house; people before their representatives, and the creation before the creature. The steward lives by preserving the estate; the house stands by reason of its foundation; the representative depends upon the people, as the creature subsists by the power of its creator. Every representative may be called the creature of the people, because the people make them, and to them they owe their being."[1] Penn was also an ardent champion of freedom of religious worship. "Liberty of conscience," he said, "we ask as our undoubted right by the Law of God, of Nature, and of our own country." "Nothing is more unreasonable than to sacrifice the liberty and property of any man (being his natural and civil rights) for religion, where he is not found breaking any law relating to natural and civil things."[2] Again he says: "I ever understood an impartial liberty of conscience to be the natural right of all men; and that he that had a religion without it, his religion was none of his own. For what is not the religion of a man's choice, is the religion of him that imposes it: so that liberty of conscience is the first step to have a religion."[3]

Another book produced during the colonial period showing the influence of Natural Law, and consequently remarkable for its democratic principles, is the work of John Wise, a very prominent minister of Ipswich, entitled *A Vindication of the Government of New England Churches.* This book was written in defence of the Congregational system of church government. It

[1] Penn, *England's Present Interest Considered*, Select Works, p. 382.

[2] *Ibid.*, pp. 200, 386.

[3] *Ibid.*, i, xvi.

is characterized by clear logic, breadth of view, and excellent literary style. In its day the book was widely read. In 1772 a new edition was issued. On the list of subscribers is found the name of John Adams and of many of the most influential persons in New England. What makes this brief treatise so interesting to us is the fact that it contains the leading political principles afterward embodied in the documents of the Revolution. It is highly probable that, appearing in a new edition just at the right time, this book exerted great influence upon the fathers of the Republic. Wise applies the principles of Natural Law to the Constitution of the Congregational churches. "Under Christ," he says, "the reason of the constitution of these and the primitive churches, is really and truly owing to the original state and liberty of mankind, and founded peculiarly in the light of Nature."[1] The excellence of this system he deems such that it seems to him "as though wise and provident Nature, by the dictates of right reason, excited by the moving suggestions of humanity; and awed with the just demands of natural liberty, equity, equality, and principles of self-preservation, originally drew up the scheme."[2]

Wise enters into a consideration of the natural and the civil state. He wishes "to disclose several principles of natural knowledge; plainly discovering the Law of Nature; or the true sentiments of Natural Reason, with respect to man's being and government."[3] He names Pufendorf as his chief authority. Wise believes that man is in the natural state a free-born creature, owing homage to no one save God. Man is governed by the Law of Nature, which is the immutable standard God has stamped upon the nature of man to guide him in all

[1] Edition of 1772, p. 20.   [2] *Ibid.*, p. 21.   [3] *Ibid.*, p. 22.

his actions. It is the law of both justice and morality. Morals are the "dictate of right reason founded in the soul of man." With Grotius and Pufendorf he ascribes to man a sociable disposition. Man is guided by self-love and the instinct of self-preservation, but has a love for his fellows. Interference with the natural liberty of man is a violation of the Law of Nature. "Every man must be regarded as equal to every other man, since all subjection and all command are equally banished on both sides." [1] He holds that all men are born free by natural right. Civil government is not of divine institution, but is formed by a voluntary compact. If formed by nature, governments would be everywhere alike. That government is best which agrees with the temper and inclinations of a people. There are several covenants necessary to form political society. The first is a covenant to form society. Then a particular form of government must be set up. Lastly, there must be a covenant between rulers and subjects, the former promising to care for the common peace and welfare, the latter to yield faithful obedience. The State is a compound moral person whose will is the will of all. The common welfare or happiness of the people is the chief end of the State. Sovereignty is either original or delegated. Originally all power is in the people. [2] The people may establish any form of government they wish. Power always reverts to them. Wise prefers the democratic form of government. "A democracy in Church or State," he says, "is a very honorable and regular government according to the dictates of right reason." [3] It is repugnant to the Law of Nature to hold that any man may enslave himself. "The end of all good government is to cultivate humanity, and

[1] *Vindication*, p. 25.   [2] *Ibid.*, p. 28.   [3] *Ibid.*, p. 44.

promote the happiness of all, and the good of every man in all his rights, his life, liberty, estate, honor, etc., without injury or abuse done to any." No other form of government is so likely to preserve the peculiar good of the whole and of every individual member as a democracy.[1]

Such are the political doctrines of this remarkable treatise which was used by the colonists as a kind of political text-book. It is a proof of the democratic sentiments generated by the theory of Natural Law. It shows likewise that these liberal doctrines were particularly congenial to Congregationalists. Not only to them, but to the colonists in general, did the theories of Natural Law possess great fascination, because their conditions seemed to support the truth of them. The contract theory appeared to fit the circumstances exactly. A number of persons set out to found a colony. They seem to be in a state of nature, under no government whatever, until they assemble, draw up a compact, and organize a government. At first a pure democracy prevails, all having a hand in governing. Representation becomes necessary as the colony increases in size. The colonists chose certain of their number to act for the whole body. Sovereignty is, as it were, conferred by the people upon the magistrates. If any one wishes to withdraw from the jurisdiction of the State, he needs but to cross the borders of the colony and strike out into the forests to find himself in the state of nature.

To take Plymouth as an example. Here the entire body of the freemen who were church-members at first exercised legislative power. A democratic theocracy existed. There was no delegation of power. The num-

[1] *Vindication*, p. 40.

ber of colonists having increased, the participation of all in regulating public affairs became impracticable. Representation was accordingly established in 1639. The deputies of the people and all officers of the colony were chosen annually.[1] Providence also was originally a pure democracy. The settlers met monthly in town meetings. Here, as in Massachusetts, representation was established.[2]

As we have seen, many factors worked together to generate a democratic spirit in the colonists. They were really republicans before they declared themselves to be so. To them the principle that all power is derived from the people was more than a mere theory. Because the political principles of the American Revolution had been embodied in their institutions their influence was intensified. The ideas of Milton, Sidney, Hooker, and Locke were familiar to them as Englishmen; but they had among themselves since the beginning of their history ardent champions of democratic views, viz.: Hooker, Roger Williams, Penn, and others.

In the American colonies the conditions existed which engendered democratic views and enabled the liberal political doctrines of the time to bear fruit. The Puritan principles of government, as we find them expressed in the works of Milton, Sidney, Locke, and others, of little actual influence upon the constitution of the mother country, were destined here to give birth to a form of government which is the admiration and hope of the world. Nowhere did there exist a people so devoted to their liberty, so independent in spirit, so

[1] Hutchinson, *History of Mass.*, II. p. 463; Hazen *Coll.*, I. 404, 408, 411, 412, 414.

[2] *Rhode Island Col. Rec.*, I. pp. 14, 42; Arnold, *Hist. of Rhode Island*, I. pp. 102, 103.

free from the bondage of custom and tradition, as these American colonists. To no other people did the notion that all men are created free and equal seem so true as to them, and nowhere else did freedom and equality exist to the same extent. Inhabiting a new land, separated from the motherland by a wide and treacherous ocean, with new problems pressing for solution which could not be settled by precedent, what was more natural than that they should break away from traditions and apply reason to their affairs? The Law of Nature, being the Law of Reason, must have attracted them greatly. In struggling for liberty of conscience they had grown accustomed to look beyond the positive laws of the State and appeal to what they believed to be their Natural Right.[1]

The character of the colonists, their surroundings and form of life, their free political institutions, their democratic form of church government, as well as their past history, bred in them a spirit of individualism. The theory of the sovereignty of the people lay at the basis of their institutions—the doctrine which, as a ray of white light contains the various prismatic colors, embraces in itself all the so-called Rights of Man. Before individual rights could become secure, the last traces of feudalism had to be destroyed and the doctrine of the divine right of kings supplanted by the conception that the sovereignty resides in the people.

It must not be forgotten that many of the colonists were men of excellent education, who compare favor-

[1] See Jellinek, *Die Erklaerung der Menschen- und Buergerrechte*, translated by Prof. Max Farrand. It seems to me that this otherwise very valuable and suggestive little treatise, in trying to account for the democratic views of the colonists, overemphasizes the importance of the struggle for religious toleration and oversees the greater influence of Natural Law.

ably with the most accomplished men of the mother-land. Much care was bestowed upon the establish-ment of good schools. The sons of well-to-do families not infrequently went abroad to finish their education. The desire for culture was general. There was a large demand for books. Next to religious books, treatises on legal and political subjects were most eagerly read. To quote the words of Edmund Burke: "In no country, perhaps, in the world is the law so general a study. The profession itself is numerous and powerful, and in most provinces it takes the lead. The greater number of deputies sent to the Congress were lawyers. But all who read, and most do read, endeavor to obtain some smattering in that science. I have been told by an eminent bookseller, that in no branch of his business, after tracts of popular devotion, were so many books as those on the law exported to the plantations. The colonists have now fallen into the way of printing them for their own use. I hear that they have sold nearly as many of Blackstone's 'Commentaries' in America as in England."[1] It was especially works on Natural Law which were carefully studied, the favorite writers being Grotius, Pufendorf, Locke, Vattel, and others. The fruits of this study showed themselves in the wonderful skill with which the colonists stated and defended their rights during the struggle with the motherland. With this conflict, and especially the documents to which it gave birth, we must now concern ourselves.

[1] Burke's *Works*, II. 124, 125. See also Schlosser, *Geschichte des 18. Jahrhunderts*, 3d. ed., III. 438 *sq.*

CHAPTER IX

THE AMERICAN REVOLUTION AND THE BILLS OF RIGHTS

WHILE resisting the aggressions of the motherland the colonists at first appealed to the common law of England and their rights as English subjects. They would not be treated as subject-colonies and dependencies, but claimed the same rights and immunities their brethren in England enjoyed. These rights and liberties they declared to be their birthright as Englishmen. Not finding their grievances redressed they sought for another standard to which to appeal. Being denied their rights as English subjects they appealed to their rights as men. What they could not obtain by the laws of the land they now demanded according to Natural Right and the Law of Nature.

Massachusetts began the Revolution. She, also, first of all the colonies, appealed to Natural Right. Three persons, James Otis, John Adams, and Samuel Adams were instrumental in bringing this about. The writers on Natural Law which they quote are Hooker, Locke, Harrington, Grotius, Pufendorf, Vattel, and Burlamaqui. Of James Otis, John Adams writes: "This classic scholar was also a great master of the Law of Nature and Nations. He had read Pufendorf, Grotius, Barbeyrac, Burlamaqui, Vattel, Heineccius. . . . It was a maxim which he inculcated in his pupils . . . that a lawyer ought never to be without a volume of natural or public law, or moral philosophy, on his table or in his pocket." [1]

In his celebrated speech on the writs of assistance, delivered at Boston, February, 1761, Otis spoke of the Rights of Man in the state of nature, asserting that in the natural state every man was his own independent sovereign, subject to, and guided by, the law written in his heart, and revealed to him by God through reason and conscience. He declared that man had an inherent and inalienable right to his life, liberty, and property. The reason why men associated to form a government he declared to be mutual defence and security of life, liberty, and property. For this end alone had the people given up their primitive rights. These principles he held to be fundamental laws of the British constitution. He declared all men to be free and equal, including even the negroes. John Adams relates that he shuddered to hear doctrines whose import was so far-reaching, and considered American independence to have been born then and there.[2] Otis's pamphlet on *The Rights of the British Colonies*, first published in the beginning of the year 1764, created a sensation throughout the colonies. It expressed the views afterward embodied in the "Bills of Rights" and exercised a great influence.

This celebrated pamphlet begins with the consideration of the origin of government. Otis considers government to be founded on the necessities of man's nature, and to have an everlasting foundation in the unchangeable will of God, the author of nature, whose laws never vary. He seems to be favorably inclined to

[1] Adams's *Works*, X. 275; Tudor, *Life of Otis*, p. 10.
[2] Adams's *Works*, X. 315, 317; Minot's *Hist. of Mass.*, II. p. 92 *sq.*

the compact theory, saying that though many objections had been raised to it, its opponents might after all not be able to prove "that the doctrine is a piece of metaphysical jargon and systematical nonsense." For a fuller consideration of the subject he refers to Locke, Vattel, and the "divine" writings of the "great and incomparable" Harrington. Of the supreme power, Otis says that it is originally and ultimately in the people, and that they never did in fact freely, nor can they rightfully, make an absolute unlimited renunciation of this divine right, which is ever in the nature of the thing given in trust and on a condition, the performance of which no mortal can dispense with, viz.: that the person on whom the sovereignty is conferred by the people shall incessantly consult their good. He says that the principle of the *salus populi* is part of the law of nature and of that grand charter which God, to whom alone belongs the right to absolute power, has given to the human race. The object of government he considers to be to provide for the security and the quiet and happy enjoyment of life, liberty, and property.[1]

The people may choose any form of government they please. Every alteration may and ought to be made by express compact.[2]

"There can be no prescription old enough to supersede the Law of Nature and the grant of God Almighty; who has given to all men a Natural Right to be free, and they have it ordinarily in their power to make themselves so, if they please." [3]

Every form of government is alike subject to the Law

[1] *Rights of the British Colonies*, p. 14.
[2] *Ibid.*, p. 16.
[3] *Ibid.*, p. 17.

of Nature and of Reason.   No king has absolute power.
Nothing but life and liberty are naturally hereditary.

Otis believed with Locke that the Legislature has
supreme power, but that this power is only fiduciary,
and that the people may remove or change the legislature when it disregards the will of the people, who in
that case have a right to assume their original liberty.[1]

Otis next treats of colonies in general.   He considers
the colonists to "be entitled to as ample rights, liberties, and privileges as the subjects of the mother country
are, and in some respects to more." [2]

Then follows a consideration of the Natural Rights of
the colonists.   By the Law of Nature they are born
free, as all men are, without distinction of color.   Here
again Locke is quoted as asserting that all men are
equal because they are all of the same species and
rank, possessed of the same faculties and entitled to
the same advantage of nature.   The colonists being
men, are equally entitled to all the Rights of Nature
with Europeans.   The Law of Nature was made by
God.   Man has no power to mend it or alter its course.
He can only obey or disobey it.

Should the charter privileges of the colonists be dis-
regarded or revoked, there are natural, inherent, and
inseparable rights as men and as citizens that would
remain after the so-much-wished-for catastrophe, and
which, whatever became of charters, can never be
abolished *de jure*, if *de facto*, till the general conflagra-
tion.

In his *Vindication of the British Colonies*, published
in 1765 in defence of the principles contained in his previous pamphlet, Otis divides the Rights of Man into

[1] Locke, *Of Civil Gov.*, Ch. 9 and 13.
[2] *Rights of the British Colonies*, p. 38.

natural and civil, and divides the latter again into absolute and relative, declaring the natural, absolute, personal rights of the individual to be the basis of positive laws and to form the essence of political and civil liberty.

The absolute liberties of Englishmen he declared to be: 1. The right of personal security; 2. Personal liberty; and 3. Private property.

The secondary rights which he meant to preserve from attack are: 1. The constitution or power of Parliament. 2. The limitation of royal power. 3. The regular administration of justice. 4. The right of petition. 5. The right of having and using arms for self-defence.

In the *Considerations on Behalf of the Colonists in a Letter to a Noble Lord*, Otis praises the works of Selden, Locke, and Sidney, and censures the views of Hobbes.

He says that when the members of a society united from a state of nature and assembled in order to regulate their affairs, they were all equal and on the same level. The minority must obey the decisions of the majority. If their number be too large, they may delegate the governing power to whom they please. The persons chosen to act for the whole, are the trustees or agents of the entire society, and have a right to act for it so long as chosen. Every branch of government derives its power originally from the whole community. *Jus divinum*, the indefeasible inheritance, the indelible character, are only for the entertainment of old women. We have here the ideas of the Declaration of Independence and of the American Bills of Rights.

In 1765 John Adams had written his *Dissertation on the Canon and the Feudal Law*. It was directed against the Stamp Act, and was one of a number of pamphlets sent to England and published there under the title

The True Sentiments of America. It speaks of "rights antecedent to all earthly government—rights, that cannot be repealed or restrained by human laws— rights, derived from the great Legislator of the universe." [1]

The people have an "indisputable, unalienable, indefeasible, divine right" to know how their government is being conducted. Rulers are the attorneys, agents, and trustees of the people. If they violate the trust reposed in them, the people have a right to revoke the authority that they themselves have deputed " and to constitute abler and better agents, attorneys, and trustees." "British liberties are not the grants of princes or parliaments, but original rights, conditions of original contracts, coequal with prerogative and coeval with government." "Many of our rights are inherent and essential, agreed on as maxims, and established as preliminaries even before a Parliament existed." [2]

Human nature is the foundation of government. Truth, liberty, justice, and benevolence are its basis. [3]

During and after the year 1765 Massachusetts Colony frequently appealed to the Law of Nature. This was without doubt due to the influence of Otis, John and Samuel Adams, all three of whom were men of great preeminence and influence, and actively engaged in the events that brought on the Revolution. Already in his youth Samuel Adams possessed those republican opinions for which he contended in manhood. In 1749, while but twenty-six years of age, he contributed an essay on Liberty to the *Public Advertiser* of Boston, a weekly paper maintained by a political club of which he was one of the foremost members, whose purpose

[1] *Works*, III. p. 449.   [2] *Ibid.*   [3] *Ibid.*, pp. 456–463.

it was to "state and defend the rights and liberties of mankind." In this essay Adams considers the Rights of Men in the state of nature. No man, he maintained, has a right to relinquish these rights or to permit their curtailment, except in so far as is necessary for their preservation, for they are the gift of God. Neither a man's life nor his liberty is his own to such an extent that he may destroy it or submit it to the wanton pleasure of another.[1]

In September, 1765, while the excitement over the Stamp Act was at its height, Samuel Adams was chosen a representative from Boston to the legislature of Massachusetts Bay.[2] He drafted the famous fourteen resolves which were passed by the House October 29, 1765, as the assertion of the inherent and inalienable rights of the people. These resolutions created a sensation throughout the country and were universally applauded by the friends of liberty. They speak of the essential rights of the British constitution, which are founded in the law of God and Nature, and are common Rights of Mankind, to which the colonists are entitled, and of which they cannot be deprived. Security of property and voting of taxes by the representatives of the people are asserted as inherent rights. All taxes not imposed by the representatives of the people are declared to be infringements of their inherent and inalienable rights as men and British subjects. The right of trial by jury is the only security of life, liberty, and property.[3]

On September 21, 1765, the Pennsylvania Assembly at Philadelphia, in a series of resolutions on the Stamp

[1] Wells's *Life of Samuel Adams*, I. pp. 16–23.

[2] *Ibid.*, p. 70.

[3] *Ibid.*, pp. 73–77; Bradford's *State Papers*, p. 50.

Act, declared that the constitution of government in that province was founded on the Natural Rights of Mankind and the noble principles of English liberty, and therefore is, or ought to be, perfectly free.

On the same occasion Connecticut declared that all power is from the people and granted with certain bounds, reverting to the people if these bounds are exceeded.[1]

The Assembly of Massachusetts, which met in May, 1769, declared that the "establishment of a standing army in the colony in time of peace, without the consent of the General Assembly of the same, is an invasion of the Natural Rights of Man, as well as those which they claim as free-born Englishmen." [2]

Most important of all appeals made to Natural Rights was the report written by Samuel Adams, which was presented by James Otis to a town meeting in Boston, convoked at Faneuil Hall, November 20, 1772. Drawn up as a protest against the infringement of the rights of the colonists by the attempt to make the salaries of the governor and the judges of the Superior Court dependent upon the crown instead of upon the people, this " Declaration of the Rights of the Colonists as Men, as Christians, and as Subjects " attracted wide attention, both in America and in England, and probably served as a model for the Declaration of Rights by the first Congress in 1774, for the Declaration of Independence, and for the Virginia Bill of Rights.[3]

The right to life, liberty, and property is declared to be a Natural Right, and, together with the right of supporting and defending them, a branch of the first Law

[1] *Conn. Col. Records*, XII. p. 653 *et seq.*

[2] Pitkin, I. p. 237; *Mass. State Papers*, pp. 170–171.

[3] Wells's *Life of S. Adams*, pp. 500–501.

of Nature, the duty of self-preservation.   No man can
be compelled to leave the state of nature, nor prevented,
in case of civil or religious oppression, from entering
another society.   Men enter society by their own voluntary consent.   The compact they form must be
observed in every particular.   They reserve to themselves every right not expressly ceded.   The Law of
Natural Reason is the standard to which all positive
laws should conform.   Every man has a right to worship God as his conscience dictates.   To just and true
liberty, equal and impartial liberty, all men have a
right according to the eternal and immutable laws of
God and Nature.   The natural liberty of man is absolute freedom from control and subjection to any law
except that of Nature.   In the state of Nature every
man is his own judge, subject only to God.   When man
enters society this natural liberty is not abridged any
further than is necessary for the good of the whole.   It
is absurd to suppose that men would renounce their
essential Natural Rights or the power to protect or preserve them.   It is for the very protection of their
rights that government is instituted.   Being given to
man by God, the right to freedom cannot be yielded up
to another.   Man cannot enslave himself.   Should he
through fear, fraud, or mistake relinquish any one of
his essential rights, the renunciation would be void
according to the eternal law of reason and the grand
end of society.

The colonists are, by the laws of God and nature, and
by the common law of England, exclusive of all charters, declared to be entitled to all the natural, essential, inherent, and inseparable rights, liberties, and
privileges of natural-born Englishmen.   Among the
rights which no man can either relinquish or take away

from others are: 1. The establishment of the legislative power, which itself cannot subvert the fundamental natural law of the preservation of society. 2. The power of the legislative is not an absolute or arbitrary disposal over the lives and fortunes of the people and must be just and equal for all. 3. No man can be justly deprived of his property without his own consent or that of his representative.[1]

The principles of Samuel Adams, embodied in these resolutions of 1772, are the principles of the Revolution. All the documents of that period merely repeat them. "He had brought them triumphantly forward, keeping the public attention ever fixed upon them, till they were not only adopted by a town, but established as the guide of a people in its march to freedom."[2]

"Without the character of Samuel Adams," says his relative, John Adams, "the true history of the American Revolution can never be written. For fifty years his pen, his tongue, his activity, were constantly exerted for his country without fee or reward."[3]

At the close of the year 1774 the Council and House of Representatives of Massachusetts Bay adopted a proclamation composed by John Adams which was sent to all the town meetings and to all the ministers in the colony. Among the principles which it contained the following are noteworthy: "As the happiness of the people is the sole end of government, so the consent of the people is the only foundation of it, in reason, morality, and the natural fitness of things. And, therefore, every act of government, every exercise of sovereignty against or without the consent of the peo-

[1] Wells's *Life of Samuel Adams*, I. pp. 500–508.

[2] *Ibid.*, p. 509.

[3] Adams's *Works*, X. pp. 263, 264.

ple, is injustice, usurpation, and tyranny. It is a maxim that in every government there must exist somewhere a supreme, sovereign, absolute, and uncontrollable power; but this power resides always in the body of the people; and it never was, or can be, delegated to one man or a few; the great Creator having never given to men a right to vest others with authority over them unlimited either in duration or degree."

"When kings, ministers, governors, or legislators, therefore, instead of exercising the powers intrusted with them according to the principles, forms, and proportions stated by the constitution, and established by the original compact, prostitute those powers to the purposes of oppression; to subvert, instead of supporting a free constitution; to destroy, instead of preserving the lives, liberties, and properties of the people, they are no longer to be deemed magistrates vested with a sacred character, but become public enemies and ought to be resisted." [1]

Many other books and pamphlets might be mentioned showing how usual a custom it had become at the outbreak of the Revolution to employ the doctrines of Natural Law in defending the rights of the colonists. Thus, the young Alexander Hamilton, when still a student at college, evinced not only his learning in the positive laws of England, but also his familiarity with the chief writers of Natural Law, in his vigorous and able pamphlet, *The Farmer Refuted*, which appeared February 5, 1775. He believes that the Deity is the author of an eternal and immutable law which takes precedence over all human regulations and binds mankind prior to any human institution. The Natural Rights of Mankind depend upon this law. Civil liberty

[1] Adams's *Works*, I. p. 193.

is founded upon natural liberty, and is but such a modification of it as civil society makes necessary. "The sacred rights of mankind are not to be rummaged for among old parchments or musty records. They are written, as with a sunbeam, in the whole volume of human nature, by the hand of the Divinity itself, and can never be erased or obscured by mortal power." [1] Hamilton holds that "in a state of nature no man had any moral power to deprive another of his life, limbs, property, or liberty." [2] Civil government is formed by compact. This compact is liable to such limitations as are necessary for the security of absolute rights. The only title upon which any man or set of men can base their claim to govern is the consent of the governed. "To usurp dominion over a people in their own despite, or to grasp at a more extensive power than they are willing to entrust, is to violate that law of nature which gives every man a right to his personal liberty, and can therefore confer no obligation to obedience." [3]

After having studied the political principles of the chief writers who touched upon the subject we are considering, let us now investigate the public documents, especially the Bills of Rights, in which these ideas found expression.

The papers drawn up by the various general congresses and by the States were printed in many European newspapers and eagerly read abroad. They were almost universally admired because of their clearness, moderation, and their elevation of thought. Schlosser states that they became the gospel of a new system of public law. [4]

[1] Hamilton's *Works*, edited by Lodge, I. p. 108.

[2] *Ibid.*, p. 60.

[3] *Ibid.*, p. 61.

[4] Schlosser, *Geschichte des 18. Jahrhunderts*, Dritte Aufl., III. p. 440.

Of the members of the Congress of 1774 Lord Chatham said in the English Parliament that for genuine sagacity, for singular moderation, for solid wisdom, manly spirit, sublime sentiments, and simplicity of language, for everything respectable and honorable, the Congress of Philadelphia stood unrivalled.[1]

One of the first acts of this Congress was to appoint a committee consisting of two delegates from each colony, to draw up a Declaration of Rights and to point out the violations of these rights which had taken place.[2]

John Jay, James Duane, Richard Henry Lee, John Rutledge, John Adams, and Samuel Adams were the leading members of this committee. It is unfortunate that our knowledge of the discussions which arose concerning these rights is so meager, our only source of information being the sparse notes of John Adams. Evidently a dispute arose regarding the basis of these rights. From what we know in regard to the views of John and Samuel Adams, as expressed in their writings, it is probable that they advocated an appeal to the Laws of Nature, such as had been made by Massachusetts. The biographer of John Adams says that he advocated "tracing effects to their ultimate causes. Quite averse to resting the justice of the American claims upon the mere offspring of man's will, upon the construction put upon an unwritten local law, or upon grants and charters derived from an equivocal sovereignty, he preferred to include an appeal to the general ideas of Natural Right."[3]

Mr. Jay thought it necessary to "recur to the Laws of Nature and the British constitution to ascertain their

[1] Cobbett, *Parliam. History*, XVIII. 155, 156.
[2] *Journal of Congress*.
[3] *Works*, I. p. 160.

rights." Colonel Lee advocated that the colonists lay their rights upon the broadest bottom, the ground of Nature, since their ancestors found no government here. But Mr. Rutledge thought their claims were founded on the British constitution and not on the Law of Nature. Mr. Duane thought the Laws of Nature would be too feeble a support.[1] In a report, no copy of which exists, though twelve, one for each colony, were ordered to be prepared, the matter was referred to Congress itself. It was decided, contrary to the views of Adams and others, that no mention be made of Natural Rights and that no grievances be stated whose origin went before 1763.[2]

Through the thorough discussion of the principles of Natural Law and of the Rights of Men the various delegates to Congress must all have become familiar with these theories. This discussion may, after the connections with the mother country had been completely severed, and there was no longer an excuse to appeal to the British constitution, have led to the "Bill of Rights" drawn up by Virginia, some of whose delegates had opposed the appeal to Natural Rights in 1774, and may also explain in some measure why the other colonies imitated the example of Virginia by prefixing such declarations to their constitutions. The rights to which the colonists are entitled, according to the declaration of Congress as agreed upon October 14, 1774, "by the immutable Laws of Nature, the principles of the English constitution, and the several charters or compacts," are: The right to life, liberty, and property; the rights, liberties, and immunities of free and natural-born subjects of England which were possessed by their ancestors before they emigrated and which they did not for-

[1] Adams, *Works*, II. pp. 371–373. [2] *Ibid.*, I. p. 160.

feit, lose, or surrender by their emigration; to a free and exclusive power of legislation in their several provincial legislatures in all cases of taxation and internal policy. They are entitled to the common law of England, especially to the right of trial by jury; to the English Statutes which existed at the time of their colonization; to the privileges and immunities granted by their charters and provincial laws; to the right of petition and assembling to consider their grievances. The keeping of a standing army in the colonies in times of peace without the consent of the legislature is unlawful. The constituent branches of government should be independent of each other. It is declared unconstitutional, dangerous, and destructive to American legislation that a council appointed at the pleasure of the crown exercise the legislative power.[1]

The basis of all these rights is still the British constitution. After independence had been declared another basis was necessary. "Virginia," as Bancroft says, "moved from charters and customs to primal principles; from the altercation about facts to the contemplation of immutable truth. She summoned the eternal laws of man's being to protest against all tyranny. The English petition of rights in 1688 was historic and retrospective; the Virginia declaration came out of the heart of nature and announced governing principles for all peoples in all time. It was the voice of reason going forth to speak a new political world into being. At the bar of humanity Virginia gave the name and fame of her sons as hostages that her public life should show a likeness to the highest ideas of right and equal freedom among men."[2]

The old Virginia House of Burgesses had been dis-

[1] *Journals of Congress.*   [2] Bancroft, IV. p. 419.

solved on the 6th of May, 1776, to make way for the new convention. The instruction given by the county of Buckingham to its delegates is indicative of the spirit and the purpose of this body. "We intrust you to cause a total and final separation from Great Britain, to take place as soon as possible; and a constitution to be established with a full representation, and full and frequent elections, the most free, happy, and permanent government that human wisdom can contrive and the perfection of man maintain."

We have here indicated the spirit from which grew the Bill of Rights. It was to be the work of this body to separate from the mother country, and to create an entirely new government based upon the sovereignty of the people and realizing the highest degree of perfection human wisdom could devise. Reason, not custom, must be their guide; the Law of Nature, not that of England, their standard.

A committee of thirty-two was appointed to draw up a Declaration of Rights. Archibald Cary, Richard Bland, Edmund Randolph, Patrick Henry, and James Madison were among its members.

It was George Mason who drew up the famous document known as the Virginia Bill of Rights. The ideas contained therein were by no means new, but in this paper they received a classic expression. They were presented to the Convention on the 27th of May, 1776, by Archibald Cary. For two weeks that body deliberated upon them. They were finally adopted without alteration except as regards the last article, which refers to freedom of conscience.

Mason's article favored granting full toleration of worship. James Madison objected to the word toleration, declaring it to imply a concession, while it was a sacred Right of Man to worship God according to his conscience.[1]

As Virginia was at the time the most aristocratic colony, so it was the one in which the principle of religious toleration had received least recognition. The Anglican Church was the established Church. Young Madison had himself suffered from religious persecution. In a letter to William Bradford, written January 24, 1774, he writes: "If the Church of England had been the established and general religion in all the northern colonies as it has been among us here, and uninterrupted tranquillity had prevailed throughout the continent, it is clear to me that slavery and subjection might and would have been gradually insinuated among us. Union of religious sentiments begets a surprising confidence, and ecclesiastical establishments tend to great ignorance and corruption, all of which facilitate the execution of mischievous projects." [2] "That diabolical, hell-conceived principle of persecution," he continues, "rages among some; and to their eternal infamy, the clergy can furnish their quota of imps for such a business. This vexes me the worst of anything whatever. There are at this time, in the adjacent country, not less than five or six well-meaning men in close jail for publishing their religious sentiments, which, in the main, are very orthodox. . . . So I must beg you to pity me and pray for liberty of conscience to all." [3] In another letter of April 1, 1774, he wrote: "Religious bondage shackles and debilitates the mind, and unfits it for every noble enterprise, every expanded prospect." [4]

The Bill of Rights was adopted June 12, 1776. It

---

[1] Bancroft, IV. p. 417.
[2] Madison's *Works*, I. p. 11.
[3] *Ibid.*
[4] *Ibid.*, I. p. 14.

declares "that all men are by nature equally free and independent." The compact theory of government is presupposed. Men are conceived as having inherent rights of which they cannot deprive or divest their descendants. These natural or inherent rights are designated as "the enjoyment of life and liberty, with the means of acquiring and possessing property, and pursuing and obtaining happiness and safety." [1] The doctrine of the sovereignty of the people is clearly expressed. All power is asserted to be vested in and derived from, them. "Magistrates are their trustees and servants, and at all times amenable to them."

The object of government is defined as the "common benefit, protection, and security of the people." Of possible forms of government, that is best which ensures the greatest degree of happiness and safety and the best administration. The people may change the government if these purposes are not realized. This is said to be "an indubitable, inalienable, and indefeasible right."

Public service alone is declared to be the title to exclusive emolument or privilege. No offices ought to be hereditary.

The doctrine of separation of powers which had been developed by Hooker, Milton, and Montesquieu is stated. There are to be frequent, certain, and regular elections. There ought to be no caste of public officials. All officers of the State are to be taken from the body of the people and shall return to private station. Elections ought to be free. The right of suffrage should be given to all who have common interest with and attachment to the community. No one ought to be taxed without his consent or deprived of his property

[1] Art. I.

involuntarily. All laws are to issue from the people or their representatives, and to have for their object the public good.

The suspension of laws or their execution by an unlawful authority is affirmed to be contrary to the rights of the people. Then follow four clauses which are judicial in their nature, to the effect that every man has a right to demand the cause of his accusation in all capital or criminal prosecutions; to be confronted with accusers and witnesses; to call for evidence in his favor; to be tried by an impartial jury of twelve men; that he cannot be compelled to give evidence against himself, nor can be deprived of his liberty except by the law of the land or the judgment of his peers.[1] "Excessive bail ought not to be required, nor excessive fines imposed, nor cruel and unusual punishments inflicted." [2] General warrants ought not be granted. The trial by jury in cases affecting property should be held sacred.

The freedom of the press is declared to be one of the great bulwarks of liberty which no free government will restrain.

The proper, natural, and safe defence of a free State is considered to be a well-regulated militia of the citizens. Standing armies are dangerous to liberty. The civil power should control the military.

Government should be uniform. It is only by adhering to justice, moderation, temperance, frugality, and virtue, and by keeping fundamental principles in mind, that liberty can be preserved.

Madison's article closes the list. It affirmed "that religion, or the duty which we owe to our Creator, and the manner of discharging it, can be directed only by

[1] Magna Charta, Art. 39.
[2] The Bill of Rights of 1689, Art. 10.

reason and conviction, not by force or violence; and therefore all men are equally entitled to the free exercise of religion, according to the dictates of conscience; and that it is the mutual duty of all to practise Christian forbearance, love, and charity towards each other." [1]

The Declaration of Independence, composed after the Virginia Bill of Rights, declares that the Laws of Nature and of Nature's God entitle one people to sever their connection with another and make themselves independent. It holds certain things to be self-evident truths, that is, to be true according to the Law of Nature. One of these truths is that all men are created equal. Wherein this equality consists we are not told. It is also asserted that men possess certain unalienable rights, among which are the right to life, to liberty, and to the pursuit of happiness. Governments are held to be instituted for the purpose of securing these rights. The principle of the sovereignty of the people is also asserted. The people may change or abolish a government that becomes destructive to the ends for which it is instituted. They may "institute new government, laying its foundation on such principles and organizing its powers in such form as to them shall seem most likely to effect their safety and happiness."

There is not a single principle among these of which Jefferson was the originator. Some of these doctrines had been put forth centuries before. There can be no doubt, however, that the influence of the Declaration of Independence was greater than that of any other similar document.

[1] Poore, *Federal and State Constitutions, etc.*, II. pp. 1908–1909. Facsimile copy of original draft in Mason's handwriting in *Life of Mason*, by Kate M. Rowland, I. pp. 240–41.

The example of Virginia was followed by the other American States. The Virginia Bill became the model for other Bills of Rights which the various States prefixed to their constitutions to guarantee the rights of the citizens.

The preamble to the constitution of Massachusetts considers the body politic to be formed by a voluntary association of individuals and to be "a social compact, by which the whole people covenants with each citizen, and each citizen with the whole people, that all shall be governed by certain laws for the common good." The constitution declares all men to be born free and equal. It empowers the people to provide for the institution of the public worship of God and "the support and maintenance of public Protestant teachers of piety, religion, and morality in all cases where such provision shall not be made voluntarily." [1]

The Declaration of Rights of Connecticut declares "That all men when they form a social compact are equal in rights." It provides that "the exercise and enjoyment of religious profession and worship, without discrimination, shall forever be free to all persons in this State, provided that the right hereby declared and established shall not be so construed as to excuse acts of licentiousness, or to justify practices inconsistent with the peace and safety of the State." [2]

The constitution of New Hampshire affirms: I. "All men are born equally free and independent; therefore, all government of right originates from the people, is founded in consent, and instituted for the general good." III. "When men enter into a state of

[1] Poore, I. p. 956 *et seq*. The constitution of Massachusetts was adopted in 1780.

[2] Poore, I. p. 258.

society, they surrender up some of their Natural Rights to that society, in order to ensure the protection of others; and, without such an equivalent, the surrender is void." IV. "Among the Natural Rights some are in their very nature unalienable, because no equivalent can be given or received for them. Of this kind are the rights of conscience." [1]

The North Carolina Declaration of 1776 states "that perpetuities and monopolies are contrary to the genius of a free State and ought not to be allowed."

The Pennsylvania constitution of 1776 contains the statement "that all men have a natural inherent right to emigrate from one State to another that will receive them, or to form a new State in vacant countries, or in such countries as they can purchase, whenever they think that thereby they may promote their own happiness." Another article says "that the people have a right to assemble together, to consult for their common good, to instruct their representatives, and to apply to the legislature for redress of grievances, by address, petition, or remonstrance." [2]

The importance attached by Americans to these Bills of Rights is shown by the fact that all the States have incorporated some such a Declaration of Rights into their constitutions, the newer States having in most cases copied from the older.

Comparing these Bills of Rights with the famous English documents, such as Magna Charta, the Bill of Rights of 1689, and others, we notice that the English declarations contain no allusions to Natural Justice nor any abstract principles whatever, but name certain concrete rights to which individuals are entitled, not as men, but as English subjects. In the American Bills

[1] Poore, II. p. 1280. [2] Ibid., p. 1542.

of Rights, on the other hand, we find statements of abstract principles; such as the natural freedom and equality of men, the purpose of government, the doctrines of the sovereignty of the people, of the separation of powers, and the like, associated with statements of concrete rights; such as the right of trial by jury, freedom of speech and of the press, freedom of elections, security against excessive fines, cruel and unusual punishments, general warrants, and others. While the first class of statements are based upon the doctrines of Locke, Blackstone, Vattel, Pufendorf, and in a few instances of Montesquieu and Rousseau, the concrete rights are taken in most cases, and often copied verbatim, from Magna Charta or the English Bill of Rights.

In severing the ties which bound them to the motherland, the colonists could no longer regard rights which were granted by king and Parliament as applying to them. They must find another support for their rights. The political philosophy of their age came to their relief. They proclaimed the Rights of Man and founded them in Nature. But it was only natural that the well-known clauses of the English documents should still possess attraction for them. Indeed, it was for definite rights they cared most. Sober Englishmen as they were, there was but little likelihood of their attempting to carry abstract statements of equality and liberty to their logical conclusions, as did the French people during their Revolution. In France these selfsame ideas became a mass of dynamite which shattered the entire social and political order of things and gave rise to the worst excesses of the Reign of Terror. In America no disturbances of any sort arose as a result of the proclamation of these principles. The difference of consequences is attributable to a difference of circumstances, of past history, and above all, a difference in the character of the American and the French people. What has been called the "Revolutionary spirit" was totally lacking in America. Again, while the American Revolution had few further results than that of recognizing the independence of the colonies, the French Revolution was a social, political, and administrative upheaval, which meant the arrival of a new era, not only for France, but for the world.

It must not be supposed, however, that these doctrines have had no influence in America. On the contrary, it is impossible to overestimate their influence in promoting that love of individual liberty which, it is true, is characteristic of the entire Anglo-Saxon race, but which is nowhere so strong as in this country. American enterprise and independence of character cannot be matched the world over. It is this trait of character which, more than any other, has made our country what it is to-day. This American spirit is the spirit of the Bills of Rights. The American States have proclaimed and guaranteed the rights of the individual. Indeed, the Bill of Rights is everywhere, perhaps, regarded as the most important part of the State constitution. Judges have frequently declared laws unconstitutional because they were contrary to the spirit of the Bill of Rights.

But what necessity is there for such declarations of rights in a republic?

Magna Charta and the other English papers were intended primarily as a protection of the individual against the arbitrary exercise of power on the part of the king. They were to serve as a check upon the king. Since to-day the king has become a mere figurehead, however, and Parliament has become omnipotent, these documents no longer have a purpose. They do not protect the individual against Parliament, for the power of Parliament is unlimited. Parliament possessing full sovereignty can grant or take away individual rights as it chooses. There is therefore, in the British constitution, no means of protecting the individual against the government.

The American Bills of Rights are intended to serve as a check upon the government, restraining it from interference with the rights the individual is to enjoy. But is such a safeguard necessary in a government where the power is in the hands of the people? To answer this question it is necessary to bear in mind that democracy and liberty are by no means synonymous. The fact that the people rule is no guarantee that personal liberty must prevail. Public liberty does not imply civil liberty. The inhabitants of the Greek and Roman republics possessed extensive public rights, but no individual rights in the modern sense. It is true that in the last few centuries the struggle for liberty has been at the same time the struggle for democracy. But unlimited sovereignty, whether exercised by one, a few, or the many, is always liable to lead to tyranny. It is doubtful whether any tyranny can be worse than that exercised in the name of the sovereignty of the people. France experienced the truth of this during the Reign of Terror. The Bills of Rights are intended as a limitation of the sovereignty of the people in favor of the liberty of the individual.

PART IV

THE FRENCH DECLARATION OF THE RIGHTS OF MAN AND OF THE CITIZEN

THE FRENCH DECLARATION OF THE RIGHTS OF MAN AND OF THE CITIZEN

CHAPTER X

FRANCE AND THE PRINCIPLES OF THE AMERICAN REVOLUTION

THE struggle of the American colonies for independence was watched by Europeans in general, and by the French in particular, with intense interest.

One must consider the views of the French in the eighteenth century in order to understand the sympathy they entertained for the Americans.

In the new world the ideas of Rousseau and of the other philosophers of that century seemed to be realized. There reason, simplicity, naturalness, and virtue were thought to reign.

The Count of Ségur tells us in his memoirs how intense the excitement was at Spa, a fashionable watering-place frequented by the aristocracy of Europe, when the news of the events in Boston in 1775 became known. "The first shot of the cannon fired in the new hemisphere," he writes, "resounded throughout Europe with the rapidity of lightning. . . ." "The courageous daring of the Americans electrified all spirits and excited a

207

general admiration. . . . And in this little city of
Spa . . . I was singularly surprised to see so lively
and general an interest manifest itself for the revolt of
a people against a king. The American insurrection
spread everywhere like a fashion . . . and I was far
from being the only one whose heart throbbed at the
news of the awaking of liberty, striving to throw off
the yoke of arbitrary power." [1] He tells us that he
found the same agitation prevailing in Paris, and that
the envoys of the Americans, Deane, Lee, and Franklin, seemed to be the sage contemporaries of Plato, or
republicans of the time of Cato and Fabius.[2]

Many members of the noblest families of France
hastened to the scene of conflict and fought with distinction at the side of Washington. Covered with
glory they returned to their native land, ardent advocates of the American views of liberty and equality.
These ideas spread widely, for they fell upon prepared
ground.[3]

Ségur tells us that as a result of the American Revolution "Everybody occupied himself with public affairs,
and, seeing to what a point under monarchical forms
views had become republican, it was not difficult for
Rousseau to predict the approach of the epoch of great
revolutions." [4] Franklin had the constitutions of the
several States, the Declaration of Independence, and
other papers relating to American affairs, published and
spread throughout the country in 1783.

A number of books had been written by Frenchmen

[1] Ségur's *Mémoires*, I. pp. 51, 52.

[2] *Ibid.*, pp. 53, 69.

[3] Jefferson's *Memoir*, by Randolph, I. p. 56; Ségur, *Mémoires*,
pp. 149, 165; Campan, *Mémoires*, I. p. 233, III. pp. 96, 116;
De Staël, *Considérations*, I. p. 88.

[4] Vol. I. p. 129.

which show what interest they took in American affairs. In 1787 was published a book entitled *De la France et des États-Unis*, by Clavière and Brissot. It deals with the prospects of commerce between France and America. In the introduction Brissot says that the American Revolution had occasioned the discussion of many points important for the public welfare, such as the social contract, civil liberty, the things that can render a people independent, and the circumstances which legitimatize an insurrection and cause a nation to take a place among the powers of the world. "What good," he writes, "have not done and will not do the codes of Pennsylvania, Massachusetts, New York, published and spread everywhere? They are not to be taken completely as models, but despotism, either through necessity or reason, will henceforth respect the Rights of Man so well known and so well established. Enlightened by this revolution the governments of Europe will be forced to reform their abuses and diminish their burdens." [1]

The Abbé Mably had written an *Impartial History of the Late War*, which referred to American affairs.

The Abbé Raynal published in 1785 a series of letters he had written to John Adams, at the time the American ambassador to Paris, under the title, *Observations on the Government and the Laws of the United States.*

He does not agree on all points with the work of the Americans, but in general he speaks of the constitutions of the several States with great enthusiasm. "While nearly all the nations of Europe ignore the constitutive principles of society," he says, "and do not regard citizens as better than the beasts of a farm, which are governed for the particular good of their

[1] Intro. xxx, xxxi.

owner, it is surprising and edifying that the thirteen American colonies have recognized the dignity of man, and have drawn from the sources of the wisest philosophy their principles of government.[1]

" These constitutions have gone to the principles of nature. They have established it as an axiom that all political authority derives its origin from the people, and that magistrates are but the agents of the people. The Americans know the Rights of Men and of Nations. The delegates who have framed the constitutions have adopted the wise principles of Locke regarding natural liberty and the nature of government."

Raynal says he has thoroughly studied the legislation of America. "All Europe," he declares, "having feared that the Americans would not be able to resist the forces of Great Britain, is enchanted with the courage and constancy they have shown, and with the happy success they have obtained." [2]

It was but natural that the great Mirabeau should take an interest in the affairs of the colonies. The political theories put forth by the Americans were hailed by him with enthusiasm. In 1777 he wrote: "When a government becomes arbitrary and oppressive, when it attacks property which it ought to protect, when it breaks the compact which assures rights, though limiting them, resistance becomes a duty and cannot be called rebellion. . . . Whoever seeks to regain freedom and fights for it, exercises but a natural right. . . . The people stand as much above the sovereign as he does above individuals." [3]

At the suggestion of Franklin, Mirabeau published

[1] *Lettre* i. p. 5.
[2] *Lettre* iv.
[3] In his *Réponse aux Conseils de la Raison.*

the *Considerations on the Order of Cincinnatus*, which appeared in London in 1785. He regrets that this order was established "at the end of the eighteenth century, at the moment when America seemed to open an asylum to the human race; at the moment when the most surprising revolution, the only one, perhaps, which philosophy approves of, has turned the attention of all to the other hemisphere." [1]

"The delegates, representatives, and legislators of the American people," Mirabeau says, "have made equality the basis of their insurrection, their work, their demands, their rights, and their code. For this reason they occupy among the powers of the world the rank and separate position to which they are entitled by virtue of the Laws of Nature and of Nature's God." [2] He then enters into a consideration of the Bills of Rights of the various States. "All the States of the Confederation have declared in their constitutions that men are born free and equal; that they possess natural, essential, and unalienable rights, of which they can by no compact deprive or despoil their posterity; that all government derives its right from the people; that no authority can be exercised over the people except that which emanates from them or is accorded by them; that the various officers of the government clothed with any legislative, executive, or judicial authority, are the substitutes, the agents, the servants of the people, and accountable to them at all times; that government is established for the common welfare, for the protection and security of the people, and not for the profit or interest of a single person, family, or assemblage of men who are but a part of the community; that government shall ensure the existence of the body

[1] P. 1.   [2] Pp. 31, 32.

politic, protect it, and procure for the individuals who compose it, the enjoyment of their Natural Rights in security and tranquillity; that every body politic is formed by the voluntary association of individuals mutually bound to each other by a social compact, by which the whole people contract with each citizen and each citizen with the entire people; that all be governed by certain laws in a uniform manner and for the common good; that the enjoyment of the right of the people to participate in legislation is the foundation of liberty and of all free government; that the whole people have a right to change the government when these ends are not realized, the doctrine of non-resistance against arbitrary power and oppression being absurd, servile, and destructive of the welfare and happiness of the human race." [1]

"America," Mirabeau declared, "can, and is going to, determine with certainty whether the human race is destined by nature to liberty or slavery. No republican government has ever found in any part of the globe such favorable circumstances." America is destined to show whether or not the beautiful ideas of Sidney, Locke, and Rousseau are to remain superb theories, whose realization is impracticable. Mirabeau appended to his *Considerations* a letter written by the famous Turgot to Dr. Price, an Englishman who possessed great enthusiasm for America, and also Price's *Observations on the Importance of the American Revolution*.

In his letter Turgot wrote: "America is the hope of the human race and ought to become the model for humanity. She ought to prove to the world in fact that men can be free and tranquil and dispense with

[1] *Considerations*, pp. 32–34.

the chains of all kinds which tyrants and charlatans have imposed on pretext of the public good. . . . She ought to be an example of liberty of all kinds: political, civil, religious, commercial, and industrial. The asylum she opens to the oppressed ought to console the world. The facility of profiting therefrom to escape the results of bad government, will force all governments to be just and to enlighten themselves." [1]

Price speaks of the American Revolution as opening a new era in the history of the world and of presenting a grand perspective. He regards it as having spread among the nations healthful principles concerning the Rights of Mankind and the nature of government, and of having given rise to a general spirit of resistance to tyranny. The Revolution, he says, gave to America the most equitable and free government in existence. He thinks that in America all the nations of the world will be blest. This vast continent will become a refuge for the oppressed of all nations. A republic has been established which will become the seat of liberty, the sanctuary of science and of virtue. He hopes that America will preserve this sacred treasure until all peoples enjoy it and the infamous servitude which degrades the earth will have terminated forever. Since the introduction of Christianity no epoch has been of equal influence upon the advancement of the race as has been that of the American Revolution. He believes that this revolution will diffuse among all nations the principles of the Rights of Man, and will afford the means of throwing off the yoke of superstition and tyranny. [2]

Great interest was also taken in American affairs by Condorcet, the famous French author, who wrote a

[1] *Considerations*, p. 95.   [2] *Ibid.*, pp. 212–16.

number of pamphlets which contain references to the Natural Rights of Mankind and to the services of America to the race in asserting them.[1] He says that "The first Declaration of Rights which really merits the name, is that of Virginia, issued June 1, 1776; and the author of this production has claims to the everlasting gratitude of the human race. Six other American States have imitated the example of Virginia."[2] These declarations do not entirely satisfy him and he indicates several omissions. Nevertheless there is no doubt in his mind that such a declaration, which contains a clear statement of the Rights of Man, is the only means of preventing tyranny, and will be a work useful to mankind as a safeguard of public tranquillity and liberty. According to his view, the best method of obtaining such a declaration is to encourage enlightened men to draw up models and then to have these drafts published, a course which was afterward pursued by the Constituent Assembly. Condorcet himself composed a lengthy Declaration of Rights in several sections, distinguishing between the Rights of Man relative to personal safety, to personal liberty, to safety of property, to liberty of property, and to natural equality. Condorcet took an active part in the French Revolution. Eventually siding with the Girondists, Condorcet presented to the convention the constitution, in which was incorporated a Declaration of Rights, which had been drawn up according to the principles of the Girondist party. He was likewise one of the most energetic opponents against the attempts of the Mountain to attack individual rights on the ground of promoting the public welfare.[3]

[1] Most of these are in Vol. IX. of Condorcet's *Œuvres*.

[2] *Œuvres*, IX. p. 168.

[3] *Ibid.*, VI. p. 556.

Mirabeau drew up a Declaration of Rights for the people of Holland in a pamphlet which he wrote in 1788, at the suggestion of the Dutch republicans, and which bears the title, *Address to the Batavians Concerning the Stadtholdership.*

He proposes to enumerate the rights to which this people are entitled as men—rights which are inherent, prior to and above all written laws, unalienable, and the eternal foundation of political society. He considers these rights to be fully carried out only in the American constitution. Without these rights mankind cannot maintain its dignity, cannot perfect itself, or enjoy peace. Every nation desiring freedom must be in possession of them.

Mirabeau's paper agrees with the American Bills of Rights in most of its articles, and is interesting not only because it shows American influence, but also because it forms, as it were, the political confession of faith of this great statesman. The Declaration contains such statements as that of the freedom and equality of all men; the sovereignty of the people; universal toleration; freedom of the press, of speech, of public meeting, and of elections; the separation of powers; abolition of exclusive privileges; the subordination of the military to the civil power; establishment of the militia system rather than having standing armies; freedom from attack upon person, house, papers, and property; independence of judges; right to speedy, free, and unbiassed justice; freedom from banishment or deprivation of life, liberty, or property, without a valid legal sentence.

We have seen that Mirabeau was well acquainted with the leading papers issued by the American general government as well as by the individual States. He took a very prominent part, as a member of the Constituent Assembly, in the discussions regarding the Declaration of the Rights of Man, and was one of the committee of five appointed by that body to prepare this Declaration.

There can be no doubt that the American Revolution seemed to Europeans to signify the dawn of liberty. This explains the interest they took in American affairs. The Marquis of Chastellux, who travelled in America during the years 1780–82, assured a number of farmers who were surprised to see a map of their country in the hands of a Frenchman, that his countrymen were as well acquainted with America as they were with their next neighbors. In the preface to his *Travels* he says that the French hailed with the greatest eagerness all information about America, and that the few copies of his journal, which he had sent to his most intimate friends, though not intended for the public, passed rapidly from hand to hand and were read with avidity.

Nor was this interest in American affairs confined to France. Of the influence of our Revolution on the Germans a writer says: "The republican sympathies of the educated and wide-awake classes in Germany were increased and strengthened by the War of American Independence, and especially by the surprisingly happy termination of that war. The long extracts from the Congressional debates, the addresses of the rebellious colonies, the Declaration of the Rights of Man by Congress, the orations of the leaders in Congress and the army, were zealously spread by German newspapers, and of necessity powerfully influenced the people. Yes, the governments even, inasmuch as England was at the time greatly hated by them, sided with the Americans and their principles, though the latter contrasted greatly with German conditions. Frederick the Great especially favored the colonists. The victory of the young republic was hailed with general and sympathetic rejoicing." [1] There was great indignation throughout Germany at the shameless traffic with Hessian soldiers. As the French officers returned to their native land filled with enthusiasm for American institutions and principles, so these German soldiers acquainted their countrymen with American ideas, not only by their written accounts, but also, and more especially, by their glowing accounts after their return.[2]

A German nobleman in the American service wrote to his friends in the old world enthusiastic accounts of the "beautiful and happy land, without kings, priests, farmers of taxes, and lazy barons, the land where every one is happy and where poverty is unknown." [3]

In 1783 there appeared in a Berlin journal an ode which contains these words: "And thou, Europe, raise thy head. Soon will shine the day when thy chains shall break. Thy princes expelled, thou wilt hail a happy free state." Addressing America the poet says: "Thy example speaks loudly to the farthest nations, free is he who wills it and is worthy to be so. Yet ever-raging despotism, which, breaking God's laws, serves but the great, frightens the nations." The writer blesses "the better hemisphere, where sweet equality reigns, and Europe's curse, nobility, does not simplicity's custom stain, wrongly defying worthier men, feasting on the sweat of the peasant.[4]

[1] Philippson, *Geschichte des preussischen Staatswesens*, II. pp. 4–6.

[2] Brandes, E., *Ueber einige bisherige Folgen der franz. Rev. mit Rücksicht auf Dschld.*, 1792.

[3] Schlözer, *Briefwechsel*, VII. 333.

[4] *Berliner Monatsschrift*, 1783.

The years preceding the outbreak of the great French Revolution were a time of great ferment in Europe, especially in France. The masses were becoming enlightened. The revolutionary teachings of such writers as Condillac, Holbach, Diderot, Voltaire, Rousseau, and others were beginning to bear fruit. In America these principles had conquered. Their success in that country increased their popularity and influence. It was hoped that they would overthrow tyranny in the old world likewise. The calling of the States General filled the French people with hope that a new order of things would soon result. The instructions prepared by the French districts for their representatives, which were called Cahiers, give expression to the hopes and desires of the French people on the eve of the Revolution. These papers show that the American idea of enumerating individual rights in a declaration had met with great favor. Several Cahiers suggest that a similar Declaration of the Rights of Man should be drawn up by the States General.

The Cahier of the Third Estate of Paris contains a declaration which states that all men have equal rights; that all power emanates from the people and should be exercised only for their welfare; that the general will makes the law and public power assures its execution. All subsidies are declared to be conceded by the nation, which has the right to determine their amount, to limit their duration, to designate the use to which they shall be put, to demand an account of their employment, and to insist upon their publication. The object of the law is to protect property and ensure personal security. No citizen should be arrested or punished without legal judgment, nor be arbitrarily deprived of any office he may hold. Each citizen has the right to be admitted to any office, possession, or dignity. The natural, civil, and religious liberty of every man, his personal security, his absolute independence of all authority except that of the law, excludes every enquiry into his opinions, his speech, his writings, and his actions, so long as they do not disturb the public order and injure the rights of another. The declaration of natural, civil, and political rights was to become the national charter, and the basis of the French government.

The Cahier instructed the deputies to demand a number of reforms as a consequence of the principles of this Declaration of Rights; namely, the abolition of all forms of servitude; of all unnecessary offices; of the violation of public faith by searching letters sent through the mails; and of all exclusive privileges, except a limited privilege to inventors. Liberty of the press was likewise demanded, subject to legitimate restrictions.

Perhaps the most remarkable of these Cahiers is that of the bailliage of Nemours, among the deputies of which district was the Viscount de Noailles, one of the young officers who had fought in America. This paper affirms that the preservation of rights is the sole object of political society, and holds that the knowledge of these rights ought to be the basis of all laws and institutions. The States General ought to determine these rights. A public Declaration should then be made by the king, which is to be registered in all the courts, published several times a year in all the churches, and inserted in all books intended for the education of children. No person is to be entrusted with any charge, place, or office, unless he has repeated this Declaration from memory, and has sworn to conform his actions thereto.[2]

[1] *Archives parlementaires*, V. 281, 282.   [2] *Ibid.*, IV. 161-3.

The electors of Nemours suggest certain truths which ought to be inserted in this Declaration. Some of these ideas are quite fanciful. Every man is said to have the right to do that which does not injure others. Every man has a right to the assistance of others, and to a reciprocal service from any one who has claimed his aid. Every helpless person has a right to the gratuitous assistance of others. No man ought to be interrupted or hindered in his work. No authority can compel any person to labor without salary, or with insufficient salary. These maxims are very wise, no doubt, but scarcely belong in a Declaration like the one intended. Other demands are: Freedom of contract; inviolability of person and property; no imprisonment without conviction; speedy trial; taxes to be levied in proportion to income; no authority to supplant that of the taxpayers or their representatives in levying taxes; freedom of speech, of petition, and of the press. This is the gist of the thirty articles this draft contains.

But already this draft seems to contain the germs of that spirit which eventually destroyed individual liberty in France; namely, the desire for a falsely conceived equality. Such appears to be the tendency of statements like the one that every person is entitled to the assistance of others; that every person in a state of infancy, helplessness, or infirmity has a right to the gratuitous help of others; that any person who has no income ought not be obliged to contribute to the payment of the public expenses, but has a right to gratuitous aid.

It was, as we have seen, an injunction of several districts of France upon the States General to enumerate and guarantee the Rights of Man and of the Citizen after the American fashion. It was universally felt that the insecurity of the individual was one of the chief evils from which the French were suffering, that *lettres de cachet*, Bastille, seignorial rights, ought to be abolished.

The members of the States General, those representing the Third Estate at least, were not likely to forget this behest.

It is true that in regard to the form of government the majority of the members of the Constituent Assembly took England, rather than America, as their model. Scarcely any one thought of the republic as a possible or desirable form of government for France. Almost without exception the monarchy was regarded as essential, even by such men as Lafayette. But it was to become a constitutional monarchy.

But nevertheless the American idea of a Declaration of the Rights of Man met with almost universal favor. It accorded perfectly with the tendency of thought. Madame de Staël speaks of the democratic declarations which found such applause in the Assembly, and states that this body was seized by an enthusiasm for philosophy, of which the example of America was a cause, the people of France believing that they might take as a basis the principles which the people of the new world had adopted.[1]

[1] Madame de Staël, *Considérations sur la Revolution Française*, I. 238, 239.

CHAPTER XI

THE CONSTITUENT ASSEMBLY AND THE DECLARATION OF THE RIGHTS OF MAN AND OF THE CITIZEN

JULY 9, 1789, there was presented to the French Constituent Assembly the report of the committee which that body had selected to draft a constitution for France, regarding the plan according to which the constitution should be framed. It was Mounier who acted as reporter of the committee. He declared the sole end of government to be the maintenance of the rights of man. In order to keep this object constantly in view, there should be prefixed to the constitution a Declaration of the Natural and Unalienable Rights of Man.[1]

Three days later, Lafayette, of American fame, addressed the Assembly. As commander of the National Guard he had no right to vote in that body, but might participate in its deliberations. He now wished "to offer the tribute of his thoughts." [2]

While in America Lafayette had imbibed the principles put forth during the Revolution. On his return to France he enclosed a copy of the American Declaration of Rights in a valuable frame. Beside the Declaration there was an empty column headed: Declaration of the Rights of the French people.

Lafayette regarded the American Revolution as having inaugurated a new social era. This new social order he held to be, properly speaking, the period of the

[1] *Arch. Parl.*, VIII. p. 216.   [2] *Ibid.*, p. 221.

Declaration of Rights.[1] He said that only since the American Revolution had the idea prevailed of defining the rights which nature gives to each man and which are independent of all preexisting order, rights which are to such an extent inherent in man's existence that not even the entire society has the right to deprive him of them.[2] He believed that the opportunity had now come for France to imitate the example set by the Americans. In his address to the Assembly, Lafayette affirmed the double purpose of a Declaration of Rights as being: 1. To recall the sentiments which nature had engraved on the heart of each individual, and to facilitate their development, a task which is the more interesting because of the fact that in order that a nation love liberty, it suffices that it know what liberty is; and that in order to be free, it need only wish to be so. 2. To express the eternal truths to which all institutions ought to conform and which ought to be a guide to the representatives of the nation, leading them to the source of Natural and Social Law. He said that a Declaration of Rights should be true and precise, and should express what the whole world knows and feels. As an attempt at such a Declaration Lafayette presented a bill which contained the following stipulations: 1. Nature has made men free and equal; distinctions necessary for the social order are founded on general utility alone. 2. Every man is born with unalienable rights, such as liberty of opinion, care of honor and of life, the right of property, the entire disposition of his person, of his business, and of his faculties, the communication of his thoughts in all ways possible, the pursuit of happiness, and resistance to oppression. 3. The only limits to the exercise of Natural Rights are

[1] *Mémoires*, II. p. 303.   [2] *Ibid.*, p. 304.

those which are necessary to ensure their enjoyment to other members of society. 4. No man can be subjected to any other laws than those consented to by himself or his representatives, and these laws must have been previously promulgated and must be legally applied. 5. The origin of all sovereignty is in the people. 6. No individual or corporation can have any authority which does not expressly emanate from the people. 7. All government has for its sole end the common welfare. This interest demands that the legislative, executive, and judiciary powers be distinct and defined, and that their organization assure the free representation of the citizens, the responsibility of agents, and the impartiality of judges. 8. The laws should be clear, precise, and uniform. 9. The subsidies should be freely voted and proportionally divided. 10. As the introduction of abuses and the rights of succeeding generations necessitate the revision of all human establishments, it ought to be possible for the nation to have, in ecrtain cases, an extraordinary convocation of deputies, whose sole object be to examine and correct, if necessary, the faults of the constitution.[1]

It is evident that the project of Lafayette is modelled after the Virginia Bill of Rights.[2] It is clear and precise, and is surely as good as many other Declarations that were subsequently submitted to the Assembly. Its adoption would have prevented much precious time from being wasted by foolish debates on the value and composition of a perfect Declaration of Rights. There were long debates as to whether the Declaration should precede the constitution, establishing the Rights of Man previous to those of society, or be placed at the end, as a result of the constitution. No agreement

[1] *Arch. Parl.*, VIII. pp. 221, 222.　[2] *Mémoires*, II. 305.

was reached at that time; it was only decided that the constitution should contain such a Declaration. The question having been raised on the 14th of July, but not then definitely decided, it was again raised on the 1st of August. For several days a lively discussion was carried on as to whether or not a Declaration of Rights should be drawn up, and whether it should follow or precede the constitution.

On the 27th of July Champion de Cicé, Archbishop of Bordeaux, the reporter for the committee of the constitution, said that the committee had judged it necessary "that the constitution be preceded by a Declaration of the Rights of Man and of the Citizen; not because it was necessary to impress upon these first truths a force they already derived from morals, from reason, and from nature, which had engrafted them in all hearts, but because these ineffaceable principles should be constantly before the eyes and in thought." This Declaration, he said, "would be a constant guarantee against the fear of any disregard of its principles." "If in the course of ages any power should attempt to impose laws upon the people that were not an emanation from these principles, this original and enduring type would instantly denounce crime or error to all citizens." "This noble idea," he proceeded, "conceived in another hemisphere, ought to be, because of its excellence, at once transplanted among us. We have participated in the events that gave to North America her liberty; she has shown us upon what principles the conservation of our own should rest; and it is the new world, whither we had formerly carried only weapons, which to-day teaches us to secure ourselves against the misfortune of betaking thither our persons." [1]

[1] *Arch. Parl.*, VIII. p. 281.

The Bishop of Auxerre, Champion de Cicé, thought the Declaration useless, and said the example set by America was not conclusive, since that country possessed only proprietors and cultivators of land, citizens who were in fact equal. Before telling men they were free, as was done in the United States, it is necessary that the laws be passed which placed them on an equality.[1]

Malouet expressed inquietude and regret on account of the time consumed and the disorders that were accumulating. He thought that action rather than talk was necessary. Though believing that the Rights of Man should be held in view, and that they were not only the guide of the legislator but also the object he should aim to realize, he thought these principles ought to be presented as they are restricted by positive law. If the Americans had not taken this precaution it was because they found man in the natural state, and presented him to the universe in his primitive sovereignty. The Americans were already accustomed to equality. They were strangers to luxury as well as to indigence, free from the yoke of imposts, of prejudice, and of feudal customs. But in France a multitude of men were without property and dependent upon assured labor and constant protection, irritated also by the spectacle of luxury and opulence. The oppressed ought rather to be restored to their rights. Wise institutions should bring together the happy and the unhappy classes of society. Immoderate luxury should be attacked at its source, for it assails all Natural Rights.[2]

Malouet said that the domestic spirit which recalls man's Natural Rights, and patriotism which consecrates them, should supplant the spirit of caste and the love

[1] *Arch. Parl.*, VIII. p. 322.   [2] *Ibid.*

of prerogative and of all vanities that are irreconcilable with enduring liberty and with the elevation of true patriotism. These reforms should be effected, or at least attempted, before proclaiming to suffering men who are destitute of enlightenment and of means, that they have equal rights with the most powerful and most fortunate. He showed that each natural law was modified by positive law, and that the moment a particular form of government was chosen, the natural man and his rights were restricted. He asked why a man should be taken to the top of a high mountain and shown an unlimited empire that was said to belong to him, when, on descending, he finds himself shut in at each step; why a man should be told that he has the free disposition of his person, when he must enter the army or the navy against his will; why he should be assured that he may dispose of his property as he wishes, when custom and law force him to dispose of it against his will; why it should be said to him that if he is indigent he has a right to the assistance of all, when he invokes in vain the pity of the passers-by. He said that since every man whose rights were declared was a member of society, there was therefore no reason of speaking of him as if he were separated from society.

Malouet pointed out the danger that might result from interminable metaphysical discussions, saying that under the circumstances of the time, when the government was without force and means, when authority was weakened and the courts inactive, when the people alone were in motion, when there was no public income, but rather an increase of expenditure, and all onerous obligations seemed unjust, a declaration expressing in general and absolute terms natural liberty and equality, might sever the bonds uniting the citizen and the government, and that under existing circumstances only the constitution could prevent universal anarchy.[1]

Delandine argued that it was not the duty of the deputies to establish principles, as Locke, Cumberland, Rousseau, and others had done, but to promulgate their results; not to lay down the preliminaries of the law, but to make the laws themselves. He said that the time had arrived to create; that the law should be simple and concise, so that even children could remember it. It was his opinion that the framers of the constitution should reserve for themselves the study of principles as bases of their labor, giving to the people only the fruits of their work. In this case the vast foundation of the palace would be hidden in the bosom of the earth, while to the eye of the citizen only the majesty of the edifice would be visible. "Let us," concluded Delandine, "hasten to erect this edifice, and may it merit the contemplation of the wise and the regard of posterity."[2]

The Abbé Grégoire believed that a Declaration of Rights would be incomplete without being at the same time a Declaration of Duties, since rights and duties were correlative, and one could not exist without the other. A man should be shown the circle within which he might move and the barriers which ought to restrain him.[3]

The wise views of Malouet, Delandine, and Grégoire were not regarded. On the 4th of August the excitement over the matter reached the climax.

An amendment proposed by Camus in accordance with the view of Grégoire and many of the clergy, that there be also a Declaration of Duties, was lost.

[1] *Arch. Parl.*, VIII. p. 323.
[2] *Ibid.*, pp. 323–325.
[3] *Ibid.*, pp. 340, 341.

The Assembly decided almost unanimously that the Declaration be prefixed to the constitution.

In the evening of the same day took place the celebrated abolition of titles of nobility and feudal customs.

The deliberation on the Declaration of Rights was thereby suspended for several days, but it was again resumed on the 14th of August.

A splendid opportunity offered itself to the members of the Constituent Assembly to try their hands at framing a Declaration of Rights of Man, and to demonstrate how well they were versed in political philosophy. About fifty projects were presented to the Assembly. A committee of five, consisting of Mirabeau, De La Luzerne, De Desmenniers, Tronchet, and Rédon, was appointed to consider the various projects and to present their conclusions to the Assembly. The three chief ones were those of Lafayette, Sieyès, and Mounier. The first two had been written before the convocation of the Constituent Assembly.[1]   That of Lafayette was the shortest and simplest.

The Declaration framed by Mounier differed but slightly in its nature from that of Lafayette. Some of its articles agreed almost *verbatim* with those of Lafayette's draft. But Mounier added several additional clauses, to the effect that no *ex post facto* laws should be passed; that all individuals be entitled to the prompt succor of the law when their rights are infringed; that they be secure from arbitrary arrest or imprisonment and from arbitrary fines; that religious toleration and freedom of the press be guaranteed, and that the civil authority alone have control over the military forces for the maintenance of public tranquillity.   The project

[1] Jefferson's Letter to J. Madison, Jan. 12, 1789.   *Memoir*, ed. by Randolph, I. p. 422.

enjoined but one duty upon each member of society—
that each pay his proportional share toward defraying
the public expenses.[1]

Mounier afterward regretted that he had participated in the Declaration of the Rights of Man. Later
events, especially those of the 5th and 6th of October,
showed him that abstract ideas on the Rights of Man
might be wrongly interpreted, and lead to dangerous
consequences.[2]

The Abbé Sieyès drew up a Declaration which was
quite different in character from any other. This
expert constitution-maker, who considered himself to
have mastered the science of politics, presented a very
elaborate project in which each metaphysical principle
followed its predecessor in logical continuity. In order
to facilitate the retention of the eternal truths which
this pamphlet professed to embody, and to make them
lucid for all classes, Sieyès likewise composed a short
extract of its main principles.[3]

In his Declaration Sieyès considers society to have
resulted from a compact between all the associated, the
purpose of this compact being the greater good of all.
Liberty is more extensive and secure in the social,
than in the natural, state. Every man is the sole
proprietor of his person and is free in the exercise of
personal faculties. He may think what he pleases and
publish his thoughts in any manner whatsoever. He
may engage in any occupation, may go or remain any-
where he pleases, and dispose of his property as seems
best.

[1] *Arch. Parl.*, VIII. pp. 289, 290.

[2] *Considérations sur les causes qui ont empeché les Français
de devenir libres*, 1792.

[3] *Arch. Parl.*, VIII. pp. 256–261.

A public force should exist to protect each individual in the enjoyment of his rights. The liberty of each should be rendered so secure by a wise constitution of government that there need be no necessity for the military force except against a foreign enemy. Each citizen is alike subject to the law. There should be an abolition of all privileges, the object of the law being the common interest. Sieyès declared that even if men are not equal in means and differ as regards wealth, intelligence, power, etc., they are equal in rights. The law should protect all without distinction, for no person possesses greater freedom than another. No one ought to be called to justice, seized, or imprisoned except according to the forms prescribed by law. Every arbitrary or illegal order is void; they who demand, sign, or execute such an order are culpable; the citizen against whom it is directed may repel violence by violence. Each citizen is declared to have a right to prompt justice. He is entitled to the common advantages which come from the state of society, and if in need, to the succor of his fellow citizens. The law is said to be the expression of the general will. Unlike Rousseau, Sieyès believed in representation.[1]

Sieyès distinguishes in his draft between natural and civil rights on the one hand and political rights on the other. The purpose of society is to develop and maintain the natural and civil rights of men, but society is itself produced by the political rights of the citizens; that is, while the former are passive rights, the latter are active.[2]

He also distinguishes between passive and active citizens. All inhabitants of a country, men, women, strangers, or children, are passive citizens, because all

[1] *Arch. Parl.*, VIII. 260, 261.   [2] *Ibid.*, p. 259.

are entitled to the rights of citizens.   Active citizens are those who contribute to public establishment. The equality of political rights is a fundamental principle.   Every privilege is unjust, odious, and contradictory to the true end of society.   The social order necessarily presupposes unity of purpose.   Sieyès says that a political association is the work of the unanimous will of the associated.   Its public establishment is the result of the will of a plurality of those associated, inasmuch as it is impossible to attain unanimity in a body of many millions.   The general will is therefore the will of the plurality.   He maintains that all authority comes from the people, and that all public powers, without distinction, are an emanation from the general will.   Every public function is a commission, not property; a duty, not a right.   All public officers except the king are responsible for their conduct.   He asserts that a people has the right to revise its constitution.   It is even good that at fixed periods such a revision take place if necessary.[1]

On the 17th of August Mirabeau, the reporter of the committee of five appointed to draft the Declaration, submitted their project to the Assembly.   In his introductory speech he said that it was a difficult task to draw up a Declaration destined for an old and infirm political body, since many local considerations must be regarded; and that the difficulty was so much the greater because the constitution to which this Declaration should form the preamble was not known.   What made the task still more arduous was that twenty projects had to be revised in three days.[2]   He said that the committee had clothed the principles in a popular form, which would recall to the people not what they

[1] *Arch. Parl.*, VIII. 259, 260.   [2] *Ibid.*, p. 438.

had read in books, but what they themselves experienced. Accordingly, the instrument was written in the language used by the people to express their ideas rather than composed after the nature of a science to be taught them. He considered this an important matter because liberty was never the fruit of philosophical deductions, but rather of every-day experience and of the simple ideas arising from facts. Mirabeau thought a Declaration would be better understood in proportion as it expressed these popular ideas. He said that the Americans had proceeded thus, having purposely omitted science and presented political truths which could be easily apprehended by the people, for whom alone liberty is intended, and who alone can maintain it. In attempting to imitate them, continued Mirabeau, a great difficulty was encountered in distinguishing what belonged to the nature of man from the modifications his nature had undergone in a particular society, and in declaring the principles of liberty without entering into details and assuming the form of laws. It was hard to resist the temptation to denounce the abuses of despotism, and compose, not a Declaration of the Rights of Man, but a declaration of war against tyrants. Mirabeau said that an ideal declaration must be simple, evident, and fruitful of consequences. He thought circumstances and men in France were not prepared for anything but a feeble attempt at such a Declaration.[1]

Mirabeau then read the draft framed by the committee, which had either entirely avoided the use of metaphysical generalizations that might be put to a dangerous application, or if it did employ an abstraction, restricted it in a way that limited its scope. This

[1] *Arch. Parl.*, VIII. p. 438.

was due to the foresight and carefulness of Mirabeau. Thus, while declaring all men free and equal, equality was in another article defined as meaning, not an equality of property or distinctions, but an equal submission to the law and an equal right to its protection.   While asserting that the citizen had the right to employ his powers, his industry, and his property as he pleased, the right was reserved to the law of modifying this liberty if the general welfare necessitated it.   Liberty of thought and expression was granted, but with the restriction that the rights of others be regarded.   Every political organization was affirmed to be instituted by a social compact by which an individual put his person and property under the supreme direction of the general will.   The stipulations of this project were: That all powers emanate from the nation; that the common welfare is the end of government, and that no laws are valid that were not consented to by the people or their representatives; that the law, being the expression of the general will, should be general in its object and ensure to all liberty, property, and civil equality; that the liberty of the citizen consisted in his being subject to the law alone, and to the authority established by law; that the citizen might resist unlawful oppression; that he should enjoy the right of public trial; that accusation, arrest, and imprisonment should be according to legal forms; that punishment should be legal, graduated according to the nature of the offence, and equal for all.   It declared further that the citizen might travel or migrate whither he pleased, with legal reservations; that all citizens should have the right of petition, of public meeting in a legal form; that the State alone could demand a sacrifice of private property, and should exercise this right only in case of necessity, and on condition of indemnifying the owner.[1]

While a contribution to the public expenses, according to the amount of property, was demanded of each citizen, it was stated that every contribution was contrary to the rights of men if it discouraged industry, excited cupidity, corrupted morals, or deprived the people of their means of subsistence. Accountability of the employment of finances and economy of administration were set down as rigorous duties of the government. The army was to be under the direction and control of the civil authorities.

Mirabeau, continuing his address, predicted that the laws passed by the Constituent Assembly would, if they were worthy laws, become the laws of Europe, and that its members were laboring not only for themselves, but also for their descendants and for the whole world.[2]

On the following day, the 18th of August, the Declaration presented by Mirabeau was laid before the Constituent Assembly for discussion. Rabaut de Saint Étienne said that the Assembly, in occupying itself with a Declaration of Rights, obeyed the demand made in various cahiers, and that these cahiers had spoken of the matter, America having served as a model. He thought that the circumstances in France were not quite the same as in that country and therefore there need be no servile imitation of what had been done by the United States. According to his idea the draft of the committee lacked plan, development, clearness, truth, and precision. He thought the whole world should be able to grasp the principles embodied in an instrument of this kind; that it should become the

[1] *Arch. Parl.*, VIII. pp. 438, 439.
[2] *Ibid.*, VIII. p. 439.

alphabet of children and be taught in the schools. A patriotic education would give birth to a strong and vigorous race of men who would know how to defend their liberties and repulse despotism, which extended from the foot of the throne to the various ramifications of government.[1]

He thought the draft presented, by aiming to be pure and simple, had become insufficient; and therefore demanded that the principles and preservatives the Abbé Sieyès had inserted in his project, which protected the citizen against the most concealed usurpations of tyranny, be embodied in the Declaration of the committee.[2]

Mirabeau arose to defend the work of the committee. He said that if the circumstances were calm, minds peaceable, and sentiments of accord, general maxims might be employed without fear of opposition or of dangerous consequences. But when the most obvious principles attacked a multitude of pretensions and prejudices there would arise such a violent opposition against any particular exposition of rights as would amount to an opposition against every declaration of this kind. Self-love and self-interest would lead to the composition of a mass of declarations. Difficulties would increase infinitely. A Declaration of Rights would be but the almanac of a single year.[3]

Inasmuch as the draft of the committee did not meet with the favor of the Assembly, Reynauld proposed that a plan be chosen, after which a consideration of the details should take place.

Mirabeau said there could be no question as to the

[1] *Arch. Parl.*, VIII. pp. 452, 453.
[2] *Ibid.*
[3] *Ibid.*, pp. 453, 454.

other projects, since they had been disposed of by the committee, but that the draft of the committee alone must serve as the basis for the discussion. It might be altered or even rejected, but until judgment had been passed on it, there could be no talk of another. He dwelt on the difficulties the committee had encountered, and said that it would be still more difficult for so large a body as the Assembly to choose among so many projects as had been presented.

Another long discussion ensued. Again no conclusion was reached. Maulette then proposed that the Assembly separate into bureaux and proceed to choose a particular draft; that having the plurality of votes to be submitted for discussion, article by article.

To put an end to these interminable disputations Mirabeau at this juncture made a motion that aroused the greatest excitement.

No man in France had suffered more than Mirabeau from the evils of the old *régime*. His first published work had been a bitter denunciation of despotism.[1] In this book he had demanded free instruction, freedom of the press, restitution of the parliaments, abolition of the *lettres de cachet*, of standing armies, and of the *lits de justice*. He had said man is born for freedom as he is for the air he breathes. He had translated and edited Milton's *Areopagitica*, that famous production demanding liberty of the press. He had likewise published a book on Moses Mendelssohn, that ardent champion of religious toleration.[2] He hailed with delight the American Bills of Rights. In his pamphlet *Aux Bataves* he had drawn up a Declaration of Rights for the Belgians. He had advocated a like Declaration for

[1] *Essai sur le Despotisme*, 1775.
[2] *Sur Moses Mendelssohn*, London, 1787.

France.   As the reporter of the committee of five, most of the work of drawing up a project devolved upon him.

Now he proposed that further action on the Declaration be deferred until the provisions of the constitution were known.[1]

We learn from Dumont, one of a number of exiled Genevese who assisted Mirabeau in his labors and often composed his speeches, that the latter entrusted his faithful friends with the task of drawing up the Declaration on behalf of the committee of five.[2]   Dumont says the quartet set to work to compose the draft, disputing, now adding a word, now erasing four, and wearying themselves in the attempt to write down Natural Rights which had never existed.   He says that the work brought to his mind reflections which he had not made before, and that he saw the undertaking to be ridiculous and a mere puerile fiction, inasmuch as rights can only be declared after the constitution is known, since they are the result of the laws.   He had come to the conclusion that the maxims to be embodied in the Declaration were not only untrue, but might become dangerous.[3]

Whether Mirabeau had been influenced by the opinions of his friend and had changed his views on the value of the Declaration, whether he only wished to prevent the waste of more time because more important problems were pressing, or whether he realized that such a Declaration could only be framed after the terms of the constitution were known, cannot be definitely ascertained.   His motion contained nothing to indicate that he was opposed to the Declaration as such. On the contrary, he proposed anew that it form an

[1] *Arch. Parl.*, VIII. p. 454.

[2] *Souvenirs sur Mirabeau*, pp. 96, 97.

[3] *Ibid.*

integral and inseparable part of the constitution.   He only desired to adjourn further deliberation until the provisions of the constitution had been determined. But many of the deputies believed he wished to prevent the framing of the Declaration entirely.   There was a violent opposition to his motion.   He was accused of using his superior talents to guide the Assembly toward contrary ends.[1]   His proposal was voted down.   The Constituent Assembly decided not to make the draft of the committee the basis of its discussions, but to proceed independently.

Lally-Tollendal pointed to the great variety of drafts that had been presented, to the difficulty of deciding upon any one of them, and to the endless debates that had already taken place.   He asked how the Assembly could hope that twenty-four millions would interpret a Declaration alike if two hundred could not agree upon the sense of its articles.   He said that the English, who of all peoples best understood the science of government, had in the various acts which state their liberties, avoided metaphysical questions and general maxims susceptible of denial or dispute, and merely stated facts which no one could deny.   He said it was without doubt a great and beautiful idea to expose principles in order to draw consequences from them; to take men to the source of their duties; to inspire them with the dignity of their being before assuring them of the enjoyment of their faculties; and to show them nature before giving them happiness; but he demanded that the Declaration be short and clear; that immediately after a principle was stated its true consequence be drawn, in order to prevent others from drawing false conclusions; and that after having transported man to the

[1] *Arch. Parl.*, VIII. p. 458.

forests he be immediately returned to France. Of all
the drafts he preferred that of Mounier. He recom-
mended various changes, especially the addition of an
article defining the relation of man to a Supreme
Being, for in speaking of Nature, he said, one should
also speak of its Author; and one ought not forget the
first base of all duties, the bond of society, the bridle
of the wicked, and the only consolation of the unhappy.
Rather than spend much more time upon the Declaration, Lally-Tollendal preferred a postponement of the
discussion upon these general maxims. The principles
of fact the Assembly was enjoined upon to establish,
he said, were independent of the principles of reason
from which it was proposed to derive them. It would
be better to give the people liberty and tranquillity—to
have them enjoy effects, and teach them causes later.[1]

On the 19th of August the Constituent Assembly
chose the draft of the sixth bureau for discussion.
On the 20th the preamble of the Declaration and the
first three articles, which were those of Mounier, were
adopted.[2]

The preamble declares ignorance, neglect, or contempt of the Rights of Man to be the sole causes of public misfortunes and of the corruption of government.
In order to keep the rights and duties of all the members of the social body constantly before their minds,
the representatives of the French people have resolved
to set forth the natural, unalienable, and sacred rights
of man in a solemn declaration. This declaration is
to serve as the standard with which the people are to
compare the acts of the government. Inasmuch as
these acts of the government can at any moment be
compared with the end of every political institution,

[1] *Arch. Parl.*, VIII. pp. 458, 459.   [2] *Ibid.*, p. 463.

they will be more respected. If the claims of citizens are founded on simple and incontestable principles, they will always tend to the maintenance of the constitution and the general happiness. From the preamble it is evident that the Constituent Assembly was influenced by the noblest motives in undertaking to declare the Rights of Man. The members of that body did not believe that they had discovered truths which were now put forth for the first time. These truths were set forth to reveal corruption in the officers of the State, to remind the citizens of their rights and duties, to make them patriotic and law-abiding, to ennoble the spirit of the people. These rights received a religious sanction by being declared in the presence of the Supreme Being.

The doctrines promulgated in this Declaration are by no means metaphysical generalities or unrestricted rights, as many writers consider them to be. They are no more general or abstract than those contained in the American Bills of Rights.

Art. I. affirms that men are born and continue free and equal in respect to their rights. Civil distinctions can be founded on public utility only.[1]

II. The end of all political associations is the preservation of the natural and imprescriptible rights of man. These rights are liberty, property, security, and resistance to oppression.[2]

III. The source of all sovereignty resides essentially in the nation; no body of men, no individual, can exercise any authority that does not emanate expressly from it.[3]

[1] Compare Virginia Bill, Arts. I., IV.; North Carolina, III.
[2] Compare Vermont Bill, Preamble, Art. I.
[3] Virg. Bill, II.; Vt., V.

The next two articles were presented by Alexander Lameth, one of the young noblemen who had been in America.[1]

IV. Liberty consists in the power of doing whatever does not injure another.[2] The exercise of the natural rights of every man has no other limits than those which are necessary to secure to every other person the free exercise of the same rights; and these limits are determinable only by the law.

V. The law ought to prohibit only such actions as are hurtful to society. What is not prohibited by law cannot be hindered, and no one can be constrained to do that which the law does not ordain.

The definition of liberty gave rise to a discussion concerning natural right and civil right. Some believed that political, not natural, liberty ought to be spoken of in this connection, for, while the previous articles had referred to man prior to his having entered society, as soon as the law is spoken of, society is already formed. In accordance with this view André proposed the following definition of liberty: "The liberty of the citizen consists in being subject to the law alone, and in being bound to obey no other authority except that established by the law; to be able to use his faculties in every respect the law does not forbid, without fear of punishment." This definition was not adopted.[3]

Next the discussion turned upon the law and the privileges of the citizens.

Barrère proposed that the right to exercise public

[1] *Arch. Parl.*, VIII. p. 464.

[2] This is the definition given by the Marquis d'Argenson in his *Considération sur le gouvernement ancien et present de la France*, printed in 1764, quoted in a foot-note of the *Contrat Social*, IV. 8.

[3] *Arch. Parl.*, VIII. p. 464.

functions be neither arbitrary nor exclusive. "By like expressions," he said, "the Americans have in their Declarations of Rights extirpated all germs of aristocracy." Others wished the laws to be considered as compacts made by society. The article proposed by Talleyrand was accepted after being amended in several particulars. The definition of the law is that of Rousseau. The article is as follows:

VI. The law is the expression of the general will. All citizens have a right to concur, either personally, or by their representatives, in its formation. It should be the same for all, whether it protects or punishes; and all being equal in its sight, are equally eligible to all honors, places, and employments, according to their ability, without any other distinction than that of their virtues and talents.[1]

This article is entirely democratic in its nature. It is a manifesto against all political privilege.

The next point taken up was arbitrary punishment. Mirabeau insisted that the responsibility of each officer of the State be declared, save that of the head of the nation. He believed this to be the guarantee of liberty. The public force, he said, should be subject to the forms determined by law.[2]

The three articles relating to judicial affairs which were decided upon, meant a radical reform of the judicial system. They were the answer of the people to the abuses of the ancient *régime*—to *lettres de cachet*, Bastille, etc.[3]

VII. No man can be accused, arrested, or held in confinement except in cases determined by law, and

---

[1] *Arch. Parl.*, VIII. pp. 465, 466.
[2] *Ibid.*, p. 472.
[3] *Ibid.*

according to the forms which the law has prescribed. All who promote, solicit, execute, or cause to be executed, arbitrary orders, ought to be punished, but every citizen called or seized by virtue of the law, ought to obey immediately, and renders himself culpable by resistance.[1]

VIII. The law ought to establish no other penalties but such as are absolutely and evidently necessary; and no one ought to be punished except by virtue of a law promulgated before the offence was committed and legally applied.[2]

IX. Inasmuch as every man is presumed innocent till he has been declared culpable, whenever his detention becomes indispensable, all rigor against him, more than is necessary to secure his person, ought to be provided against by law.

A long and interesting discussion took place in the Constituent Assembly concerning religious liberty. Some deputies did not consider religious liberty a right. Others thought the question of religion should be treated in the Constitution, not in the Declaration. Bonnal, Bishop of Clermont, considered religion the base of empires, the eternal reason watching over the order of things, and demanded that the principles of the constitution rest on religion as an eternal basis.[3] Laborde pleaded for tolerance, regarding the attempt to control religious opinions as the most cruel despotism. He thought liberty of religion a sacred good belonging to every citizen, and urged that strange cults be respected. Mirabeau said that in his eyes the most unlimited liberty of religion was so sacred a right that

[1] North Carolina, Bill of Rights, XII.
[2] *Ibid.*, XIII.
[3] *Arch. Parl.*, VIII. p. 472.

the word toleration itself seemed to him tyrannical. This was exactly what Madison had said in the Virginia Convention. Diversity of opinions, Mirabeau continued, results from a diversity of minds, and cannot be prevented. Against those who spoke of a dominant cult, he said the word dominant was tyrannical and ought to be banished from legislation. Nothing should dominate except justice. No one should do that which might harm another.[1] Rabaut de Saint Étienne made an eloquent plea for full religious toleration. He said that one-third of his constituents were Protestants, who enjoyed but imperfect toleration. He attacked those who held that liberty of opinion should be granted, provided the public order were not disturbed by the manifestation of these opinions. He declared this view extremely dangerous. He proposed "that each citizen be free in his opinions, that he have the right to profess his cult freely, and ought not be inquieted for his religion." He said that liberty ought to belong to all Frenchmen equally and in the same manner. Liberty of thought and opinion he held to be the most sacred of rights. It escapes the rule of men, he said, and takes refuge in conscience as a sanctuary whither no mortal has a right to penetrate. It is the only right which men have not put under the laws of the common association: to constrain this right is an injustice, to attack it a sacrilege. He demanded for all non-Catholics equal liberty and equality of rights with the Catholics. He pointed to the "generous" Americans who had put universal religious liberty at the head of their civil code; to the Pennsylvanians who had declared that all who adored a Supreme Being, in what manner soever, should enjoy

[1] *Arch. Parl.*, VIII. pp. 472, 477.

all the rights of citizens. The article as definitely declared, contained the restriction against which Rabaut had spoken.[1] It reads thus:

X. No man ought to be molested for his opinions, not even on account of his religious opinions, provided their manifestation does not disturb the public order established by the law.[2]

XI. The unrestrained communication of thoughts and opinions being one of the most precious rights of man, every citizen may speak, write, and publish freely, but is responsible for the abuse of this liberty, in cases determined by the law.[3]

XII. A public force being necessary to give security to the Rights of Man and of the citizen, that force is instituted for the advantage of all, and not for the particular benefit of those to whom it is entrusted.[4]

XIII. A common contribution being necessary for the support of the public force, and for defraying the other expenses of administration, such a contribution ought to be apportioned equally among all the citizens according to their abilities.[5]

XIV. Every citizen has a right, either by himself or through his representative, to a free voice to determine the necessity of the public contributions, to consent to them freely, follow their employment, and determine their amount, mode of assessment, collection and duration.[6]

XV. The community has the right to demand of all its agents an account of their conduct.[7]

[1] *Arch. Parl.*, VIII. pp. 478–80.
[2] *Ibid.*, p. 480; Maryland, XXXIII, VIII.
[3] *Arch. Parl.*, VIII. p. 483; Vermont, XIV.; Maryland, VIII.
[4] Maryland, XXV.
[5] *Arch. Parl.*, VIII. p. 484; Vermont, IX.; Maryland, XIII.
[6] North Carolina, XVI.
[7] Vermont, V.; *Arch. Parl.*, VIII. p. 487.

Lameth said that without a separation of the powers of government there would be despotism. Target shared this view. The principle was thus expressed:

XVI. Every community in which the possession of rights is not assured nor the separation of powers determined, lacks a constitution.[1]

XVII. The right of property being inviolable and sacred, no one can be deprived of the same, unless the public necessity, legally determined, makes this unavoidable, and then a just indemnity must previously be paid.[2]

[1] North Carolina, IV   [2] Vermont Declaration, II.

CHAPTER XII

THE EFFECTS OF THE DECLARATION OF THE RIGHTS OF MAN

THERE is a tendency on the part of some, notably English, writers, to ridicule all political theorizing. Scientific and historical, rather than philosophical studies, have most attraction for the English mind. Thinkers of that nation are inclined to regard it as a fruitless task to grapple with philosophical questions. It is not accidental that Bacon, the man who did perhaps more than any other person in developing the spirit of inductive research to which modern science owes her wonderful triumphs, was an Englishman. To collect facts, rather than build up systems, is characteristic of English intellectual activity. And in accordance with this tendency political theories have been utterly discarded in the English system of government; indeed it is doubtful whether the word system can be legitimately used in speaking of the English constitution, for this constitution is not the product of logical construction, as French constitutions have invariably been, but consists rather of devices dictated by the necessities of the moment. The British government has never recognized those ideas which form the political creed of the American and French Revolutions. Although England has since the earliest days of her history been the example of a free country to the

rest of the world, the doctrine of the sovereignty of
the people is not recognized. Although almost every
adult male can in England acquire the right of suffrage
if he desires, full manhood suffrage has not been proclaimed, but the idea of property, rather than that
of equality, is still adhered to. The existence of the
peerage, which still possesses great social and political
privileges, further disagrees with the doctrines of
equality and popular sovereignty. Neither is there
any recognition of the rights of the individual as a
man, although nowhere, with the possible exception of
America, is the importance of personal liberty more
esteemed. Though written safeguards after the American fashion are lacking, the force of custom is so strong
that the rights of the citizen are nowhere more secure.

While these considerations apply to England they
do not apply to other nations, especially not to the
American and the French nations, among whom ideas
of this sort have been a force in influencing historical
development, whose importance can hardly be exaggerated. It is impossible to comprehend the French
Revolution without understanding the effects of the
so-called "Principles of 1789." It may be said that
these ideas form the essence of that movement. De
Tocqueville, whose acute and luminous observations
have so greatly broadened our views regarding the
Revolution and its antecedents, distinguishes between
the accidental and transitory features of this period
on the one hand, and its essential and permanent
characteristics on the other. The antagonism to the
Church and hostility against religion he regards as
subordinate, while the substance of the Revolution,
the most fundamental, the most durable, the truest
portion of its work, seems to him to be " the doctrines

of the natural equality of man, and the consequent abolition of all caste, class, or professional privileges; popular sovereignty; the paramount authority of the social body; the uniformity of rules." [1]

The most necessary and abiding reforms effected during the Revolution were but the results of applying the doctrines of the Declaration of the Rights of Man to the existing order composing the ancient régime, which was founded upon royal prerogative, social and political inequality, and submission. The consequences of this application of principles to conditions were the reform of the monarchy, of the educational system, abolition of feudal privileges, a radical change in the system of administration and in the judicial organization, as well as a reform of the civil and criminal laws—reforms demanded by the doctrines of equality, liberty, and popular sovereignty, and this work was done logically, yes, mathematically, in accordance with the tendency of the French mind.

But let us inquire what the opinions of the men were who drew up this Declaration, regarding the importance of the principles it contained.

To Bailly, the famous astronomer, member of three academies, president of the Constituent Assembly, and at one time mayor of Paris, this Declaration seemed both necessary and dangerous; dangerous because of the abuses which wicked and seditious men might commit, forgetting that rights entail duties and that liberty is not license; necessary, because the Rights of Man had been forgotten, otherwise there would have been no Revolution. The first work of the Revolution should be the Declaration of Rights. The first measure of the legislators should be their recognition and procla-

[1] *L'Ancien Régime et la Révolution*, Ch. 2.

mation. They should form the basis of the constitution, the thread put into the hand of the legislators to guide them constantly. It was worthy of the wisdom of the Assembly, Bailly holds, not to hesitate in recognizing these rights, and to begin its work upon the constitution with this solemn act, which is the prize of possessing liberty, "an act made by us, for ourselves, but belonging to all mankind as well." [1]

Condorcet regards the declaring of the Rights of Man as the only means of preventing tyranny, which is according to him, simply a violation of these rights.[2]

Rabaut de Saint Étienne, the Protestant minister, who is one of the most influential of the actors in the early part of the Revolution, considers the Declaration of Rights the most important achievement of the Revolution. When all other parts of the constitution have perished, this will survive; although it may be submerged it will always come to the top again,—a prediction which has come true. It has established itself easily in America, Rabaut continues, because neither kings, nor priests, nor doctors, nor nobles exist in that country to attack it; but crossing the ocean to the old continent, with its populous cities, its overnumerous cathedrals, towers, monasteries, and dungeons, it has been exposed to the bitterest insults. But he regards this as the new gospel, which will naturally be opposed because it is the good tidings of the lowly and foolishness according to the world. Its mysteries were long hidden, because they attacked the priests and the great.[3]

[1] *Mémoires de Bailly* (Edition of Berville and Barrière), II. pp. 211, 212.

[2] Condorcet, *Idées sur le Despotisme*, Œuvres, IX. p. 168.

[3] Rabaut, *Précis historique de la révolution française; Réflexions politiques*, 14, 15, pp. 415, 416.

In the preamble to the Declaration, the Constituent Assembly consider ignorance, neglect, or contempt of human rights the sole causes of public misfortunes and corruptions of government. They anticipate as results of the Declaration, that the members of the social body will be kept attentive to their rights and duties; that the acts of the government will be more respected; and that the claims of the citizens will tend to the maintenance of the constitution and the general happiness.

The members of the Constituent Assembly felt certain that they were legislating for all mankind. They believed that the eyes of the entire race were upon them; that their work, especially the Declaration of the Rights of Man, would survive the vicissitudes of the ages. And indeed they were hardly mistaken in holding this view, for the effects of their work are still to be felt. The Principles of 1789 have in reality transformed the structure of European government and society. The seeds of liberty have sprung up again and again, despite all exertions to destroy them. While the conquests made by the French during this most brilliant period of their military history have been lost, and almost everything else that was attempted by the leading actors in that great drama has vanished, these ideas still survive as a living force. Despite the numerous political upheavals in France that have occurred since the close of the Revolution, the French people have always returned to these principles. Ideas which have exerted such a fascination in the past, and have been prized by some of the noblest of the race ever since the time of the Stoics, can hardly be regarded as fallacies, and are on no account to be held in derision.

It is but natural that ideas which have exerted such

tremendous influence as have the Principles of 1789, should not only find enthusiastic adherents but also bitter opponents. The most famous attack, perhaps, upon the Rights of Man, as upon the influence of the French Revolution on the whole, was that of Edmund Burke, the noted English parliamentarian, in his *Reflections on the Revolution in France*—a dissertation full of the most striking observations expressed with an unexampled wealth of language, but one in which truth and falsehood, sound judgment and unpardonable prejudice, are strangely mixed. Though Burke's views have been often discussed, at least a brief consideration of them must here be given because of their bearing on our subject.

Though Burke, in accordance with almost all of the political philosophers of his age, accepts the theories of Natural Law and a state of Nature, he is really a forerunner of the Historical School of politics, anticipating the notions of Savigny by a quarter of a century. The organic theory of the State could scarcely be expressed more clearly than it is in the following words of Burke's, in which he lays bare the leading error of the Natural Rights School: "Society is, indeed, a contract. Subordinate contracts for objects of mere occasional interest may be dissolved at pleasure; but the State ought not to be considered as nothing better than a partnership agreement in a trade of pepper and coffee, calico or tobacco, or some other such low concern, to be taken up for a little temporary interest, and to be dissolved by the fancy of the parties. It is to be looked on with other reverence; because it is not a partnership in things subservient only to the gross animal existence of a temporary and perishable nature. It is a partnership in all science, a partnership in all art, a partnership

in every virtue and in all perfection.   As the ends of
such a partnership cannot be obtained in many generations, it becomes a partnership not only between those
who are living, but between those who are living, those
who are dead, and those who are to be born." [1]   The
idea of the continuity of the State is thus plainly emphasized.   Burke repeatedly attacks the fallacy of sup-
posing that the foundations of the State might be torn
up at any moment and replaced by a more suitable sub-
structure.   He looks "with horror on those children
of their country who are prompt rashly to hack that
aged parent in pieces and put him into the kettle of
magicians, in hopes that by their poisonous weeds and
wild incantations they may regenerate the paternal
constitution and renovate their father's life." [2]   He
censures French politicians and writers for their over-
confidence in their own wisdom and lack of respect for
the wisdom of others; for their love of the new and
hatred of the old simply because it is old; for their
assumption that governments may vary like modes of
dress; for their forgetfulness of the fact that they have
duties to perform as well as rights to enjoy.[3]   Concerning the participants in the Revolution he says that they
despise the ancient, permanent sense of mankind and
set up a scheme of society on new principles.[4]

Burke maintains that if civil society is the result of
a convention or contract, laws and constitutions of
government framed are the creatures of this convention, and that men have abdicated their Natural Rights,
such as the right of self-defence and the right of judg-

[1] Burke's *Works*, Edition of Little, Brown & Co., III. p. 359.
[2] *Ibid.*, III. pp. 358, 359.
[3] *Ibid.*, pp. 347, 348.
[4] *Ibid.*, p. 450.

ing for oneself or asserting one's own cause for securing the liberty of the civil state. Government is not made in virtue of Natural Rights, but is a contrivance of human wisdom to provide for human wants. Men have a right that these wants should be provided for. But the inclinations of men must be frequently thwarted, their will controlled, and their passions brought into subjection, by a power out of themselves. "In this sense, the restraints on men, as well as their liberties, are to be reckoned among their rights. But as the liberties and the restrictions vary with times and circumstances, and admit of infinite modifications, they cannot be settled upon any abstract rule." [1]

With respect to the Rights of Man Burke says that they are extreme metaphysical rights, which are morally and politically false. He considers the real rights of men to be a sort of middle, incapable of definition, but not of discernment. "The rights of men in government are their advantages; and these are often in balances between differences of good,—in compromises sometimes between good and evil, and sometimes between evil and evil." The intricacy of man's nature and of the objects of society, the gross and complicated mass of human passions and concerns, makes innumerable modifications of the primitive Rights of Man unavoidable. [2]

Burke endeavors to prove that the notions he attacks are repugnant to English tastes and have no place in the English system of government. He denies that the people of England have the right to choose their own governors, to cashier them for misconduct, or to frame a government for themselves. He asserts that England will ever preserve "an established church,

[1] *Works*, III. pp. 309–11.   [2] *Ibid.*, pp. 312, 313.

an established monarchy, an established aristocracy, and an established democracy, each in the degree it exists, and no greater." [1] "We have not been drawn and trussed," he says, "in order that we may be filled, like stuffed birds in a museum, with chaff and rags, and paltry, blurred shreds of paper about the Rights of Man." [2]

The views of Burke are shared by Bentham, Austin, and Maine.

Fully as hostile as these English writers against the Rights of Man, is Taine, the brilliant French historian and philosopher. [3] According to Taine the articles of the Declaration are poniards directed against human society. In the absence of a supreme court after the American fashion, or of a similar tribunal to interpret the Declaration and apply its principles, the local club in each city or village becomes the champion, the judge, the interpreter, the minister of the Rights of Man. He shows how the people might draw such conclusions from these principles as would result in the destruction of all law and order. Whenever they considered themselves oppressed they would rise up in arms and resist; they might claim the right of demanding personal account of the magistrates, of supervising the legislators; the proletariat might demand the right of suffrage; all might claim the privilege of carrying arms or of serving in the National Guard; royalty, being an hereditary office, might be declared unlawful and the king hurled from his throne; and in general the mob would try to legitimize the worst excesses, by appealing to the Declaration.

[1] *Works*, III. p. 352.

[2] *Ibid.*, p. 345.

[3] Taine, *La Révolution*, I. pp. 273–277.

He calls the larger part of the articles "abstract dogmas, metaphysical definitions, axioms more or less literary, that is, more or less false, now vague, now contradictory, susceptible of various and opposite senses, good for a pompous harangue and not for effective use, a simple decoration, a sort of flaring standard, unuseful and heavy, which, fastened to the front of the constitutional structure and shaken daily by violent hands, cannot fail soon to fall upon the head of the passersby." [1]

Taine must have been unfamiliar with the constitutions of the American States, for he says that the American constitution has nothing resembling statements of the Rights of Man.   He states that Jefferson's Declaration of Rights was refused, and that merely eleven amendments were added affirming the fundamental liberties of the citizen.

Stahl, whose Philosophy of Law still enjoys considerable popularity in Germany, is acquainted with the Bills of Rights of the American States, and rates them very highly, but is hardly fair toward the French Declaration.   He says: "The French Constituent Assembly was entranced with the philosophical procedure of North America and imitated it with the greatest exaggeration.   While disclaiming any intention of drawing up metaphysical, and not practical rights, hollow and erroneous deductions from Natural Law were placed at the head of the Declaration of the Rights of Man and of the Citizen." [2]

A careful comparison of the French and the American Declarations will show that the nature of both classes of papers is essentially the same.   It seems to me there is scarcely any warrant for calling the French Docu-

<hr />

[1] *La Révolution*, I. 274.
[2] Stahl, *Philosophie des Rechts*. II. Ch. 17.

ment a collection of unrestricted metaphysical principles. That instrument recognizes the fact that the exigencies and needs of civil society make a restriction of individual rights necessary. The language is quite carefully guarded. Thus, the limit to the liberty of any person consists in the equal rights of others; freedom of opinion is granted, but the public order must not be disturbed; freedom of speech and of the press is granted, but the citizen is responsible for the abuse of this liberty. There is nothing incendiary about any of these principles. While in some cases an attempt was made to palliate the crimes committed during the Revolution by appealing to the Rights of Man, it is exceedingly probable that these excesses would have occurred even if there had never been a Declaration of the Rights of Man. It is not this Declaration which caused the September massacres or the Reign of Terror, but the danger threatening the French from the invasion of the foreign foe, the opposition of a large portion of the country against the Revolution, the desire of ambitious individuals to retain their power, and other considerations of like nature. It seems to me that the wholesome effects of these principles far outweighed their evil influence. It is impossible to deny that on the whole the Rights of Man contain good doctrine, and have been productive of incalculable good. Believing that the political development of the French people had been kept back by the misrule of autocratic kings, selfish nobles, worldly churchmen, and grasping magistrates, the Constituent Assembly thought it wise to proclaim the principles they regarded as forming the basis of society, hoping that these principles would guide the legislators in framing the constitution and laws of the state; that they would remind the citizens of their rights and duties; and that they would serve as a bridle upon all magistrates, restraining them in the exercise of unlawful power. The purposes, there can be no doubt, were noble. But why did the Rights of Man fail to accomplish what was anticipated? There seem to me to be several reasons for this failure.

While the Rights of Man had been asserted by the Americans against an external foe, these same doctrines, proclaimed by the French people, became a declaration of war against the privileged classes. The conditions which the Declaration of Man presupposed did not exist in France, as they did, to a considerable extent at least, in America, and therefore liberty, equality, and popular sovereignty had first to be won. This could not happen without exciting the bitterest opposition of the interests threatened. The Rights of Man became a mass of dynamite which shattered the entire social and political fabric. A strong central government might have prevented this upheaval, but that was lacking. Too much inflammable material had been heaped up by centuries of oppression, to which fire was applied by declaring the Rights of Man.

Out of the ruins arose a new structure whose foundation was the Declaration of the Rights of Man. It is the constructive, rather than the destructive, side of the Revolution, which ought most to be considered. It cannot be denied that the Rights of Man had much to do in regard to rendering the Revolution a benefit to mankind. The wholesome influence of these ideas might have been still greater, had they been rightly understood.

The French people prized equality more highly than liberty. In trying to bring about absolute equality, which will ever remain a dream, they sacrificed liberty.

They failed to see that liberty can exist where considerable inequality prevails, as has been the case in England. The French desired not only equality before the law, but also social and economic equality, which cannot be procured, and which would scarcely be beneficial if it could be obtained. Thus it happened that not only the nobles were proscribed, but the levelling propensity eventually attacked every one whose birth, wealth, or intellect distinguished him above the mob. Liberty seemed to the French to be synonymous with equality of conditions. It was not equality of rights, but equality in fact after which they chased. In the pursuit of this chimera the real Rights of Man were sacrificed. They were entirely unfamiliar with the real nature of liberty. It was to them merely an idea—something existing on paper, but something which they had never tasted and which had not entered the nature of the people.

The French did not only confuse liberty and equality, they likewise believed liberty to be identical with democracy, thus committing the same error as the Greeks and Romans. We have seen that among the ancients the State was everything, the individual nothing, and that in the city-state of antiquity individual rights were constantly overridden by the general will. It was shown that though wielding sovereign power the people may yet be slaves, providing there is nothing to limit the interference of the government with individual rights. The same development occurs in France, even though the Declaration of the Rights of Man was intended to shield the individual against tyranny, whether this tyranny be exercised by the king or by the people themselves. The liberty of the individual is safe only when the sovereignty of the State finds its limits in the rights of the citizen.

The error of the ancients again manifested itself. The views of Locke and others, who had asserted that the State must not interfere with the Natural Rights of Man, even though these views had given birth to the idea of a declaration of the rights which are reserved to the individual, were nevertheless supplanted by the notion to which Rousseau had given expression, that the power of the people is unlimited. It was the prevalence of this latter view which caused liberty to perish. The doctrine of the public welfare becomes destructive of the rights of the individual. The spirit of the Declaration is violated though its principles are on everybody's lips.

This victory of the principle of sovereignty over the principle of liberty was not solely due to the influence of Rousseau, great as that influence was upon Robespierre, Saint Just, and other assassins of French liberty. Rousseau himself but represented a deep tendency of the French character—the tendency, namely, toward centralization, which to this day is inimical to individual liberty in France. Whatever our view regarding the origin of this inclination toward centralization may be— whether we regard it as a victory of the Roman influence over the Germanic; whether we ascribe it to the revival of Roman Law and the influence of the legists, who were constantly asserting that what the king wishes is Law; or whether we attribute it to the deliberate creation of the French kings; this tendency can be clearly traced through French history, down to the very present. It was not created by the revolutionists but was inherited from the old *régime*.

It is the conception of the omnipotence of the State, of the supremacy of the public welfare, which the Mountain takes up as the justification of the Terror. Robespierre says that the revolutionary government is not to be permanent. Its purpose is to establish the victory of liberty, after which it will be followed by the constitutional *régime*, which will concern itself principally with civil liberty. The revolutionary government is entirely legitimate, for "it is founded upon the most sacred of all laws, the public welfare, upon the most irrefragable of all titles, necessity."[1] "The government of the Republic," Robespierre again says, "is the despotism of liberty against tyranny."[2] A famous revolutionary journal expressed the matter thus: "The welfare of the people is the supreme law. This is the grand principle before which all others incline and lower themselves. When a nation is in danger, the rights of the individual disappear, there remain only the rights of the people, and their first right, without doubt, is that of physical and political preservation. In moments of peril or of crisis, a people may and ought to do whatever it believes will conduce to its safety, without being hindered by any personal consideration, or by the fear of violating justice."[3] It was in the name of the public welfare that the excesses of the Terror were committed. The despotism of an energetic and unscrupulous minority utterly destroyed liberty. A more execrable tyranny never existed than that which was now exercised in the name of the people. Robespierre and his consorts were attempting to establish the triumph of liberty by the violation of liberty. They confounded true liberty with a false liberty, namely

---

[1] Robespierre, *Rapport sur les principes du gouvernement révolutionnaire*; Buchez et Roux, *Histoire parlementaire de la Révolution française*, XXX, pp. 459, 460.

[2] Buchez et Roux, *op. cit.*, XXXI, pp. 276, 277.

[3] *Les Révolutions de Paris*, No. 180, 15th of December, 1792.

with the sovereignty of the people. The Rights of Man are trampled upon because the welfare of the State demands it; centralization supplants the self-direction of the individual; the tendency begun by Philip the Fair, continued by Louis XIV., is again taken up by the Mountain, only to be completed by Napoleon; paternalism encroaches more and more upon individual rights until liberty is practically destroyed. Everything is managed from one centre by the ever active and interfering bureaucracy. Everything is done for the people, in the name of the people, but nothing by the people. The people are considered children whom the government must protect and direct. It is due to the peculiar fascination of the doctrine of the sovereignty of the people, and to the confusion of democracy with liberty, that the Rights of Man were forfeited. Centralization and paternalism are the bane of the French people to this day. France presents the spectacle of a country which is democratic in principle, but which knows little of individual liberty. The celebrated Dreyfus case was a flaring confirmation of the truth of this statement. That the tendency toward centralization is responsible for many evils from which France has long been suffering and is still suffering, has been felt by many of her best men—men of the stamp of Laurent, De Tocqueville, and Laboulaye. It is only by placing the individual upon his own feet, by cultivating individual initiative and self-reliance, by refraining from an excess of legislation and administrative control, by granting to the individual a large measure of liberty and by protecting him in the enjoyment of this liberty; and finally by allowing the people to govern themselves, not only in national, but also in local affairs, that a nation can become and remain strong and great. Under these conditions only can the development of the individual citizens reach its highest stage, and this means likewise the maximum of national power and greatness. "It is in the respect of the person that one can measure the true grandeur of civilization." [1] The history of mankind is the record of the gradual enfranchisement of the individual. Experience has demonstrated the wisdom of freeing the individual from all unnecessary restraint. Freedom of thought (*Lehr— und Lernfreiheit*) has given the world German science. Religious freedom has not caused, but prevented, civil disturbances; has not resulted in a decline, but rather in an increase, of religious fervor, as the religious condition of the United States plainly shows. Freedom of trade has not diminished the wealth and commercial power of England. The restriction of the right of public meeting and of public speech has not diminished, but rather increased, the political power of the Social Democrats in Germany, while in the United States, where these rights are unrestricted, socialism and kindred movements are almost unknown. It is precisely those nations in which the individual enjoys the greatest freedom which are to-day in the lead. If France is lagging somewhat behind, that is due to the fact that she still clings to the paternal system. It is not Anglo-Saxon race superiority, but rather Anglo-Saxon liberty, to which the greatness of the Germanic powers is due. France can only regain her former power and glory and the station to which the wealth of her resources and the genius of her people entitle her, by forsaking her pernicious system, and returning to the spirit of the Declaration of the Rights of Man.

[1] Laboulaye, *L'État et ses limites*, p. 32.

We have assigned two reasons for the failure of the Declaration of the Rights of Man to result in the triumph of personal liberty in France; namely, the undue emphasis put upon actual equality, and the identification of sovereignty with liberty. A third cause of this failure deserves attention. Though the Declaration contains a clause stating that every society in which a guarantee of rights and a separation of the powers of government is wanting, lacks a true constitution, yet the French people neglected to provide for such a guarantee as well as for the separation of the three departments of government. This separation is also lacking in the British constitution, and among any other people but the English, the omnipotence of Parliament might prove disastrous to personal freedom. But in England the force of custom and the respect of personal liberty are such, that they really act as restraints upon Parliament. In the American system of government it is by means of a territorial diffusion of sovereignty among the States and the national government; by means also of our system of "checks and balances"; and especially by the importance of our courts, that the sovereignty of the people is with us restrained and the individual protected in the enjoyment of his rights, not only against the infringement of these rights by other individuals, but also by the government.[1] In France safeguards of this sort were, and are still, entirely lacking. Sovereignty there is concentrated; no system of courts exists to protect the individual from the government. In the administrative courts the government, not the individual, is favored. In the absence of a tribunal whose function it is to interpret

[1] See the excellent essay of A. L. Lowell on "Democracy and Liberty" in his *Essays on Government*.

and apply the doctrines of the Declaration of Rights, that function must be exercised either by the administration itself, which would result in despotism, or else the people themselves would interpret the Declaration, in which case mob rule would be the consequence. Both of these eventualities have occurred in France, both have contributed toward rendering liberty nugatory. That which still further fostered the tendency toward direct government by the mob, was the pernicious view of popular sovereignty which Rousseau inculcated. If the general will is but the sum of the individual wills; if this general will, strictly speaking, cannot be delegated, it follows that the people have a direct share in the government, that the legislators and magistrates are on the same level with the people, that the people have the right to see that their will is carried out; mob rule thus received a philosophical foundation. Hereby the respect for law and authority was still further undermined and the pernicious influence of the revolutionary spirit, which has worked such havoc in France, still further aggravated. Seeking liberty, the French people conferred sovereignty upon Napoleon, the Bourbons, Louis Philippe, Napoleon III., only to find that they had, in every case, been deluded.[1] The French have yet to learn that it is not paper constitutions which form the basis of liberty, but that liberty must have its foundations in the customs of the people, and above all, in that reverence for law and order, without which liberty can never exist.

The Principles of 1789 are not yet dead in France. The influence of those ideas, which has been so wonder-

[1] See Laboulaye, *Histoire des États-Unis*, III., Intr. pp. vii., viii.; Laurent, *Études sur l'histoire de l'humanité, La Révolution Française*, I. p. 103 *et seq.*

ful in the past, is destined still to increase, not only in that country, but throughout the world. These principles are the basis of modern liberty. This liberty, the fruit of a struggle between people and their rulers which had been carried on for centuries, will not be forsaken. History shows, as Buckle points out, that there is "an intimate connexion between knowledge and liberty; between an increasing civilization and an advancing democracy." [1]

Those who hold that public expediency determines the measure of individual rights, believe in a principle which no sound thinker will doubt. If the alternative were between the good of the whole State and the good of an individual, it would be foolish to deny that the good of the whole is of greater significance than that of an infinitesimally small part of the whole. But this alternative does not arise. There is at present a tendency, now that the organic conception of the State is universally accepted, to forget that the State consists of individuals and has no interest apart from theirs. Many persons who are continually speaking of public expediency forget that what we hold to be for the good of the whole may after all be only our own individual view of public expediency. It was in the interests of public expediency, falsely understood, that censorships, the inquisition, repressive measures of all sorts, were established. It was avowedly for the public good that Socrates was put to death; that the Puritans were driven from England; that the Huguenots were oppressed; that Robespierre and his consorts sent thousands to the guillotine; that the English government, during the French Revolution, adopted that wretched

[1] Buckle, *Hist. of Civilization in England*, I. p. 438.

system of repression which brought the country to the verge of civil war. There can be no hostility between personal liberty and public expediency, rightly understood.

BIBLIOGRAPHY

ABBOT, LYMAN. The Rights of Man. Boston, 1901.

ADAMS, JOHN. Works, edited by C. F. Adams. Boston, 1856. 10 vols.

ADAMS, SAMUEL. Life and Public Services of, by W. V. Wells, Boston, 1865. 3 vols.

ÆNEAS SILVIUS. De concilio Basilensi, in FLACIUS ILLYRICUS, Catalogus testium veritatis.

—— Tractatus de ortu et auctoritate imperii Romani, in GOLDAST, Monarchia, II. 1558 sq.

ALTHUSIUS, JOHANNES. Politica methodica digesta. Herborn, 1603.

ARCHIVES PARLEMENTAIRES, de 1787 à 1799. Edited by Mavidal and Laurent. First series. Paris, 1867–80. 11 vols.

ARNOLD, MATTHEW. Essays on Democracy and Equality in Mixed Essays. N. Y., 1880.

ARNOLD, S. G. History of Rhode Island. N. Y., 1859–60. 2 vols.

AUSTIN, JOHN. Lectures on Jurisprudence, the Philosophy of Positive Law. London, 1873. 2 vols.

BAILLIE, ROBERT. Letters and Journals. Edinburgh, 1841–42. 3 vols.

BASTWICK. The Utter Routing of the Whole Army of the Independents, etc. London, 1646.

BANCROFT, GEORGE. History of the United States. N. Y., 1888. 6 vols.

BAUDRILLART, HENRI. Jean Bodin et son temps. Tableau des théories politiques et des idées économiques au seizième siècle. Paris, 1853.

BAUMANN, J. J. Die Staatslehre des heiligen Thomas von Aquino. Leipzig, 1873.

BAXTER, RICHARD. Narrative of the most memorable Passages of his Life and Times. London, 1676. Also abridged by Calamy.

BEBENBURG, LUPOLD VON De Juribus Regni et Imperii Romani. 1338–40.

BEDA VENERABILIS. Historia ecclesiastica gentis Anglorum; in MIGNE, Patrologia, v. 6.

BELLARMIN. De membris ecclesiæ militantis, in Opera omnia. Venetiis, 1721–28. 7 vols.

BERTRAND, ALEXIS. La Déclaration des Droits de l'Homme et du Citoyen. Paris.

BERVILLE ET BARRIÈRE. Collection des Mémoires relatives à la Révolution Française. Paris, 1821. 68 vols.

BEZOLD, F. VON. Die Lehre von der Volkssouveranität im Mittelalter. SYBEL's Histor. Zeitschrift, XXXVI. 324 sq.

BLAKEY, ROBERT. The History of Political Literature from the Earliest Times. London, 1855.

BLANC, LOUIS. Histoire de la Révolution Française. Paris, 1847–62 12 vols.

BLAND, RICHARD. An Enquiry into the Rights of the British Colonists. 1776.

BLUM, E. La Déclaration des Droits de l'Homme et du Citoyen. Paris, 1902.

BLUNTSCHLI, J. K. Geschichte der neueren Staatswissenschaft. Allgemeines Staatsrecht und Politik. Leipzig, 1881. 3. Aufl.

BLUNTSCHLI und BRATER. Deutsches Staatswörterbuch. Stuttgart, 1857–70. 11 Bde.

BODIN, JEAN. De la République. Paris, 1576.

BONAR, J. Philosophy and Political Economy. London, 1893.

BORGEAUD, CHARLES. The Adoption and Amendment of Constitutions in Europe and America. N. Y., 1895.

—— The Rise of Modern Democracy in Old and New England. London, 1894.

BOURNE, H. E. American Constitutional Precedents in the French National Assembly. Amer. Histor. Review, VIII. 466 sq.

BOUTMY, E. La Déclaration des Droits de l'Homme et du Citoyen et M. Jellinek. Annales des Sciences Politiques, 15e juillet, 1902.

BRADFORD, GAMALIEL. The Lesson of Popular Government. N. Y., 1899.

BRADFORD, WILLIAM. History of Plymouth Plantation. Boston, 1856.

BRANDES, E. Ueber einige bisherige Folgen der franz. Revolution. 1792.

BRISSOT ET CLAVIÈRE. De la France et des États-Unis. London, 1787.

BROWNE, ROBERT. Booke which sheweth. 1582.

—— True and Short Declaration. 1584.

—— Treatise of Reformation. 1582.

BRUNNER, H. Deutsche Rechtsgeschichte. 1887–1893. 2 vols.

BRUNS, C. J. Fontes iuri Romani antiqui. 6th ed., Mommsen and Gardenwitz. Freiburg, 1893.

BRYCE, JAMES. Studies in History and Jurisprudence. N. Y., 1901. 2 vols.

—— The American Commonwealth. 3d ed., N. Y., 1895.

BUCHANAN, GEORGE. De Jure Regni apud Scotos Dialogos, in his Rerum Scoticarum Historia. Edinburgh, 1583.

BUCKLE, H. T. History of Civilization in England. London, 1872. 3 vols.

BURGESS, J. W. Political Science and Comparative Constitutional Law. Boston, 1890. 2 vols.

BURKE, EDMUND. Works. 4th ed., Boston, 1871. 12 vols.

CÆSAR, JULIUS. Commentarii de Bello Gallico.

CALVIN, JOHN. Institutio Religionis Christianæ. Antwerp, 1536. 9 vols.

CHALMERS, GEORGE. Political Annals of the Present United Colonies from their Settlement to the Peace of 1763. London, 1780.

CICERO. Opera, edited by Mueller, Klotz, etc. 10 vols.

CLARENDON, EDWARD, Earl of. The History of the Rebellion and Civil Wars in England. Oxford, 1849. 7 vols.

CLARKE PAPERS, THE. Edited by C. H. Firth. Camden Society Publications. London, 1891–1901. 4 vols.

CLEMENS ALEXANDRINUS. Opera, edited by Klotz. Leipzig, 1830–34.

COBBETT. Parliamentary History of England. 36 vols.

CONDORCET, J. A., MARQUIS DE. Œuvres. 12 vols. Paris, 1847–49.

CONNECTICUT COLONIAL RECORDS. Edited by Trumbull and Hoadley. 15 vols.

CONSTANT, BENJAMIN. Cours de Politique Constitutionnelle. Paris, 1836. 2 vols.

CORPUS IURIS CANONICI. Ed. by Richter and Friedberg. 2 vols.

CORPUS IURIS CIVILIS. Ed. by Krueger and Mommsen. 2 vols. Berolini, 1882–84.

DEUX AMIS DE LA LIBERTÉ. Histoire de la Révolution de France. Paris, 1792–1800. 20 vols.

DEXTER, H. M. The Congregationalism of the last Three Hundred Years, as seen in its Literature. N. Y., 1880.

DIOGENES LÆRTIUS. Edited by Hübner. Leipzig, 1828–31. 2 vols.

DOYLE, J. A. The English Colonies in America. London and N. Y., 1882–89.

DOCUMENTS INÉDITS SUR HISTOIRE DE FRANCE.

DUMONT, E. Souvenirs sur Mirabeau. La Haye, 1832.

DUNNING, W. A. A History of Political Theories Ancient and Mediæval, N. Y., 1902.

—— Jean Bodin on Sovereignty. Polit. Sc. Quart., II. p. 82 sq.

EDWARDS, THOMAS. Gangræna. London, 1647.

EICHHORN. K. F. Deutsche Staats- und Rechtsgeschichte. 5th edition, Goettingen, 1843–44. 4 vols.

FESTER, R. Rousseau und die deutsche Geschichtsphilosophie. Stuttgart, 1890.

FISCHER, KUNO. Geschichte der neueren Philosophie. Heidelberg, 1897. 6 vols.

FISKE, JOHN. The Beginnings of New England. N. Y., 1889.

FOWLER, W. W. The City State of the Greeks and Romans. London, 1893.

FRANCK, A. Réformateurs et Publicistes de l'Europe. Paris, moyen age, 1869; dix-septième siècle, 1881.

FREDEGAR. Chronicon.

FRIEDBERG, E. Lehrbuch des katholischen und evangelischen Kirchenrechts. 4th ed., 1895.

FROTHINGHAM, RICHARD. The Rise of the Republic of the United States. Boston, 1872.

FUSTEL DE COULANGES. La Cité antique. 7th ed., Paris, 1878. Am. Edition, Boston, 1894.

GAIUS. Institutiones, edited by Krüger and Studemund, 3d ed., 1891.

GARDINER, S. R. History of England from the Accession of James I. to the Outbreak of the Civil War, 1603–42. London, 1883–84. 10 vols.

GARDINER, S. R. History of the Great Civil War, 1642–49. 2d ed., London, 1888–91. 3 vols.

—— The Constitutional Documents of the Puritan Revolution. Oxford, 1889.

GEFFKEN, H. Church and State, their Relations Historically Developed. London, 1877. 2 vols.

GENTILIS, A. De Jure Belli Libri Tres. Hanoviæ, 1612.

GERSON, JOHANNES. Opera. Antwerp, 1706. 5 vols.

GIDDINGS, F. H. Democracy and Empire. N. Y., 1900.

GIERKE, OTTO. Johannes Althusius und die Entwickelung der naturrechtlichen Staatstheorien. Breslau, 1880. 2. Aufl., 1902.

—— Das deutsche Genossenschaftsrecht. 1868–81. 3 vols.

—— Political Theories of the Middle Age. Part of Vol. III. of the above. Translated by Maitland, Cambridge, 1900.

GODWIN, WILLIAM. History of the Commonwealth of England. London, 1826.

GOLDAST, MELCHIOR. Monarchia Sancti Romani Imperii, etc. Frankfort and Hannover, 1611–1614. 3 vols.

GREGOROVIUS, F. Geschichte der Stadt Rom im Mittelalter. 4. Aufl., Stuttgart, 1889–95. 8 Bde.

GREGORY OF TOURS. Historiæ Francorum.

GRIMM, J. Deutsche Rechtsalterthümer. Göttingen, 1828.

GROTIUS, HUGO. De Jure Belli ac Pacis. Paris, 1625.

HALLAM, HENRY. Introduction to the Literature of Europe in the 15th, 16th, and 17th Centuries. N. Y., 1886. 4 vols.

HAMILTON, ALEXANDER. Works, edited by H. C. Lodge.

HANBURY, B. Historical Memorials relating to the Independents. London, 1839. 3 vols.

HARLEIAN MISCELLANY. London, 1808–11. 12 vols.

HARRINGTON, JAMES. Oceana. London, 1656.

HETTNER, H. Litteraturgeschichte des 18. Jahrhunderts. Brunswick, 4th and 5th ed., 1893–95. 6 vols.

HEMMING, N. De Lege Naturæ apodictica Methodus. Wittenberg, 1577.

HILDENBRAND, KARL. Geschichte und System der Rechts- und Statsphilosophie. Leipzig, 1860.

HINRICHS, H. F. W. Geschichte der Rechts- und Staatsprincipien seit der Reformation bis auf die Gegenwart. Leipzig, 1849. 3 vols.

HOBBES, THOMAS. Opera philosophica quæ Latine scripsit omnia, collected by Molesworth. London, 1839–45. 5 vols.

Höffding, H. Rousseau.

Holtzendorff, F. von. Encyklopädie der Rechtswissenschaft. 5th ed., Leipzig, 1890.

Holland, T. E. Elements of Jurisprudence. 4th ed., Oxford, 1888.

Hooker, Richard. Works, 5th ed., Oxford, 1865. 3 vols.

Hooker, Thomas. A Survey of the Summe of Church Discipline. London, 1648.

Hopkins, Stephen. The Rights of the Colonies Examined. 1765. Reprint in R. I. Records, VI.

Hotman, F. Franco-Gallia, sive tractatus de regimine regnum Galliæ. Geneva, 1573.

Humboldt, Wilhelm von. Ideen zu einem Versuch die Grenzen der Wirksamkeit des Staats zu bestimmen. Vol. VII. of his Werke. Berlin, 1841–52.

Hutchinson, T. The History of Massachusetts from the First Settlement thereof in 1628 until the Year 1750. 3d ed., Boston, 1795. 2 vols.

Hyslop, J. H. Democracy, N. Y., 1899.

Inama-Sternegg, von. Deutsche Wirtschaftsgeschichte. Vol. I., 1879.

Janet, Paul. Histoire de la Science Politique dans ses Rapports avec la Morale. Paris, 1887. 2 vols.

Jefferson, Thomas. Memoir, Correspondence, and Miscellanies. Ed. by T. J. Randolph. 2d ed., Boston and N. Y., 1830. 4 vols.

—— Works. Ed. by P. L. Ford. N. Y., 1892–99. 10 vols.

Jellinek, Georg. Die Erklärung der Menschen- und Bürgerrechte. Leipzig, 1895. Tr. by Farrand.

Jhering, Rudolph von. Geist des römischen Rechts auf den verschiedenen Stufen seiner Entwickelung. 4. Aufl., 3 Bde., 1874–78.

Johnston, A. History of Connecticut. N. Y., 1887.

Junius Brutus. (Languet). Vindiciæ contra Tyrannos. 1579.

Justinian. Institutes.

Kaltenborn, C. Die Vorläufer des Hugo Grotius auf dem Gebiete des Jus Naturæ et Gentium im Reformationszeitalter. Leipzig.

Kampschulte, F. W. J. Calvin: seine Kirche und sein Staat. Leipzig, 1869.

LABOULAYE, E. R. L. L'État et ses Limites. 2d ed., Paris, 1871.

—— Histoire des États-Unis. 6th ed., Paris, 1876–77. 3 vols.

LAFAYETTE, M. J. P. R. Y. G. M. Mémoires, Correspondance et Manuscrits. Bruxelles, 1837. 2 vols.

LAUD, JOHN. Works. Oxford, 1847–57. 5 vols. in 8.

LAURENT, F. Études sur l'Histoire de l'Humanité. Paris, 2d ed., 1865–80. 18 vols.

LIEBER, F. Civil Liberty and Self-government. Phil., 1853.

—— Political Ethics. Boston, 1838–39.

LOCKE, JOHN. Two Treatises of Government.

LOWELL, A. L. Essays on Government. Boston, 1889.

M'CRIE, THOMAS. Life of John Knox. London, 1854.

MACKEY, T. A Plea for Liberty. London, 1891.

MADISON, JAMES. Letters and other Writings. Phil., 1865. 4 vols.

MADVIG, J. N. Verfassung und Verwaltung des roemischen Staats. Leipzig, 1881–82. 2 vols.

MAINE, HENRY S. Ancient Law. N. Y., 1885.

MARIANA, J. De Rege et Regis Institutione. Toledo, 1599.

MARQUARDT, J., und MOMMSEN, T. Handbuch der roemischen Alterthuemer. Leipzig, 1876–88. 7 vols.

MARSIGLIO OF PADUA. Defensor Pacis. Frankfort, 1612.

MASSACHUSETTS HIST. SOC. COLL. Boston, 1795–1877. 43 vols.

MASSON, D. Life of Milton. Cambridge, 1859–80. 6 vols.

MATHER, COTTON. Magnalia Christi Americana. 1702. Hartford, 1855. 2 vols.

MATHER, RICHARD. Church Government and Church Covenant Discussed. London, 1643.

MELANCHTHON, P. Epitome Philosophiæ Moralis, v. 16 of Opera, Halis Saxonum. 1834–60. 28 vols.

MERRIAM, C. E. A History of American Political Theories. N. Y., 1903.

MICHEL, H. L'Idée de l'État. 2e ed., Paris, 1896.

MIGNE, J. P. Patrologiæ Cursus Completus ab Ævo Apostolico ad Tempora Innocentii III. Paris, 1844–64. 221 vols.

MILL, JOHN STUART. On Liberty. 3d ed., London, 1864.

MILTON, JOHN. Prose Works. London, 1868–71. 5 vols.

MIRABEAU, H. G. R., COMTE DE. Adresse aux Bataves sur le Stathouderat, 1788.

—— Considérations sur l'ordre de Cincinnatus. Londres, 1788.

—— Essai sur le Despotisme. 1775.

MOHL, R. VON. Die Geschichte und Litteratur der Staatswissenschaften. Erlangen, 1855–58. 3 Bde.

MONTESQUIEU, BARON CH. DE SECONDAT. Œuvres complètes. Paris, 1843.

MONUMENTA GERMANIÆ HISTORICA.

MORLEY, JOHN. Rousseau. London, 1873. 2 vols.

NEAL, D. The History of the Puritans. London, 1732. N. Y., 1844. 2 vols.

NICOLAUS CUSANUS. Opera Omnia. Basel, 1565.

OLDENDORP, J. Juris Naturalis, Gentium et Civilis Eisagoge. Cologne, 1539.

OSGOOD, H. L. The Political Ideas of the Puritans. Political Science Quarterly, 1891.

OTIS, J. The Rights of the British Colonies Asserted and Proved. 1765.

—— Vindication of the British Colonies. 1765.

—— Considerations on behalf of the Colonies in a Letter to a Noble Lord.

PALFREY, J. G. History of New England, Boston, 1858–90. 5 vols.

—— Compendious History of New England. Boston, 1884. 4 vols.

PENN, W. Select Works. London, 1771.

PHILIPPSON, M. Geschichte des Preussischen Staatswesens vom Tode Friedrichs des Grossen. Leipzig, 1880–82. 2 Bde.

PICTON, ALLANSON. Cromwell. N. Y., 1882.

PITKIN, T. A Political and Civil History of the United States. New Haven, 1828. 2 vols.

POLLOCK, FREDERICK, Sir. An Introduction to the History of the Science of Politics. London, 1890.

—— On the History of the Law of Nature. Columbia Law Review, 1901.

—— Spinoza: His Life and Philosophy. London, 1880.

POORE, B. The Federal and State Constitutions, Colonial Charters, and other Organic Laws of the U. S. Washington, 1878. 2 vols.

RABAUT DE SAINT ÉTIENNE. Précis Historique de la Révolution Française. Paris, 1792.

RANKE, L. VON. Sämmtliche Werke. 54 Bde. Leipzig, 1873–90.

RAPIN DE THOYRAS, PAUL. History of England. 3d ed. London, 1743–47. 4 vols. in 5.

RAYNAL, G. T. F., L'Abbé. Révolution de l'Amérique. Londres, 1781.

REHM, HERMAN. Geschichte der Staatswissenschaft. Freiburg und Leipzig, 1896.

RHODE ISLAND COLONIAL RECORDS. Edited by Bartlett. 10 vols.

RICHTER, CARL. Staats- und Gesellschaftsrecht der Französischen Revolution. Berlin, 1865. 2 Bde.

RIEZLER, S. O. Die Literarischen Widersacher der Päpste zur Zeit Ludwig des Baiers. Leipzig, 1874.

RITCHIE, D. G. Contributions to the History of the Social Contract Theory. Polit. Sc. Quart., 1891, and in his Darwin and Hegel, London, 1893.

—— Natural Rights: A Criticism of some Political and Ethical Conceptions. London, 1895.

RITTER, A. H. Geschichte der Philosophie. Hamburg, 1836–52. 12 Bde.

ROBINSON, JOHN. A Justification of Separation from the Church of England. 1610.

—— A Just and Necessary Apology of Certain Christians no Less Contumeliously than Commonly Called Brownists or Barrowists. Latin ed., 1619. Engl. ed., 1625.

—— Essays or Observations Divine and Moral. 1625.

ROSENTHAL, L. America and France. N. Y., 1882.

ROTH, PAUL. Feudalitat und Unterthanenverband. 1863.

—— Geschichte des Benefizialwesens von den ältesten Zeiten bis in's zehnte Jahrhundert. Erlangen, 1850.

ROWLAND, K. M. The Life, Correspondence and Speeches of George Mason. N. Y., 1892.

RUSHWORTH, J. Historical Collections. (1618–48.) London, 1721. 8 vols.

SAVIGNY, F. K. VON. Geschichte des römischen Rechts im Mittelalter. Heidelberg, 1834–50. 7 Bde.

—— Vom Beruf unserer Zeit für Gesetzgebung und Rechtswissenschaft. Heidelberg, 1814.

SCHARPFF. Nicolaus von Cusa. Tübingen, 1871.

SCHLOSSER, F. C. Geschichte des achtzehnten Jahrhunderts. Heidelberg, 5. Aufl., 1864–66. 8 vols.

SCHMIDT, H. G. Die Lehre vom Tyrannenmord. Tübingen, 1901.

SCHULTE, J. F. VON. Lehrbuch der Deutschen Reichs- und Rechtsgeschichte. Stuttgart. 6. Aufl. 1893.

SCHRÖDER, R. Lehrbuch der Deutschen Rechtsgeshichte. 2. Aufl. 1894.

SCOTT, E. G. Development of Constitutional Liberty in the English Colonies of America. N. Y., 1882.

SELDEN, JOHN. De Jure Naturale et Gentium Juxta Disciplinam Ebraeorum. 1640.

SEXTUS EMPIRICUS. Opera. Leipzig, 1841–42. 2 vols.

SICKEL, W. Der Deutsche Freistaat. 1879.

SIDNEY, ALGERNON. A General View of Government in Europe and Discourses Concerning Government, in Works. London, 1772.

SOHM, R. Institutionen des römischen Rechts. 4. Aufl., 1891.

SOREL, A. L'Europe et la Révolution Française. 3d and 4th ed. Paris, 1895–98.

SPENCER, HERBERT. The Man versus the State. N. Y., 1884.

SPINOZA, BENEDICT. Opera omnia. Ed. by Bruder. Leipzig, 1843–46. 3 vols.

STAËL, Mme. DE. Considérations sur les Principaux Evénémens de la Révolution Française. Liège, 1818. 3 vols.

STAHL, F. J. Die Philosophie des Rechts. 3. Aufl. Heidelberg, 1854–56. 2 vols. in 3 pts.

STEPHEN, Sir J. F. Liberty, Equality, Fraternity. N. Y., 1873.

STEPHENS, H. M. A History of the French Revolution. N. Y., 1886–91. 2 vols.

STOBÆUS. Anthologium. Edited by Wachsmuth and Hense, 1884–95.

STORY, JOSEPH. Commentaries on the Constitution of the United States. 5th ed. Boston, 1891. 2 vols.

STUBBS, WILLIAM. Constitutional History of England in its Origin and Development. Oxford, 1875–78. 3 vols.

STUMPF, T. Die Politischen Ideen des Nicolaus von Cues. Köln, 1865.

SUAREZ, F. Tractatus de Legibus ac Deo Legislatore. Parisiis, 1841. 2 vols.

SULLIVAN, J. Marsiglio of Padua and William of Ockam. Amer. Hist. Review, II., pp. 409–426, 593–610.

TACITUS, CORNELIUS. De Germania. Ed. by Halm. Lipsiæ, 1893.

TAINE, H. A. Les Origines de la France Contemporaine. Paris, 1877–94. 6 vols.

TIEDEMAN, C. G. The Unwritten Constitution of the U. S. N. Y., 1890.

TOCQUEVILLE, ALEXIS DE. L'Ancien Régime et la Révolution. 3d ed., Paris, 1857.

—— De la Democratie en Amérique. Paris, 1835–40. 2 t.

TRENDELENBURG, F. A. Naturrecht.

TREUMANN, R. Die Monarchomachen, Eine Darstellung der Revolutionaren Staatslehren des XVI. Jahrhunderts. Leipzig, 1895.

TREVELYAN, Sir GEORGE. The American Revolution. London and New York, 1899–1903. 2 vols.

THIBAUT, A. F. J. Über die Notwendigkeit eines allgemeinen bürgerlichen Rechts für Deutschland. Heidelberg, 1814.

THOMAS AQUINAS. Opera omnia. Antwerp, 1612, and Parma, 1852–72.

THOMASIUS, C. Fundamenta Juris Naturæ et Gentium. Halæ et Lipsiæ. 1705.

—— Institutionum Jurisprudentiæ divinæ Libri tres. Halæ Magdeburgicæ, 1730.

THUDICHUM. Der altdeutsche Staat. Giessen, 1862.

TUDOR, W. Life of James Otis. Boston, 1823.

TURGOT, A. R. J. Œuvres. Paris, 1844. 2 vols.

TYLER, M. C. A History of American Literature during the Colonial Time. N. Y., 1897. 2 vols.

—— Literary History of the American Revolution. N. Y. 1897. 2 vols.

VOIGT, MORITZ. Die Lehre vom jus naturale, æquum et bonum und jus gentium der Römer. Leipzig, 1856–75. 4 Bde.

VOLTAIRE. Œuvres complètes. Paris, 1869–73. 13 vols.

WAITZ, GEORG. Deutsche Verfassungsgeschichte. 3d ed. Kiel, 1880. 8 vols.

WALKER, G. L. Thomas Hooker, Preacher, Founder, Democrat. N. Y., 1891.

WARNKÖNIG. Rechtsphilosophie. Freiburg, 1839.

WEINGARTEN, H. Die Revolutionskirchen Englands. Leipzig, 1868.

WHITELOCKE, B. Memorials of the English Affairs from the Beginning of the Reign of Charles I. to the Happy Restoration of King Charles II. Oxford, 1853. 4 vols.

WILLIAMS, ROGER. The Bloudy Tenent of Persecution. London, 1644. Reprint, Providence, 1867.

—— The Bloudy Tenent yet more Bloudy. London, 1652. Reprint, Providence, 1870.

WINKLER, B. Principiorum Juris Libri Quinque. Lipsiæ, 1615.

WOOLSEY, T. D. Political Science. N. Y., 1877.

WILLOUGHBY, W. W. The Nature of the State. N. Y., 1896.

WINSOR, JUSTIN. Narrative and Critical History of America. Boston and N. Y., 1886–89. 8 vols.

WINTHROP, JOHN. History of New England. Boston, 1853. 2 vols.

WISE, JOHN. A Vindication of the Government of New England Churches, Drawn from Antiquity; the Light of Nature; the Holy Scripture. 1717. Reprint, Boston, 1772.

WOLFF, CHR. Institutiones Juris Naturæ et Gentium. Halæ Magdeburgicæ, 1750.

XENOPHON. Works. Ed. by Sauppe. 1865–69. 5 vols.

ZELLER, E. Die Philosophie der Griechen. Leipzig, 1865–75. 4 Bde.

ZIEGLER, THEOBALD. Die Ethik der Griechen und Römer. Bonn, 1881.

ZIMMERMAN, W. Geschichte des Grossen Bauernkriegs. Stuttgart, 1856. 2 Bde.

INDEX